THE CLASSICAL GUITAR

"The guitar is a wonderful instrument which is understood by few."

Schubert

"The instrument most complete and richest in its harmonic and polyphonic possibilities."

Manuel de Falla

"I love the guitar for its harmony; it is my constant companion in all my travels."

Nicolo Paganini

"Nothing is more beautiful than a guitar, save perhaps two."

Chopin

THE CLASSICAL GUITAR

ITS EVOLUTION

AND

ITS PLAYERS

SINCE 1800

BY

MAURICE J. SUMMERFIELD

FIRST EDITION MARCH 1982

Typeset and printed in Great Britain by
Campbell Graphics Ltd., Newcastle upon Tyne NE6 1AS

ISBN 0 9506224 8 6 HARDBACK
ISBN 0 9506224 7 8 PAPERBACK

THE CLASSICAL GUITAR

CONTENTS

To Mario Maccaferri

and

Charles E. H. Smith

Great Guitarists

and

Great Friends

THE CLASSICAL GUITAR
PREFACE

I have long felt the need for a book dealing specifically with the classical guitar and its most important players and personalities since 1800. Those authors who have written books in past years about the history of the classical guitar have usually devoted a large section of their work to the lute, vihuela and early guitar. As a result in these books many important players and personalities, in particular contemporary classical guitarists, are not included or given just a brief mention.

Since the publication of my first book, 'The Jazz Guitar—Its Evolution And Its Players', in 1978 it often occurred to me the format that I applied to this work would lend itself admirably to one on the classical guitar. Amongst the many enthusiastic letters I have received from guitarists all over the world about this first book, many of the writers supported this view. With their encouragement I began to write this book early in 1980. Originally I had hoped to complete the new work early in 1981 but the task proved much greater than I expected. The book was finally completed earlier this year and I am now satisfied that 'The Classical Guitar—Its Evolution And Its Players Since 1800', is currently the most complete and up-to-date work dealing with the modern classical guitar.

As with my book on the jazz guitar, one of the most important features of this new book is its very full listing of records, music and details of books and magazine articles. Most of the items detailed are still currently in production or print. Those which are not can be obtained with a little patience by using the section 'Sources of Supply', at the back of the book. I have personally found that an advert placed in one or more of the specialist guitar magazines will often bring that elusive item. You will also be amazed, particularly if you live in a larger city, at what your local main library can offer. In regard to records you should remember that many items are available in different countries with different brands, sleeves and numbers, so be careful not to duplicate or be misled.

The collection of photographs in this book of classical guitarists, past and present, is I believe a unique one. It gives me really great pleasure to see such a collection under one cover and I wish to give special thanks to all those who have supplied them. Their contribution has been vital to the excellent illustration of this book.

I realise there is a possibility that some readers may feel that some other classical guitarists they know of and admire have been omitted. However I have sincerely tried to include all those guitarists who I believe have made an impact on the evolution of the guitar in classical music since 1800. I have not included the many great guitarists who play the classical guitar but not classical music. Therefore the great flamenco guitarists, Nashville stylists like Chet Atkins, Latin American virtuosi such as Baden Powell and Sebastiao Tapajos, and jazz guitarists like Charlie Byrd and Lenny Breau are not included. I am aware that there are many fine classical guitarists throughout the world who may well deserve a place in future editions of this book but circumstances and events have not as yet allowed them to contribute in an effective way to the evolution of the classical guitar. Some of these guitarists that I have heard play in concert or on record, or know of, are illustrated in the appendix to the players' section of this book as a tribute to their ability and important contribution to the growth of today's classical guitar world.

MAURICE J. SUMMERFIELD
June 1982

ACKNOWLEDGEMENTS

KIICHI ARAKAWA
AARON & GORDEN (USA)
WILFRED M. APPLEBY

HERBERT BARRETT MANAGEMENT (USA)
BYERS, SCHWALBE & ASSOC (USA)
GEORGE M. BOWDEN

CBS RECORDS (USA)
COLBERT ARTISTS MANAGEMENT (USA)
COLUMBIA ARTISTS MANAGEMENT INC (USA)
GEORGE CLINTON

DECCA RECORD COMPANY (LONDON)
DAILY TELEGRAPH
THEA DISKER (USA)
JOHN W. DUARTE
BASIL DOUGLAS LTD
DEUTSCHE GRAMMAPHON

EMI RECORDS (LONDON)
EVEREST RECORD GROUP (USA)

IZYDOR GEFFNER
GRAMOFON AB BIS (SWEDEN)
GENDAI GUITAR (JAPAN)
GUITAR REVIEW

IBANEZ GUITARS
ICM ARTISTS

JUDD CONCERT BUREAU (USA)

KALLAWAY LTD (LONDON)

LYRICHORD DISCS (USA)

MARIO MACCAFERRI
JORGE MOREL

JOSEPH PASTORE JNR
M. PEROTT
POLYDOR INTERNATIONAL (GERMANY)
PHILIPS RECORDS

RADIO FRANCE

SAMIRA BAROODY ASSOCIATES
SHAW CONCERTS INC
SIMONDS MANAGEMENT
C. E. H. SMITH
SUPRAPHON RECORDS

T. TAZAWA
TRANSBERG LTD

ZEN-ON CO

THE CLASSICAL GUITAR

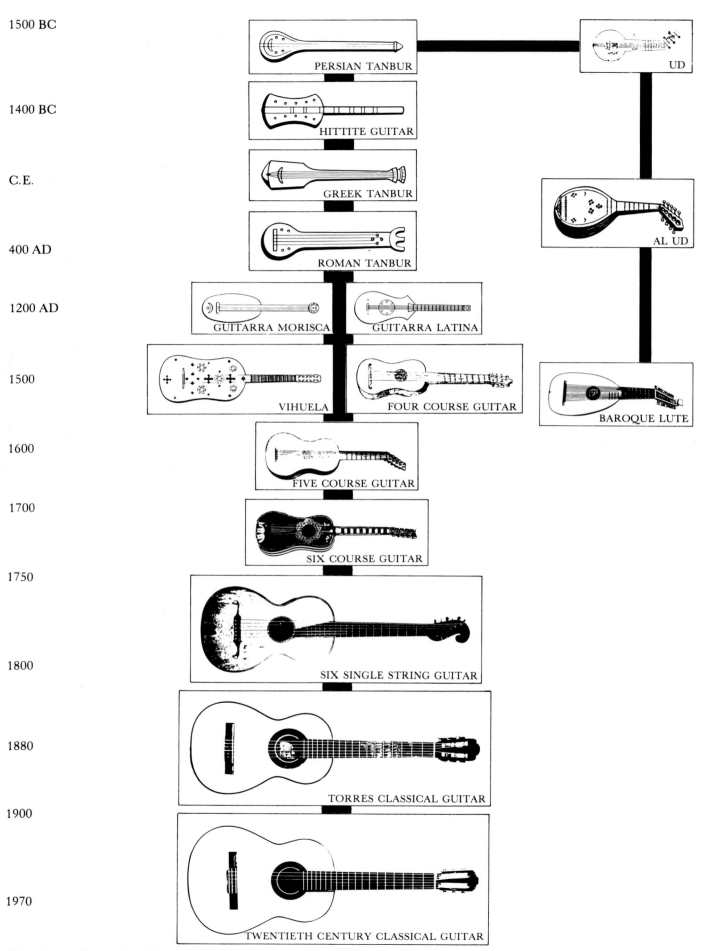

1500 BC

1400 BC

C.E.

400 AD

1200 AD

1500

1600

1700

1750

1800

1880

1900

1970

PERSIAN TANBUR

HITTITE GUITAR

GREEK TANBUR

ROMAN TANBUR

GUITARRA MORISCA   GUITARRA LATINA

VIHUELA   FOUR COURSE GUITAR

FIVE COURSE GUITAR

SIX COURSE GUITAR

SIX SINGLE STRING GUITAR

TORRES CLASSICAL GUITAR

TWENTIETH CENTURY CLASSICAL GUITAR

UD

AL UD

BAROQUE LUTE

Chart showing the evolution of the classical guitar as an instrument from 1500 BC to the present day.

THE CLASSICAL GUITAR
ITS EVOLUTION

This book deals with the evolution of the classical guitar since 1800. Many excellent books have been written in past years on the history of the guitar and its origins before that time. These are listed at the end of this chapter for those readers who wish to extend their research of this earlier period in greater detail. Nevertheless as a start to this chapter I believe it necessary to make the reader briefly aware of the origins of the guitar before 1800.

For many years several guitar scholars and historians put forward the theory that the guitar's ancestor was the Persian instrument the al'ud. They claimed that the Spanish guitar gradually evolved from this lute like instrument after the Moors brought the instrument to Spain when they invaded the Iberian peninsular around 711AD. However more recent research has shown that the six string classical guitar, as we know it today, evolved in a different manner.

The first guitar like instrument on record is shown on a 1400BC archeological object taken from the city gates of the new Hittite settlement at Alaja Huyuk. It shows a Hittite musician playing a long necked guitar shaped instrument rather than the more common tanbur. During this period of history the popular instrument of the region was the tanbur and, although having a fretted or marked neck, had a distinctive bowl shaped body as opposed to the distinctive guitar shape of today. The word guitar itself is derived from two Persian words, tar – meaning string, and char – meaning four. Therefore char-tar stood for a four stringed instrument. Many of these early stringed instruments originally had four strings. Over the years the name char-tar gradually evolved into the word guitarra in Spain and then into similar names throughout most of Europe. An exception was Portugal where the word for a guitar has always been violao which is derived

Illustration of four course guitar in 1551 music book.

from the latin word 'fidicula' (a small plucked fiddle like instrument).

From these early tanburs/chartars emerged the Greek tanbur in 300BC. Later the Romans developed their own tanbur around 300AD. These instruments were both chartars, i.e. four stringed instruments. It now seems absolutely certain that the Romans took their tanburs to the Iberian peninsular in 476AD, almost three centuries before the Moors' invasion of Spain, and it was this Roman tanbur that was later developed into the 'guitarra morisca' and the 'guitarra latina'. These were both guitar like instruments distinctly illustrated in the important historical document 'The Cantigas of Alphonso The Wise' in 1270AD. The 'guitarra latina' had a flat back, as has the modern guitar, and the soundboard had one hole over which the strings passed. It was used for playing chords and was a forerunner of the vihuela. The 'guitarra morisca' had a vaulted back, the fingerboard was large and the soundboard had several soundholes. It was used for the playing of melodies.

It was these instruments that later evolved into the aristocratic vihuela (a six double stringed instrument, tuned G,C,F,A,D,G) which dominated the courts of Spain and Portugal during the sixteenth century. The four course guitar (tuned C,F,A,D – the same as the middle four strings of the vihuela) was used mainly by troubadours to accompany songs and dancing.

The al'ud which had also evolved from early tanburs, eventually developed into the baroque lute (like the vihuela the original lutes were tuned G,C,F,A,D,C). This instrument became extremely popular in England, France, Italy and Germany during the seventeenth century. Although related to the early guitar, because of its similar origins, the lute really had little part in the evolution of the guitar. Nevertheless the technique required to play both fretted instruments had many similarities and their strings were both laid out in courses (that is two strings tuned either in octaves or unison) and both had similar tuning.

Both these instruments were also fretted – fret is derived from the old French word 'ferretté', meaning 'banded with iron'. The frets on early instruments, unlike the metal frets of the modern guitar, were made of gut and tied around the neck. The lute and vihuela had ten or eleven frets whereas the early guitar had between four and eight. This amount was dependent on whether the guitar was to be used for melody or the strumming of chords. A great deal of the music originally written for the lute

Julian Bream playing a baroque lute.

An interesting illustration from 'Pablo Minguet's Modo de taner todos los instrumentos mejores' (Method of Playing All the Best Instruments) published in Madrid 1752.

and vihuela, in later years, became successfully transcribed for the six string classical guitar and now forms a valuable part of its repertory.

The period of musical history from 1400BC to 1800AD saw a vast multitude of plucked string instruments evolving first in the Middle East, Asia and the Far East, and then later in Europe. The Greeks and Romans had, as well as their tanburs, their harp like instruments the lyra and kithara. It seems likely that the kithara, originally a four stringed hand harp, also derived its name from the Persian words char-tar. In India the sitar, surbahar, and tampura were popular stringed instruments. The Chinese had their p'i p'a and the Japanese their samisen. There is little doubt that all these early instruments are distant relatives of the guitar sharing with it their origin in the tanbur (sometimes mistakenly called the nefer). In the sixteenth century many versions of the lute also appeared. The chittarone and theorbo lute were two of the more popular versions of this aristocratic descendent of the Persian al'ud. The citterne, a mixture of the lute and four course guitar, also appeared in the sixteenth century and as did the first mandolins in Italy. Many of these had six courses of strings but as the eighteenth century drew to a close the four course mandolin, as it is known today, became established. As most of these

early fretted string instruments fell into disuse and became museum pieces the mandolin remained one of the few to survive in the guitar dominated nineteenth and twentieth centures.

In Europe both the lute and the vihuela gradually fell into disuse towards the end of the seventeenth century. The lute suffered from the addition of more and more strings so that it became virtually impossible to master (and also to tune). When the tuning of the four course guitar changed to A,D,G,B, and a fifth course (high E) was added, the vihuela began to loose its popularity. The addition of this fifth string on the four course guitar is often accredited to the Spanish poet and musician Vicente Espinel (1551-1624). By the time the six string guitar came into being towards the end of the eighteenth century the vihuela had become virtually extinct.

It is not known exactly when the sixth string was added to the guitar but most historians agree it happened around 1780 and probably almost simultaneously in Italy and Germany. The German luthier Jacob Augustus Otto has often been credited to be the first person to make a six string guitar, adding its lower E, around 1790. But it now seems probable that the first six single string guitars were being made in Italy a little after the middle of the eighteenth century.

Frontispiece of Luys Milan's "El Maestro", a collection of vihuela music, which was published in Valencia, Spain in 1535. It shows Orpheus playing a six course vihuela.

By 1800 most countries of Europe had given up the five and six course guitar in favour of the six single string guitar. In Russia a seven string guitar was developed by the guitarist Andreas Ossipovitch Sichra. This was tuned D,G,B,D,G,B,D, and was to remain very popular for many years in that part of the world. The noted Italian composer Luigi Boccherini (1743-1805) had given the 'new' guitar its first taste of musical 'respectability' by adapting several of his finest quintets to include a part for guitar. This he did in Spain under the patronage of the Marquis de Benavente, an enthusiastic amateur guitarist, around 1790. By 1800 several virtuosos of the six string classical guitar were beginning to emerge in various parts of Europe and the first golden age of the classical guitar was about to begin.

This golden age of the guitar began simultaneously in Spain and Italy around 1775. The appearance of the first six single string guitars coincided at the beginning of the nineteenth century with another important development in the internal construction of the instrument, fan strutting. This is the term used for the strips of wood attached in a particular manner to the back of the soundboard of the guitar. These strips vastly improve the tone and volume of the instrument. In time there would be many variations and extensions of fan strutting but there is no doubt that even these early simplified versions were

an important innovation. The years 1800 to 1980 were to see a gradual development of the instrument in three main areas. These were the guitarist's technique, the guitar's repertory and the construction of the instrument. These parallel developments began in Spain, and to a lesser extent in Italy, at the end of the eighteenth century. Towards the end of the nineteenth century there would be a period of decline in the progress and popularity of the guitar as it became overshadowed by orchestral and keyboard instruments. It would again be in Spain at the end of the nineteenth century that the evolution of the classical guitar would be given an enormous boost by luthier Antonio Torres de Jurado and virtuoso guitarist Francisco Tarrega.

Torres, inspired originally by the virtuoso guitarist Julian Arcas, had developed a larger bodied guitar with advanced fan strutting and also a wider fingerboard. It was with this new version of the instrument that Francisco Tarrega developed a new playing technique which would eventually make musicians aware of the enormous potential of the guitar. His work was to be extended in the first half of the twentieth century by more Spanish guitarists, in particular Andres Segovia. It was Segovia who, against extreme opposition, would embark upon a worldwide crusade lasting for almost eighty years to promote the instrument. This crusade was eventually to be so successful that today the guitar

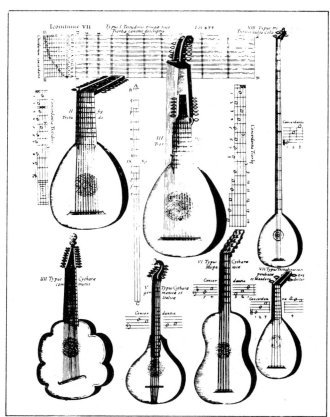

A variety of stringed instruments, including a five-course guitar (named Cythara Hispanica), from Athanasius Kircher's "Musurgia Universalis" published in Rome, 1650.

has become one of the most popular classical instruments with a vast repertory of music equal to most other instruments.

Towards the end of the eighteenth century a well known organist Father Basilio, a monk of the Citeaux order, turned his full attention to the guitar. He developed a fine solo technique on the instrument and his virtuosity on the instrument became widely recognised in Spain. He was asked to play for Charles IV of Spain, and later he was to become tutor to Queen Marie Louise. Basilio, whose real name was Miguel Garcia influenced two other important eighteenth century guitarists, Fernando Ferrandiere and Don Federico Moretti. In 1799 Ferrandiere published his method for the six string guitar in modern notation 'Arte de tocar la Guitarra Espanola' and Moretti published his 'Principas para tocar la guitarra de seis ordenes'. Both these works drew upon the earlier work of guitarist Antonio Ballestres published in 1780 'Obra para Guitarra de seis ordenes'.

It was these men who laid the foundations in Spain for a nineteenth century revival of the guitar which would be completed by two of Spain's greatest exponents of the six single string guitar, Fernando Sor (1778-1839) and Dionisio Aguado (1784-1849). These two brilliant musicians led very active careers of concertizing and teaching throughout most of Europe. Both these guitarists lived for a good part of their lives in Paris, which was one of Europe's most important centres for music and the arts. Sor in fact died in Paris, Aguado returned to Spain to spend his last years in his native city Madrid. Both men were prolific composers and their music still remains an integral part of the twentieth century guitarists repertoire. There is no doubt that Fernando Sor was the greater and more prolific composer of the two, nevertheless Aguado's contribution was also important to the then very limited repertory of the guitar.

Dionisio Aguado was also the inventor of the tripodison, an unusual guitar accessory devised to hold the guitar rather than resting it on the right thigh. However this invention did not achieve any lasting success. Both Sor and Aguado published important guitar methods which, over the years, were translated into several languages and are still used to this day.

It is interesting to note the variations in these two great guitarist's right hand technique. Whilst both agreed on the 'tirando' stroke to pluck the strings (that is the right hand fingers rise after plucking the string as against 'apoyando' in which the fingers continue past the string to rest on the string below),

Portrait of Francesco Corbetta on music 'Varii Scherzi di Sonate Per La Chittara Spagnola" published Brussels, Belgium 1648.

Aguado advocated the use of the fingernails whereas Sor used the pads of his right hand fingertips. Nineteenth century guitarists were divided on this matter and the controversy has continued to the present day. At the beginning of the twentieth century Francisco Tarrega advocated the right hand 'no nail' technique and this method of plucking the strings was continued by Emilio Pujol amongst several other important guitarists. The vast majority of twentieth century players have followed the use of the nails as advocated by Andres Segovia (and also Miguel Llobet) from the early 1920s.

The early part of the nineteenth century saw many fine guitarists but two are regarded as being the most outstanding. Fernando Sor from Spain and from Italy, Mauro Giuliani (1778-1829). Little is known of Giulani's early musical background but on his arrival in Vienna in 1806 musicians soon became aware that he was a guitarist/composer extraordinary. He associated and befriended many other fine musicians in the Austrian capital including Beethoven, Hummel, Diabelli, Moschelles and Mayseder. Giuliani has the distinction of having had the first guitar magazine in English 'The Giulianad' named in his honour. It was published in London in the early 1830s by the German born guitarist Ferdinand Peltzer. Vienna, where Giuliani made his home, was one of the great European centres for the arts, music and the guitar at the beginning of the nineteenth century. It was also the home of several other important and influential guitarists including Simon Molitor (1766-1848) and Johann Kaspar Mertz (1806-1856) as well as guitar makers like Johann Staufer.

Two other important and influential Italian guitarists were Mateo Carcassi (1792-1853) and Ferdinando Carulli (1770-1841). Although not of the stature as Giuliani, Carcassi and Carulli were prolific composers and contributed greatly to the nineteenth century repertory for the guitar. All three Italian guitarists concertized widely throughout Europe. Whereas Giuliani made Vienna his home and centre of work, Carulli and Carcassi chose Paris.

Other important nineteenth century guitarists were Giulio Regondi (1822-1874) and Napoleon Costé (1806-1883) from France, Luigi Legnani (1790-1877) and Zani De Ferranti (1802-1878) from Italy, and Don A. F. Huerta (1805-1875) and Julian Arcas (1832-1882) from Spain. In Russia Andreas O. Sichra (1772-1852) and Nicolas Makarov (1810-1890) were also important figures in the development of the guitar. The Italian violinist Nicolo Paganini (1782-1840) was also a virtuoso guitarist

Francisco Tarrega

and composed several important pieces for the instrument.

An important feature of the evolution of the instrument in the early years of the nineteenth century, and one which has continued to this day, was the co-operation between the guitarist and guitar maker in improving the quality of sound and volume of the instrument. Fernando Sor worked closely with René Francois Lacote in France and Louis Panormo in London, Luigi Legnani worked with Staufer and towards the end of the century Julian Arcas was instrumental in developing the larger bodied classical guitar with Antonio Torres de Jurado in Spain.

Although after 1860 the guitar continued to have a few outstanding soloists its acceptance in most musical circles as a serious musical instrument began to decline. There were several reasons for this. Despite the large output of compositions by guitarists themselves the instrument's repertory was limited as none of the great composers had written for it. Hector Berlioz (1803-1869) and Franz Schubert (1797-1828) were both fine guitarists but with exception of a few songs written with a guitar accompaniment by Schubert, neither wrote for the guitar. Excellent music of past centuries, written for the lute, vihuela and early guitar had not at that time been transcribed for the six string instrument. With the exception of the compositions of Sor and Giuliani, the quality of most guitar music did not compare with the vast library of fine music available for other instruments. The use of the guitar in folk music, accompanying singers and dancers (as in flamenco), and in other popular forms of music lost its respectability as a serious musical instrument in the eyes of the vast majority of serious musicians and music teachers throughout Europe. These prejudices against the guitar lasted for many years and even today still linger on in some areas of the classical music world. The original nineteenth century small bodied guitars also suffered from a lack of volume which hindered their use when played in company with other instruments.

It was the great Spanish guitarist Francisco Eixea Tarrega (1854-1909) who was to set the guitar back on an illustrious and firm course. Originally a talented pianist, Tarrega won first prize for harmony and composition at the Conservatory of Madrid. He began to play the guitar as a child and continued to develop his technique on the instrument throughout his conservatory career. It was Julian Arcas (1832-1882) who had originally encouraged the luthier Antonio Torres to make a wider bodied guitar with a wider neck, and subsequently Torres developed and improved the pattern of fan strutting and a new style bridge. Tarrega realized that to play this new shaped guitar the techniques applied to the original small bodied guitar had to be altered. With the small bodied instrument the early nineteenth century guitarists rested the instrument on their right thigh and many often supported the right hand on the guitar by fixing the little finger of the right hand into the body near the bridge. Carulli was a strong advocate of this position whereas his countryman, Francesco Molino, who also lived in Paris, taught his pupils to play without resting the little finger on the soundboard. Guitarists of that period would also sometimes bring the thumb of their left hand over the edge of the neck to play bass notes, and applied the 'tirando' stroke to pluck the strings with the right hand.

Tarrega completely revised the whole of the established guitar technique. He rested the guitar on his left thigh, the leg slightly raised by the use of a footstool. He freed the right hand from the supported position and instigated the use of the 'apoyando' as well as the 'tirando' stroke. With the wider neck he set firm rules for the placement of the fingers on the fingerboard. He also made a massive

A Nineteenth century cartoon of an imaginary 'battle' between supporters of Carulli and Molino.

contribution to the evolution of the modern classical guitar by extending its repertory. He not only composed a quantity of delightful original pieces and studies for the instrument, but also initiated the art of transcribing for the guitar music originally written for other instruments. His excellent transcriptions of the music of Bach, Beethoven, Mozart, Schubert, Haydn, Albeniz and Granados were a delight to hear and play. Through his many public performances of these transcriptions and original compositions Tarrega made musicians throughout the world aware once again of the guitar's enormous potential. Although he did give many concerts in several European countries including France, Italy and England, he was not fond of travelling and preferred to stay in Spain. As a result his influence was not as great as it possibly could have been had he extended his public performances to more countries.

With the approach of the twentieth century the second and the greatest golden age of the classical guitar was beginning to dawn. As it had been Spain that had laid the foundation of the nineteenth century classical guitar, so it was Spain once again that contributed so greatly to the twentieth century guitar through the work of Tarrega, the founder of the modern guitar school, and Torres, the father of modern guitar construction.

Early in the twentieth century Emilio Pujol (1886-1980) and Miguel Llobet (1878-1938), two of Tarrega's pupils, travelled widely and gained new audiences for the guitar both in Europe and America. Yet it was to be another Spanish guitarist Andres Segovia (1892) who led the classical guitar into its greatest years.

A self-taught guitarist, Andres Segovia's great musical talent was recognised at an early age. He disregarded the advice of other Spanish classical musicians to change to a "more serious" musical instrument and dedicated himself to establish the guitar worldwide as an instrument equal to any other classical instrument. He decided that this could only be done by presenting the guitar in concert to as many audiences as possible and by extending its repertory. This he has done with tireless energy for almost seventy years. Few would disagree that his success in achieving these goals has gone far beyond his wildest dreams.

There are now few countries in the world in which Segovia has not appeared in concert. Everywhere his audiences have been astounded not only with his incredible musicianship but also with the scope of the guitar in the hands of a master. It was in the early 1920s Segovia began his campaign to encourage leading contemporary composers to write for the guitar. His pleas were first answered by Joaquin Turina (1882-1949) and Moreno Torroba (1891) in 1924. In fact in 1920 Manuel De Falla (1876-1945), fulfilling an early promise to Miguel Llobet had been the first great composer to write a piece for the guitar. This was entitled 'Homenage pour le tombeau de Claude Debussy'. Since that time Segovia has never let up in his campaign to enlarge the guitar's repertory. He has also made many transcriptions of fine music originally written for other instruments. Within a relatively short period the guitar now has a vast library of original works. Other important composers who have written especially for the guitar as a direct result of Segovia's instigation are, Joaquin Rodrigo (1902), Manuel Ponce (1886-1948), Mario Castelnuevo Tedesco (1845-1968), Alexander Tansman (1897) and Heitor Villa Lobos (1887-1954).

Segovia has also continued the tradition of early nineteenth century guitarists by working with guitar makers to improve the quality of sound and the volume of the instrument. He worked first with the Ramirez family, and subsequently with Hauser and Fleta. He was also instrumental in the development of the nylon guitar string with luthier Albert Augustine in 1947. This development was an enormous step forward in the evolution of the guitar.

Miguel Llobet with admirers, Segovia is sitting on his right.

Andres Segovia, 1959

The years from 1930 to 1980 have seen the rise of many outstanding guitarists in most countries of the world. Although there were variations in certain aspects of the technical approach, for example the 'no nail' technique versus nails, using the right hand side of the nails or the left hand side of the nails to pluck the strings, the vast majority of guitarists have followed the technique of the instruments as developed by Tarrega and refined by Segovia.

In France Ida Presti (1924-1967) was recognised as a child prodigy in the 1930s and later with Alexandre Lagoya (1929) became the greatest guitar duo of all time. Many great guitarists have also appeared in Spain after Pujol, Llobet and Segovia. Regino Sainz de la Maza in the 1930s was followed in more recent times by Narciso Yepes, José Luis Gonzalez, José Tomas, Angel Romero and Pepe Romero.

In Great Britian two of the grestest guitarists of all time appeared in the 1950s and 1960s, Julian Bream and John Williams. They have both continued and extended the Segovia tradition in a magnificent way. Julian Bream has also been a major figure in the revival of the baroque lute and its music. John Williams in recent years has instigated a fusion of classical and rock music with his extremely successful group 'Sky'. In South America during the 1920s and 1930s Agustin Barrios Mangoré was the outstanding guitar virtuoso and composer. Nevertheless Segovia still proved, after his various concert tours there, to be the most lasting influence on guitarists in more recent generations. Maria Luisa Anido, an early pupil of Miguel Llobet, has continued this tradition and has been the teacher to many of the great guitarists originating from South America in recent years. In more recent times the world has seen many more great guitarists emerge. Italy has produced Oscar Ghiglia. In the United States, Vahdah Olcott Bickford and William Foden were two of the most influential guitarists at the beginning of the twentieth century, and in more recent years Christopher Parkening. From Cuba Manuel Barrueco, Rey de la Torre and Leo Brouwer; from Austria Konrad Ragossnig; from Japan Akinobu Matsuda and Kazuhito Yamashita; from Czechoslovakia Vladamir Mikulka. These are only a few of the most outstanding players of the twentieth century. The chart on page twenty two shows in detail the most important classical guitarists from 1800 to 1980.

Wherever he went Segovia not only encouraged leading composers to write for the guitar but he also

19

made a point of approaching music conservatories, colleges and universities to establish a seat for the classical guitar. At the beginning of the twentieth century the guitar was not accepted in any of these institutions. Today there are very few departments of music education which do not include the guitar in their curriculum and who do not have a professor of guitar.

Andres Segovia is without doubt the most important classical guitar figure of the twentieth century. There is not a classical guitarist today who does not owe a direct debt to his super-human efforts which no-one would deny have firmly established the instrument worldwide.

The classical guitar currently rides on the crest of a wave of popularity and growth, but what of the future? Recent years have seen the development of the ten string guitar played by Narciso Yepes who also instigated its production. José Tomas plays and advocates an eight string guitar and recently a seven string guitar (with an extra string above the high E rather than a low D) has been developed. In past centuries when extra strings were added to stringed instruments this usually in time spelt doom for the instrument. These current variants of the six string guitar will no doubt linger on but it seems certain that the standard six string classical guitar will be dominant for many years to come. The number of talented players of the instrument, its general acceptance in all musical circles throughout the world, and the size of its repertory, all continue to grow at a staggering rate.

Alirio Diaz

COURTESY VANGUARD RECORDS

Selected Reading

The Art and Times of the Guitar – Frederic V. Grunfeld – Macmillan (1969)

The Illustrated History of the Guitar – Alexander Bellow – Franco-Colombo (1970)

The Guitar from the Renaissance to the Present Day – Harvey Turnbull – Batsford (1974)

Guitars from the Renaissance to Rock – Tom and Mary Evans – Paddington (1977)

Traditions of the Classical Guitar – Graham Wade – John Calder (1981)

The Guitar and Mandolin – Philip J. Bone – Schott (1914 and 1954)

The Story of the Spanish Guitar – A. P. Sharpe – Clifford Essex (1954)

Guitarren-Lexicon – Josef Powrozniak – Verlag Neve Musik (1979)

The Evolution of the Classical Guitar – Wilfred M. Appleby – I.C.G.A. (1966)

Guitares – Michel Foussard – Eurydice (1980)

Diccionario Guitarras, Guitarristas and Guitarreros – Domingo Prat – Buenos Aires (1934)

The Segovia Technique – Vladimir Bobri – MacMillan (1972)

Guitar Music Index Volumes 1 and 2 – George Gilmore and Mark Pereira – Galliard (1976)

Guitar Music in the Archives of G.F.A. – Thomas F. Heck – G.F.A. (1981)

Tone Production on the Classical Guitar – John Taylor – Musical New Services (1978)

Classical Guitar, Lute and Vihuela Discography – Ronald C. Purcell – Belwin Mills (1976)

Guitar Review Magazines – 1946 through 1982 – New York

Handbuch der Gitarre und Laute – Konrad Ragossnig – B. Schott's (1978)

THE GUITAR

DEFINITIONS BY CARL SANDBURG

A small friend weighing less than a newborn infant, ever responsive to all sincere efforts aimed at mutual respect, depth of affection or love gone off the deep end.

A device in the realm of harmonic creation where six silent strings have the sound potential of profound contemplation or happy go lucky whim.

A highly evolved contrivance whereby delicate melodic moments mingle with punctuation of silence bringing "the creative hush".

A vibratory implement under incessant practice and skilled cajolery giving out with serene maroon meditations, flame dancers in scarlet sashes, snow-white acrobats plunging into black midnight pools, odd numbers in evening green waltzing with even numbers in dawn pink.

A chattel with a soul often in part owning its owner and tantalizing him with his lack of perfection.

An instrument of quaint form and quiet demeanor dedicated to the dulcet rather than the diapason.

A box of chosen wood having intimate accessories wherefrom sound may be measured and commanded to the interest of ears not lost to hammer crash or wind whisper.

A portable companion distinguished from the piano in that you can take it with you, neither horses nor motor truck being involved.

David Russell with Andres Segovia.

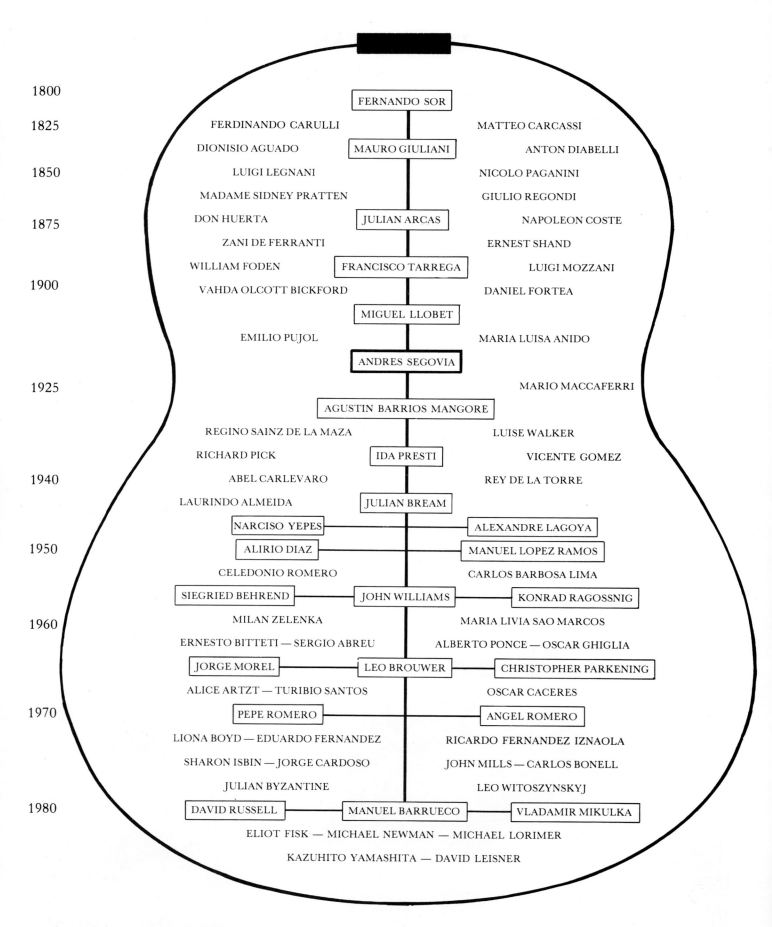

1800	FERNANDO SOR	
1825	FERDINANDO CARULLI	MATTEO CARCASSI
	DIONISIO AGUADO — MAURO GIULIANI	ANTON DIABELLI
1850	LUIGI LEGNANI	NICOLO PAGANINI
	MADAME SIDNEY PRATTEN	GIULIO REGONDI
1875	DON HUERTA — JULIAN ARCAS	NAPOLEON COSTE
	ZANI DE FERRANTI	ERNEST SHAND
	WILLIAM FODEN — FRANCISCO TARREGA	LUIGI MOZZANI
1900	VAHDA OLCOTT BICKFORD	DANIEL FORTEA
	MIGUEL LLOBET	
	EMILIO PUJOL	MARIA LUISA ANIDO
	ANDRES SEGOVIA	
1925		MARIO MACCAFERRI
	AGUSTIN BARRIOS MANGORE	
	REGINO SAINZ DE LA MAZA	LUISE WALKER
	RICHARD PICK — IDA PRESTI	VICENTE GOMEZ
1940	ABEL CARLEVARO	REY DE LA TORRE
	LAURINDO ALMEIDA — JULIAN BREAM	
	NARCISO YEPES	ALEXANDRE LAGOYA
1950	ALIRIO DIAZ	MANUEL LOPEZ RAMOS
	CELEDONIO ROMERO	CARLOS BARBOSA LIMA
	SIEGRIED BEHREND — JOHN WILLIAMS — KONRAD RAGOSSNIG	
	MILAN ZELENKA	MARIA LIVIA SAO MARCOS
1960	ERNESTO BITTETI — SERGIO ABREU	ALBERTO PONCE — OSCAR GHIGLIA
	JORGE MOREL — LEO BROUWER — CHRISTOPHER PARKENING	
	ALICE ARTZT — TURIBIO SANTOS	OSCAR CACERES
1970	PEPE ROMERO — ANGEL ROMERO	
	LIONA BOYD — EDUARDO FERNANDEZ	RICARDO FERNANDEZ IZNAOLA
	SHARON ISBIN — JORGE CARDOSO	JOHN MILLS — CARLOS BONELL
	JULIAN BYZANTINE	LEO WITOSZYNSKYJ
1980	DAVID RUSSELL — MANUEL BARRUECO — VLADAMIR MIKULKA	
	ELIOT FISK — MICHAEL NEWMAN — MICHAEL LORIMER	
	KAZUHITO YAMASHITA — DAVID LEISNER	

A general chart showing the most important classical guitarists since 1800. The most outstanding soloists are highlighted.

THE CLASSICAL GUITAR
ITS PLAYERS

CODE TO ABBREVIATIONS OF PUBLISHERS NAMES AS USED IN SELECTED MUSIC COLUMNS

BP . . . . .Brazilliance Music
UME . . . . .Union Musical Espanola
EMB . . . . .Editio Musica Budapest
SI . . . . .Belwin Mills
ZA . . . . .Zanibon
JWC . . . . .J & W Chester
ZM . . . . .Musikverlag Zimmerman
FC . . . . .Franco Colombo
UE . . . . .Universal Edition
GA . . . . .Guitar Archives-Schott
ESC . . . . .Editions Max Eschig
MB . . . . .Mel Bay
N . . . . .C. F. Peters
EMT . . . . .Editions Musicales Transalantiques
RIC . . . . .Ricordi
CO . . . . .Columbia Music Company
B & B . . . . .Bote & Bock
CG . . . . .Carl Gehrmans
B . . . . .Broekmans en Van Poppel
BA . . . . .Ricordi, Buenos Aires
B & H . . . . .Boosey & Hawkes
SY . . . . .Ricordi
EMM . . . . .Editiones Musicales Madrid
CHANT . . . . .Chanterelle

MIGUEL ABLONIZ

Born – Cairo, Egypt

29th May 1917

Miguel Abloniz

The son of a Greek father and an Italian mother, Miguel Abloniz now resides in Italy. He is regarded as one of the foremost guitar authorities and teachers in the world today.

Abloniz began teaching himself the guitar at the age of eight. Qualified teachers were not to be found in Cairo at that time, and for a period of five years the young guitarist used the methods of Carulli, Albert and Carcassi. Abloniz then managed to correspond with prominent teachers in Europe who were able to send him new guitar books and music. In 1933 he made contact with French guitarist Andre Verdier, a former pupil of Miguel Llobet. Verdier recommended the young guitarist to Emilio Pujol, who also began to correspond with Abloniz.

During the second World War Miguel Abloniz gained a lot of experience as a concert guitarist, both in recital and on the radio. Eventually he was to devote most of his time to teaching and transcribing, rather than playing in concert. In 1946 he went to the Escuela Municipal De Musica in Barcelona, Spain to study privately with Pujol. He then continued his music studies with Juan Parras Del Morral. In 1945 Abloniz travelled to Great Britain to hear and meet Andres Segovia.

In 1953 Miguel Abloniz moved to Milan, Italy, where he established a guitar school in his home which is still in existance today. Abloniz teaches at a number of Italian academies and colleges, and also spends some time each year to visit guitar courses abroad. These include one held at the Ithaca College in the USA, where he is the principal teacher.

Miguel Abloniz has not only developed a high reputation as a teacher of the guitar, but over the years he has transcribed around one thousand works for the instrument. Most of these have been published by the Italian publishing firm, Bérben of Ancona.

SELECTED MUSIC

Arietta Medievale	Bèrben	Polo	Ricordi
Blues for Rosy	Bèrben	Prelude and Guitar Bossa	Bèrben
Buleria Gitana	Ricordi	Romantic Bossa	Bèrben
Capriccio Flamenco	Bèrben	Sequential	Bèrben
Chorinho	Ricordi	Tango Andaluz	Ricordi
Cowboy Melody – based on 'Colorado Trail'	Ricordi	Tarantella Burlesca & Bossa Nova	Bèrben
Four Preludes	Ricordi	Three Gitanerías	Ricordi
Four Recreational pieces	Ricordi	Two Ricercari Moderni	Ricordi
Giga	Ricordi	Valsette and Marcetta	Ricordi
Guitar Chôro	Bèrben	Crab Fingering	Bèrben
Guitar Serenade	Ricordi	Essential Exercises for the Left Hand	Bèrben
Improvisation – Homage to Villa-Lobos	Ricordi	Fifty Arpeggios for the Right Hand	Bèrben
An Incorrigible Dreamer	Bèrben	Ten Melodic Studies	Ricordi
Moods	Bèrben	The Twenty-Four Diatonic Scales	Bèrben
Partita in E	Ricordi	Tuning & Fingerboard Rediscovered	Bèrben

---

SELECTED READING
Miguel Abloniz

Article –'Guitar Player' – October 1977

Sergio Abreu

SERGIO ABREU

Born – SERGIO REBELLO ABREU
Rio De Janeiro, Brazil

5th June 1948

Sergio Abreu showed exceptional talent from early childhood. In 1961 he and his brother Eduardo (born 19 September 1949) played for the eminent Argentinian guitarist Aldofina Raitzin Tavora, a former disciple of Andres Segovia. She was so impressed by the brothers' ability that she immediately decided to coach them in advanced technique and musical interpretation.

As a duo the Abreu brothers performed all over the world achieving great success. In the eyes and ears of many critics they were the true successors to the throne of Ida Presti and Alexandre Lagoya.

Life as a professional guitarist did not appeal to Eduardo, and for the past few years Sergio has followed a highly successful career as a soloist. His recent tours have included visits to the United States of America, Australia, the United Kingdom, and most countries of Europe. Wherever he appears Sergio Abreu's performances receive high critical praise. In recent years he has appeared at the Windsor Festival in England where he performed a duo with violinist Yehudi Menuhin, and also at the Guitar '81 Festival in Toronto, Canada. Here he appeared as a performer, judge and teacher. Sergio has also in recent years devoted much of his spare time to the construction of classical guitars, but still remains one of the finest and most active concert guitarists in the world today.

SELECTED RECORDS

The Guitars of Sergio and Eduardo Abreu	CBS	61262
The Guitars of Sergio and Eduardo Abreu	Ace of Diamonds	SDD 219
Two Concerts for Two Guitars	CBS	61469
Sergio Abreu Interprets Paganini and Sor	Ariola	201614

SELECTED READING

Sergio Abreu	Article – 'Guitar' – February 1978
Sergio Abreu	Article – 'Guitar' – January 1979
Sergio Abreu	Article – 'Guitar Player' – July 1980

Dionisio Aguado

DIONISIO AGUADO

Born – DIONISIO AGUADO Y GARCIA, Madrid, Spain
8th April 1784

Died – Madrid, Spain
20th December 1849

Dionisio Aguado was the son of a leading clergyman in Madrid. He showed an early aptitude for music and was taught the rudiments of music by a monk called Basilio in a Madrid college. But it was the renowned singer/guitarist Manuel Garcia to whom Aguado owed his thorough grounding in both music and the guitar.

In 1803 Aguado moved to a small estate which had been left to him by his father, in the village of Fuenlabrada, near Aranjuez. Aguado was there able to devote all his time to an intense study of the guitar and music. The end result was several volumes of studies for the guitar and finally his 'Method for Guitar', which was published in Madrid in 1824. Aguado took up residence once more in Madrid after the end of the French invasion. After the death of his mother, Aguado travelled to Paris in 1825 where his works for guitar were already well known. He decided to return to Spain but took up residence again in Paris, in 1835, for a period of five years. It was during this spell in Paris that Aguado met the great guitar virtuoso Fernando Sor. They developed a strong social and musical friendship, even though their technical approach to the guitar was very different. For a time they lived in the same house in Paris. A sign of the close friendship of these two virtuoso guitarists is the fact that Sor composed a duet for two guitarists, entitled 'Les Deux Amis', which was dedicated to their association.

Aguado used his right hand nails and dazzled his audiences with an amazing technique in direct contrast to the 'no nails' technique of Sor.

In late 1838 Aguado decided to return to his native Spain, and he took up residence once again in Madrid. Here he was to remain until his death in 1849 at the age of sixty-five.

The volume of Aguado's compositions was not as great as his friend and countryman Fernando Sor, but there is no doubt of Aguado's genius, and the lasting qualities of his music. Aguado was also the inventor of an unusual accessory for the guitar called the tripodison. This was a three legged stand on which the guitarist could rest his guitar whilst playing. Aguado claimed his invention increased the volume of the guitar, and also made the guitar easier to play in concert. Despite support for this contraption by several players, including Sor, the tripodison did not gain wide support, becoming extinct within a short period of time.

SELECTED MUSIC

'Allegro and Allegro Vivace'	GA 301
'Allegro brillante'	GA 302
'Easy Waltzes and Studies'	GA 303
'Fandango and Variations, ed Tarrago'	UME
'Selected Works' – facsimile edition, with introduction 'critical commentary'	Chant
'Six Selected Pieces'	GA 55
'Thirty-one little Guitar Works'	N3212
'The Selected Works'	ECH 400

SELECTED READING

'The Tripodison'	Article – 'Guitar Review' No. 39 1974

Laurindo Almeida

LAURINDO ALMEIDA

Born Santos, Brazil

2nd September 1917

Laurindo Almeida received his earliest musical training on the piano from his mother, a concert pianist. On hearing his sister Maria play the guitar, he fell in love with the instrument and decided to master it and give up the piano.

Almeida gave his first public recital on the guitar at the age of 13, and soon made his radio debut at the age of 15. Almeida then gave concerts in Brazil's main cities, following which he became a staff member of one of the country's largest radio stations. He then signed on as a musician on the ocean liner *Cuyaba* for a trip to Europe. During the voyage he heard the legendary gypsy jazz guitarist Django Reinhardt playing in France. The sound of Reinhardt's jazz music was to affect Laurindo's future attitude towards music as a whole.

In 1947 he moved to the United States spending some time in Hollywood working in the film studios. He then became an important member of the Stan Kenton Jazz orchestra. In 1950 Laurindo Almeida left the Kenton orchestra to play a series of solo concerts, and also to devote time to composing. He has now written more than 200 compositions.

Over the years Laurindo Almeida has recorded profusely on the classical guitar for the Capitol and Decca labels. In 1966, he performed two American debut recordings of Radames Gnatalli's 'Concerto De Copacabana' and the Villa Lobos Guitar Concerto.

It was Laurindo Almeida that first brought Bossa Nova to the United States in the 1960's. He has recently formed a new jazz quartet, with saxophonist Bud Shank, which is very similar to the one he had in the 1960's playing modern jazz with a delightful Latin flavour. The new group is entitled the L.A. Four and is achieving great success both in concert and in record sales.

Laurindo Almeida lives in Sherman Oaks, California, and remains one of the busiest and most popular classical guitarists in the United States. There is no doubt that through his enormous output of records, publications and also his concert appearances, Laurindo Almeida has been one of the most influential guitarists on the North American scene for over thirty years.

SELECTED RECORDS

'Guitar Music of Spain'	Capitol	P 8295
'Guitar Music of Latin America'	Capitol	P 8321
'Vista's D'Espana'	Capitol	P 8367
'Danzas'	Capitol	P 8467
'Villa Lobos'	Capitol	P 8497
'Spanish Guitars'	Capitol	P 8521
'From the Romantic Era'	Capitol	DP 8601
'Plays Radames Gnattali'	Capitol	SP 8625
'Virtuoso (With Deltra Eamon)'	Orion	ORS 7260
'Almeida Concerto for Guitar and Orchestra'	Concord	CC 2001

SELECTED READING

Laurindo Almeida	Article – 'Guitar Player' – August 1968
Laurindo Almeida	Article – 'Guitar' – July, 1974
Laurindo Almeida	Article – 'Guitar' – November 1979
Laurindo Almeida	Article – 'Frets' – June 1979

SELECTED MUSIC

Chôro Para Olga	BP 25	The One Minute Divertimento	BP 24
English Air	BP 29	Pavana for Pancho	BP 28
Gypsy Dance	BP 44	Serenata, in Memoriam to Garoto	BP 00
Gypsy Suite on Popular Motives, in 5 Movements	BP 26	Soledad	BP 500
Gypsy Suite, in 5 Movements	BP 27	Sueño	BP 35
Insomnia	BP 23	Two Spanish Folk Songs	BP 45
Lament in Tremolo Form	BP 20		
Mystified	BP 38		

Two scenes of Santiago de Compastella, Spain.

MARIA LUISA ANIDO

Born – ISABEL MARIA LUISA ANIDO
Moron, near Buenos Aires, Argentina

26th January 1907

Maria Luisa Anido

Maria Luisa Anido's father, Don Juan Carlos Anido was the publisher of a magazine 'La Guitarra', this magazine was devoted to guitarists and guitar music. Encouraged by her father she took up the guitar at an early age and studied first with Domingo Prat and then later with Miguel Llobet.

Maria Luisa Anido showed exceptional talent on the guitar at an early age and was to make her first concert debut at the age of ten on the 7th May 1918 in Buenos Aires. Since that time she has continued to give concerts throughout the world. In 1925 she gave a series of duo concerts with her renowned teacher Llobet. Over the years she has made many recordings and broadcasts, particularly in her native Argentina. She was made professor of the guitar in the National Conservatoire of Music in Buenos Aires, and over the past fifty years has taught most of Argentina's finest classical guitarists.

SELECTED RECORDS
'Grand Dame De La Guitare'   ERATO   STU 70722

SELECTED MUSIC
'Impresiones Argentinas – Nine Compositions'   Ricordi

WILFRED APPLEBY

Born – WILFRED MORRISON APPLEBY
Brighton, England

3rd July 1892

Wilfred Appleby

COURTESY WILFRED APPLEBY

For many years Wilfred Appleby was one of the leading personalities on the British classical guitar scene. As editor of 'Guitar News', he kept British guitarists well informed of International and British guitar events and its personalities for over 20 years, following the end of World War II.

Together with his wife Kay, Wilfred Appleby originally decided to take up the study of the guitar to help pass the time during the long nights of World War II. After a period of intense study of books from the public library, and also music obtained through friends in Spain and Argentina, Wilfred Appleby became a proficient player and teacher. He was also acknowledged as an authority of the guitar. He was invited by A. P. Sharpe, the editor of the long established fretted magazine 'B.M.G.', tto write a monthly column on the classical guitar. In a period of over five years he was in fact to write almost 80 articles.

Wilfred Appleby then took an active part in the revived Philharmonic Society of Guitarists in London. He was also very much involved in his own local society in Cheltenham which was formed in 1946. Together with Boris M. Perott, Wilfred Appleby helped to promote the talents of the young guitar prodigy Julian Bream.

In 1951 he decided that the established magazine, 'B.M.G.', did not cater enough for the classical guitar lover. So together with his wife Kay, and a few friends, he formed the International Classical Guitar Association (I.C.G.A.). He also produced the first copies of 'Guitar News' which was to provide an excellent service to its readers all over the world until it ceased publication in 1973. Wilfred Appleby also gave occasional recitals on the guitar, and was often called upon to give lectures about the instrument. All his work for the guitar was a labour of love, both the Guitar Society and 'Guitar News' were run on a non-profit basis.

Today Wilfred Appleby continues a very active life from his home in Cheltenham, England. Throughout his life he has been a man of many talents – a painter, poet, writer, Esperanto expert and philatelist. He still retains a great interest in all these subjects, and of course the guitar.

SELECTED READING

'B.M.G.' Regular articles
'Guitar News' Regular articles
'Guitar Review' Various articles
'The Evolution of the Classical Guitar' Wilfred M. Appleby – I.C.G.A. (1966)

JULIAN ARCAS

Born – Almeria, Spain
25th October 1832

Died Antequera, Malaga, Spain
16th February 1882

Julian Arcas

Julian Arcas, a virtuoso guitarist, was one of the most important figures in Spanish music of the nineteenth century. The music he performed was based mainly on traditional Spanish folk and flamenco melodies.

During the years 1860-70 Arcas was at the height of his career as a recitalist. He made lengthy and highly successful concert tours of Spain and the rest of Europe. In 1862 he performed for the British Royal family in Brighton, England.

In 1864 Julian Arcas made his name in Barcelona, Spain, and then appeared in several concerts throughout Spain with a young pianist called Patanas. By 1870 Arcas was tired of travelling and settled once again in his native city of Almeria. There he established a business in the Calle Granada.

Julian Arcas then became very interested in guitar construction and co-operated with the famed guitar maker Torres of Seville in developing the instrument. After ten years in business in Almeria Arcas decided to retire to Antequera, Malaga, where he died soon after, at the age of fifty, in 1832.

Julian Arcas, one of Spain's great nineteenth century guitar virtuosi, was also a highly respected and prolific composer of national melodies and dances which he arranged for the guitar.

SELECTED MUSIC

El Delirio – Fantasía	UME
El Fagot – Waltz (Oliva)	Ricordi
Jota Aragonesa	Ricordi
Los Panaderos – Bolero	Ricordi
Soleá de Concierto	Ricordi
Spanish Guitar Music, ed. Benko	EMB

Alice Artzt

ALICE ARTZT

Born – New York, U.S.A.

16th March 1943

Alice Artzt

COURTESY ALICE ARTZT

Alice Artzt showed exceptional musical talent from an early age. After studying the piano and the flute, Alice turned to the classical guitar at the age of thirteen. Her first important teacher was Alexander Bellow in New York City. She was later to study in France with Ida Presti and Alexandre Lagoya, and then in England with Julian Bream. She also studied composition with Darius Milhaud, and did graduate work in composition and musicology at Barnard College, Columbia University, N.Y.C.

Since her international debut, Alice Artzt has toured Europe extensively twice a year, and also performed throughout North America. She has also made concert tours in most other continents of the world. Alice Artzt has had works dedicated to her by several well known composers including John W. Duarte and Guido Santorsola. In recent years she was chosen to play special recitals in London, England, for the 75th birthday of Sir Lennox Berkeley, and also the 60th birthday of John W. Duarte.

SELECTED RECORDS

Classic Guitar	Gemini	GME 1018
Original Works	Gemini	GME 1019
Plays Fernando Sor	Meridian	E77 066
Plays Tarrega	Meridian	E77 026
English Guitar Music	Meridian	E77 037
'Romantic Virtuoso Guitar Music'	Hyperion	A66040

SELECTED READING

Alice Artzt	Article – 'Guitar' – August 1973
Alice Artzt	Article – 'Guitar' – November 1977
Alice Artzt	Article – 'Guitar Player' – May 1979

JOSÉ DE AZPIAZU

Born – Onante, Spain

26th May 1912

Jose De Azpiazu

Born in the Basque region of Spain, José De Azpiazu began to study the guitar at the age of thirteen. His first teacher was his uncle. Whilst a teenager, Azpiazu was asked to give recitals at the festivals in San Sebastian. He met with considerable success as a guitarist at these recitals, but still decided to devote most of his spare time to his other talent, painting. He won the first prize for designing and painting at the School of Modern Arts in San Sebastian in 1929. He was also active in the Basque Folklore Society.

It was not until he was twenty-four years old that Azpiazu made his debut on Radio Bilbao. He then started his professional career as a guitarist. Azpiazu soon gave up his other activities and devoted all his time to his career as a concert guitarist. He toured Spain extensively for many years, but due to World War II, it was not until 1950 that he performed abroad. He had a very successful concert tour of Switzerland which included several radio broadcasts.

Whilst in Geneva he befriended the painter Andres Segovia junior, who was to introduce the guitarist to his father. Segovia was so impressed with Azpiazu that on his recommendation the Professorship of Guitar at the College of Music in Geneva was bestowed upon José De Azpiazu. A prolific arranger and composer of guitar music, Azpiazu's 'Suite in C' won first prize in the 1954 International Competition held in Modena, Italy.

SELECTED MUSIC

Cachucha	Ricordi
Cubana	Ricordi
Fandanguillo de Huelva	Ricordi
Five Iberian Miniatures for Guitar	Ricordi
Jota – On Popular Themes	Ricordi
Minué del Baztán Errimina – Nostalgie	Ricordi
Six Children's Stories	Ricordi
Theme with Variations – Hommage to Sor	Ricordi
Tonadilla – Hommage to Granados	Ricordi

SELECTED READING

'Guitars and Guitarists'   José de Azpiazu, Ricordi 1960

ANTONIO CARLOS BARBOSA-LIMA

Born – San Paulo, Brazil

17th December 1944

Antonio Carlos Barbosa-Lima began to play the guitar at the age of nine. His teachers were Isaias Savio and B. Moreira. By the time he was thirteen years old Barbosa-Lima was regarded as a child prodigy, and had in fact already made a successful recording of Brazilian music.

At the age of twelve Barbosa-Lima made his concert debuts in San Paulo and Rio de Janeiro. He then travelled to the U.S.A. made his concert New York debut, in March 1972, at the Alice Tulley Hall. Since that time he has made extensive tours of North America, South America and Europe. He made his debut in Paris in March 1974, during the International week of the guitar, and in June 1979, he was the first guitarist to participate at the 'Festival Casals' in Puerto Rico, performing as a soloist and also with an orchestra.

Since that time Barbosa-Lima has continued to give concerts throughout the world. He is also now widely recognized for his transcriptions of works by Scarlatti, Bach and Handel. Barbosa-Lima has had works written and dedicated to him by well known contemporary composers including Francisco Mignone, Leonardo Balada, Guido Santorsola, Albert Harris, and John Duarte. Barbosa-Lima has also conducted over the past few years many master classes and guitar seminars in the United States, Europe and South America. He was recently artist-in-residence at the Carnegie-Mellon Institute in Pittsburgh, U.S.A.

Antonio Carlos Barbosa Lima

COURTESY SHAW CONCERTS INC.   PHOTO CHRISTIAN STEINER

SELECTED RECORDS

'Des De Dos Magicos Num Violao De Ouro'	Chantecler	CLP 1001
'O Menino E O Violao'	Chantecler	CMG 1004
'A Scarlatti Guitar Recital'		ABC/ATS 20005
'Mignone – 12 Guitar Studies'	Philips (Brazil)	6598-312

SELECTED READING

Carlos Barbosa-Lima	Article – 'Guitar' – July 1973

Agustin Barrios Mangore

AGUSTIN BARRIOS MANGORÉ

Born – San Juan Bautista De Las Misiones, Paraguay
5th May 1885

Died – San Salvador, El Salvador
7th August 1944

In recent years, almost forty years after his death, full recognition is finally being given to the genius of the Paraguayan guitar virtuoso Agustin Barrios Mangoré.

One of eight children, Barrios was born into a musical family. He began to play the guitar at an early age and was able to use the instrument to study harmony at his school. Barrios' first formal teacher was Gustavo Sosa Escalda. He introduced the young guitarist to the music of Sor, Tarrega, Aguado and other composers of the established guitar repertoire. By the time he was thirteen years old, Barrios was recognised as a prodigy. He was awarded a scholarship to the Colegio Nacional in Asuncion. There he studied calligraphy (he was a fine graphic artist), and also achieved high results in mathematics, journalism and literature.

In 1910 Barrios, already established as a guitar virtuoso, left Paraguay and went to Argentina. Over the next thirty-four years he toured the South American Continent giving concerts in the major cities and towns of Argentina, Uruguay, Brazil, Venezuela, Costa Rica and El Salvador. He also visited Chile, Mexico, Guatemala, Honduras, Panama, Columbia, Cuba and Haiti. Between 1934-1936 the great guitar virtuoso also visited Europe playing in England, Spain, Germany and Belgium.

It was in 1932 that Barrios began to call himself Nitsuga Mangore – the Paganini of the guitar. Nitsuga (Agustin spelt backwards) and Mangoré (the name of a legendary Guarani chieftain).

By the mid 1930s Barrios was suffering from a bad heart condition and could not continue long strenious concert tours. He was to live his last years in El Salvador teaching, composing and giving occasional guitar recitals.

As well as being an outstanding player, Barrios was a composer of over three hundred works for the guitar, many of which are now accepted as some of the finest guitar solos ever written.

SELECTED RECORDS

'Agustin Barrios Mangoré' – Original Recordings (2 LPs)	El Maestro	EM 8002
'Agustin Barrios Recordings' – Vol. 3'	El Maestro	EM 8002 V3
'Gentil Montana plays Barrios'	Leguiz	67-368
'John Williams plays Barrios'	CBS	CBS 76662
'Jesus Benites plays Barrios' (2 LPs)	Globo	402-403

SELECTED READING

Agustin Barrios	Article – 'Guitar' – July 1974	
Agustin Barrios	Article – 'Guitar Player' – January 1978	
Agustin Barrios	Illustrated biography – Richard Stover with El Maestro Record Set	EM 8002

SELECTED MUSIC

Barrios Mangoré	
Vol. 1, 23 selections	Zen-On
Vol. 2, 25 selections	Zen-On
Vol. 3, 25 selections	Zen-On
Chôro da Saudade	Bèrben
Contemplación	Belwin Mills – SI 157
Cueca, ed. Stover	Belwin Mills – SI 156
Danza Paraguaya, ed. Díaz	ZA 5296
El Ultimo Canto, rev. Ranalli	Bèrben
The Guitar Works of Agustin Barrios Mangoré (3 volumes)	Belwin Mills
La Catedral	Belwin Mills – SI 154
Maxime	Belwin Mills – SI 155
Medallón Antiguo – Homage to Pergolesi	ZA 5315
Oración	ZA 5263
Preludio, Op. 5, No. 1	Ricordi
Three Paraguayan Dances	Belwin Mills – SI 152
Un Sueño en la Floresta	Belwin Mills – SI 158
Vals, Op. 8, No. 3	Belwin Mills – SI 153

Manuel Barrueco

MANUEL BARRUECO

Born – Santiago, Cuba

1952

Without doubt one of the greatest guitarists of the twentieth century, Manuel Barrueco began his guitar studies, at the age of eight, under the tutelage of Manuel Puig. He was soon enrolled in the Esteban Salas Conservatory, where he continued his early training.

In 1967 Barrueco's family moved to the United States where the young guitarist continued his studies with Juan Mercadal in Miami and Rey De La Torre in New York. Four years later he entered the Peabody Conservatory in Baltimore. He was a full scholarship student (studying under Aaron Shearer), a soloist with the Peabody Orchestra, and a winner of the Peabody competition – the first

guitarist to achieve any of these three honours. As a result, his New York debut followed the same year at the Carnegie Recital Hall, and this was an enormous success.

Since that time success has followed success for Manuel Barrueco. He has given highly acclaimed concerts throughout the United States, Canada, Europe and the United Kingdom. He has recorded three outstanding records for the Vox-Turnabout record company. Since 1975 he has been on the faculty of the Manhattan School of Music, where he was one of the co-founders of the guitar department.

SELECTED RECORDS

'Works for Guitar' – Villa – Lobos, Guarnieri, Chavez'	Turnabout	TV 34676
'Albeniz/Granados – Spanish Dances'	Turnabout	TV 34738
'Manuel Barrueco plays Scarlatti/Paganini'	Turnabout	TV 347

SELECTED READING

Manuel Barrueco	Article – 'Guitar' – June 1979
Manuel Barrueco	Article – 'Guitar and Lute' – January 1981
Manuel Barrueco	Article – 'Guitarra' – July 1979
Manuel Barrueco	Article – 'Guitar Player' – October 1980

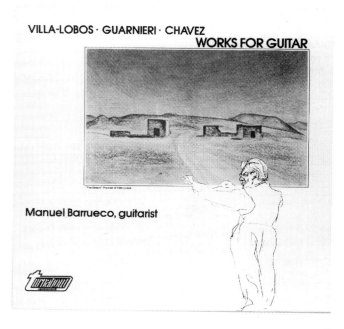

RENÉ BARTOLI

Born – Marseilles, France

1941

Rene Bartoli

The guitar was an established feature of the Bartoli household, and René Bartoli began his studies on the instrument at an early age. His first tutor was an uncle, and Bartoli made such great progress that he decided to make the guitar his career.

In 1959 Bartoli won the 'Concours Internationale De La Guitarre' competition organized by ORTF (French radio and television). Following on this success he was able to study with Andres Segovia, Ida Presti and Alexandre Lagoya.

In 1960 René Bartoli gave his first recital in his native town, Marseilles. Over the next few years he was to give many guitar recitals throughout France but was rarely heard in concert in other countries. He was appointed Professor of Guitar at the Marseilles Conservatoire in 1965, a position he still holds.

Bartoli has made several recordings for the French record company Harmonia Mundi, and is currently one of France's most influential guitarists.

SELECTED RECORDS

'René Bartoli'	RCA	LSB 4032
'Guitare 1'	Harmonia Mundi	HMV 572
'Guitare 2'	Harmonia Mundi	HMV 583
'Guitare 3'	Harmonia Mundi	HMV 751
'Music for Flute and Guitar'	Odyssey	321 60218

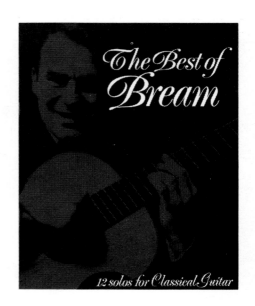

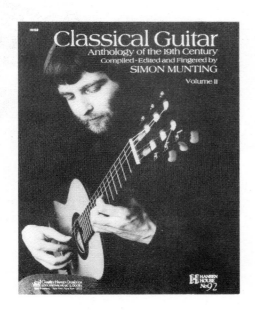

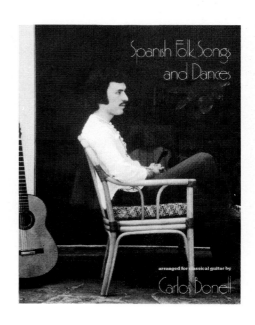

Prominent classical guitarists illustrated on six music covers.

Siegfried Behrend

SIEGFRIED BEHREND

Born – Berlin, Germany

19th November 1933

Siegfried Behrend's father was a guitarist who taught at a conservatory in Berlin. As a student at the age of sixteen, Behrend entered the same conservatory to study the piano, composition and conducting. Whilst he was there the young musician began to take a close interest in the guitar. His father recommended him to a guitar teacher and within a year Siegfried Behrend had given his first public concert.

Behrend decided to gain experience and knowledge of his instrument by embarking on an extensive concert tour of Germany. At the age of twenty-one he toured throughout Italy and two years later throughout Spain. Since that time Siegfried

Behrend has given concerts in most countries throughout the world including the Soviet Union.

Behrend has also recorded extensively for the prestigious 'Deutsche Grammophon' label and has had many of his original compositions and transcriptions published. He has taken a particular interest in Avant Garde music for the classical guitar. Regarded very highly as a teacher of his chosen instrument, Behrend holds a music festival annually at the Rosenburg Castle near Regensburg in Germany. At this festival guitarists from all over the world join in Siegfried Behrend's international master courses in the art of guitar playing.

SELECTED RECORDS

'Two Guitar Concertos – Rodrigo/Tedesco'	Deutsche Gramophon	139 166
'Siegfried Behrend Guitar'	Deutsche Gramophon	139 167
'Deutsche Guitarren Musik'	Deutsche Gramophon	139 377
'Altitalienische Guitaren Konzerte'	Deutsche Gramophon	139 417
'Guitar and Percussion'	Deutsche Gramophon	2530 034
'English Guitar Music'	Deutsche Gramophon	2530 079
'Chitarra Italiana'	Deutsche Gramophon	2530 561
'Treasures for Guitar'	Supraphon	50 780
'Guitarra Olé'	EMI Electrola	SHZE 383
'Meister Werke Fur Zwei Guitarren' (with Martin Kruger)	Acanta	DC 23 098
'Sinfonische Folklore'	Colloseum	SM 570

SELECTED MUSIC

Fantasía Malagueñita	JWC
Granadina de la Rambla	JWC
Postkarten – Suite No. 1 (7 easy pieces)	ZM 1896
Six Monodien (1974) (Modern)	ZM 1907
Three Spanish Dances	ZM 1802
Zorongo para Murao	JWC

ALEXANDER BELLOW

BORN – Russia
1912

Died – Sherman, Conneticut, U.S.A.
12th March 1976

Alexander Bellow was a Russian born, naturalised American citizen. A graduate of the Moscow Conservatory, Bellow majored in composition and conducting, and was awarded a degree of Doctor of Music with honours. Bellow also studied painting and engineering. During World War II he was imprisoned by the Germans in a concentration camp. He managed to survive and emigrated to the United States of America in 1949 with his wife Mura, and daughter Natasha.

As a classical guitarist Bellow performed in the United States and abroad both as a solo recitalist and as part of a chamber group. On the advice of Andres Segovia he decided to devote his musical talents to teaching. Alexander Bellow's greatest contribution to the guitar was as a teacher, and also as a transcriber of many early guitar compositions from the original tablature. Almost one hundred of his original compositions were published and he was also instrumental in forming the first U.S.A. Guitar Orchestra in New York.

His book 'The Illustrated History of the Guitar' (Franco Colombo Inc. 1970) is now accepted as one of the standard works for the study of the instrument, and is highly recommended reading for the guitar enthusiast.

Alexander Bellow

COURTESY C. E. H. SMITH

SELECTED MUSIC

Arpeggiato	Kerby
Cavatina	Hansen
Preludio e Toccata	Kerby
Prelude, Scherzetto and Fugue	Hansen
Scherzando	Kerby
Sonata for Guitar	FC 2794
Sonata II for Guitar	Kerby
Sonatina II	Hansen
Suite Provençale	Hansen
Tales of the Alhambra – As told by Washington Irving	Kerby
Variations on a theme of Mudarra	Kerby

SELECTED READING
'The Illustrated History of the Guitar' – Alexander Bellow Franco Colombo Inc. 1970

HECTOR BERLIOZ

Born – La Cote Saint Andre, near Grenoble, France
11th December 1803

Died – Paris, France
8th March 1869

The popularity of the music of the great nineteenth century composer Hector Berlioz continues to grow at an increasing rate, yet it is amazing how few musicians and music lovers, even today, realize that the guitar was the only instrument on which Berlioz was really proficient.

Berlioz's father encouraged him in his music studies from an early age, first on the flute and flageolet, and then the guitar. He studied, together with his elder sister, with a teacher named Dorant. At the age of eighteen Berlioz was sent by his parents to Paris to study medicine. He was soon to discover that medicine was not for him and he decided to make music his life. The decision upset his father who promptly stopped his maintenance. Berlioz was therefore forced to earn his living teaching the guitar, as well as the flute. He wrote several studies and variations for the guitar and these were published by Aulagnior in Paris during this period.

In 1830 Berlioz won the 'Prix De Rome' at the Conservatoire of Music, where he studied under Lesueur. This success earned him a government grant for three years further study in Rome.

The following years saw the full development of Berlioz the composer. He befriended Mendelssohn and Paganini amongst many other fine musicians and composers. His very distinctive style of composition and orchestration has been attributed by some authorities to the fact that the guitar and the flute were the only instruments he ever mastered.

During Berlioz's lifetime the influence of his music was mainly on Russian composers although Liszt, Wagner and their successors borrowed and developed his new orchestral sound.

In his famous 'Treatise on Instrumentation and Orchestration' five pages are devoted to the guitar and mandolin. Berlioz's last guitar is now in the museum of the National Conservatoire of Music in Paris. This guitar, made by Grobert of Mirecourt (1794-1869), was originally owned by Nicolo Paganini and bears the signatures of both its famous owners.

SELECTED READING
'Memoirs – 1865' (translated David Cairns 1969) – Hector Berlioz
'Treatise on Instrumentation and Orchestration' – Hector Berlioz

Portrait of Hector Berlioz with his guitar on a French ten franc bank-note.

GILBERT BIBERIAN

Born – Istanbul, Turkey

19th February 1944

Gilbert Biberian

Gilbert Biberian came to live in England where he studied the guitar and composition at Trinity College of Music in London graduating in 1968. In 1965 a French government grant took him to France to study with Ida Presti and Alexandre Lagoya. He continued his work with this legendary guitar duo until Ida Presti's untimely death in 1967.

After leaving Trinity College Biberian studied interpretation with pianist Anthony Kinsella for three years. Following a successful debut in the Wigmore Hall, he was invited to work with the London Sinfonietta and Pierre Boulez, Luciano Berio, the Nash Ensemble, the BBC Symphony Orchestra and many others. Biberian has also played at the Proms and at Covent Garden (where he played the guitar part in Tippett's 'King Priam') and has performed concertos and given solo recitals on numerous other occasions.

While continuing to be in demand as a soloist, Gilbert Biberian found time to create and direct two guitar ensembles, the Omega Players and the Omega Guitar Quartet. Both groups stimulated much original composition and made a substantial contribution to contemporary music. Since 1973 the Omega Guitar Quartet has gained international acclaim for its performances.

Gilbert Biberian has taught and lectured extensively, both in the United Kingdom and abroad. He has directed the ensemble workshop in Guitar '75 and Guitar '78 at Toronto – North America's most influential guitar festival – and in Guitar '78 he was also a member of the panel of adjudicators.

Gilbert Biberian studied composition with James Patten, Elisabeth Lutyens and Hans Keller. Since 1965 he has produced more than 80 compositions, not only for solo and ensemble guitar but also for the voice and for various combinations of other instruments, including a concerto, two song cycles and a sonata for flute and guitar. His guitar compositions are becoming part of the standard repertoire and are being performed widely. His works have been published in England, Italy, Holland and the U.S.A. He is currently editor of the guitar series published by publishers J. & W. Chester.

SELECTED RECORDS		
'Omega Guitar Quartet'	President	PTLS 1066

SELECTED READING		
Gilbert Biberian	Article – 'Guitar' – August 1972	
Gilbert Biberian	Article – 'Guitar' – December 1976	

SELECTED MUSIC	
Greek Suite	B1140
Monogram – to Michael Lorimer	Waterloo
Prelude & Fugue	Novello
Sonata No. 3	G 122

VAHDA OLCOTT BICKFORD

Born – ETHEL LUCRETIA OLCOTT, Norwalk, Ohio, U.S.A.
17th October 1885

Died – Los Angeles, U.S.A.
18th May 1980

As a child Vahda Olcott Bickford lived in Los Angeles where she showed an early gift for music. She began her study of the guitar at the age of eight and became one of the last pupils of the renowned teacher Manuel Ferrer (1828-1904). She proved to be an outstanding pupil and was to give many successful concerts throughout the United States of America.

Olcott went to New York in 1914, and soon became known through her concerts and teaching of the guitar. By invitation she lived for a time with the famous Vanderbilt family at Biltmore. There she taught Mrs. Vanderbilt and her daughter, Cornelia, to play the guitar. It was whilst she was in New York that Bickford became associated with world famous astrologer Evangeline Adams, and was her only assistant for nine years, adopting her new name of 'Vahda'.

In 1915 she married another outstanding North American guitarist/mandolinist and musician, Zarh Myron Bickford. They lived and worked together in New York, finally moving to Los Angeles in 1923. During her stay on the East Coast of the U.S.A. Vahda Olcott Bickford established herself as an outstanding guitar soloist and teacher.

In 1923 she was instrumental in founding the American Guitar Society in Los Angeles. There is little doubt that through her promotional efforts, and her transcriptions of music for the guitar, Bickford was one of the most influential figures in the North American classical guitar scene during the first fifty years of this century.

Vahdah Olcott Bickford

COURTESY C. E. H. SMITH

Vahda Olcott Bickford died at the age of ninety-four in 1980. She spent her last years still devoted to the guitar, both teaching and giving her expert advice to musicologists and historians of the guitar. She continued to give concerts with her husband Zarh until his death in 1961. Bickford continued as a solo artist until her last concert at an American Guitar Society meeting in 1977. She is survived by her second husband, Robert Revere.

SELECTED MUSIC
Olcott-Bickford Method for Guitar Oliver Ditson, Philadelphia, 1921

Ernesto Bitteti

ERNESTO BITETTI

Born – ERNESTO GUILLERMO BITETTI
Rosario, Argentina

1943

Ernesto Bitetti began his studies at the age of five in his native Argentina. He continued his musical education at the Instituto Superior de la Musica Universidad Nacional del Litoral, from which he graduated with the highest honours in 1964. In 1961 he was awarded First Prize in the 18th Concurso de la Sociedad Hebraica Argentina de Buenos Aires for stringed instrument playing, and in 1962 he reached the finals of the 'Coupe Internationale de Guitarre' in Paris, France. In addition to the guitar, Bitetti has also studied conducting, choral music, piano, flute and composition.

Since his initial and immediate successes, Bitetti has continued to tour annually throughout Europe, the Soviet Union, Central and South America, the United States, Canada, Japan, Israel, New Zealand, India, the Far East and South Africa.

Ernesto Bitetti has appeared as soloist with leading orchestras including the English, Israel and Munich Chamber Orchestras, and also with leading symphony orchestras throughout Europe, the Far East, North and South America, Australia and South Africa. He has given joint recitals with Teresa Berganza in Vienna, and appeared at the Festivals of Edinburgh and Aix en Provence. During his 1980-81 United States tour, Ernesto Bitetti played in concert and recitals coast to coast, including a performance at the Kennedy Centre for the Performing Arts.

Many leading composers have written works expressly for Bitetti including Mario Castelnuovo-Tedesco, Joaquin Rodrigo, John Duarte, Frederick Moreno Torroba, José Buenagu, Anton Garcia Abril, and Angelo Gilardino. With the Saint Louis Symphony Orchestra, Bitetti premiered the 'Concerto para la Guitara Criolla' by de los Rios, and in New York City's Town Hall, Bitetti also appeared with violinist Ruggiero Ricci in the world premiere of 'Dio Concerto, No. 2', a piece written specifically for the Occasion by the contemporary Spanish composer, Tomas Marco.

Now residing in Madrid, Ernesto Bitetti is a major recording artist for the Hispavox label.

SELECTED RECORDS

'Musica Contemporanea'	Hispavox	HHS 10-304
'Bach/Weiss Suites'	Hispavox	HHS 10-331
'Rodrigo Concerto'	Hispavox	HHS 10-335
'Musicas Espagnoles'	Hispavox	HHS 10-344
'Four Centuries of Spanish Guitar Music'	Hispavox	HHS 10-365
'Four Centuries of Italian Guitar Music'	Hispavox	HHS 10-400
'Halffter Concerto'	Hispavox	HHS 10-420
'Waldove De Los Rios Concerto'	Hispavox	HHS 10-429
'Encores'	Hispavox	HHS 10-450
'Albeniz'	Hispavox	HHS 10-460
'Paganini Guitare/Violin Works' (With R. Ricci)	Hispavox	HHS 10-473
'Grandes Exitos'	Hispavox	S-60-135
'Rodrigo Concerto De Aranjuez'	Hispavox	S-60-157
'Manuel De Falla'	Hispavox	S-60-207
'Ernesto Bitteti plays Vivaldi'	Hispavox	S60-687

DIEGO BLANCO

Born – Palma De Mallorca, Spain

2nd June 1951

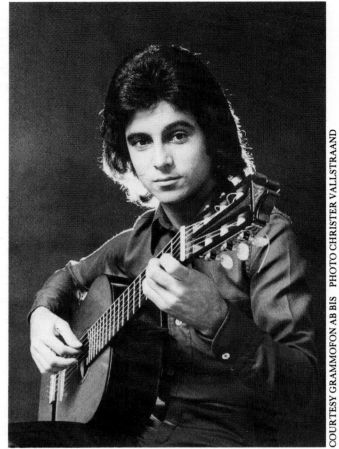

Diego Blanco

Diego Blanco started to learn the guitar at the age of eight with his uncle. Later he studied with guitarist/teacher Dan Greenholm, a pupil of Emilio Pujol and Andres Segovia.

Whilst learning the guitar Blanco was also taught the piano, and the theory and history of music, by the Spanish composer and pianist Lorenso Galmes. At the age of eleven Diego Blanco gave a series of concerts throughout Spain, but his real debut as a recitalist of importance was in Stockholm, Sweden in 1968 where he enjoyed enormous success.

Since that time Diego Blanco has given many concerts in Scandanavia, Spain, Italy, England, Eastern Europe and the Soviet Union. He has appeared in numerous television and radio programmes in these countries and several composers have dedicated works to the young guitarist including Koch, Karkoff, Ravtavayara, Santorsola and Saeverud.

In 1979 Diego Blanco won the important International Guitar competition – 'Queen Sofia's Competition' in Madrid, Spain. He has made several recordings for the Swedish company BIS.

SELECTED RECORDS

'Blanco Plays Ponce/Sojo/Lauro/Barrias'	BIS	LP 33
'Blanco Plays Fernando Sor'	BIS	LP 133
'Guitarra Espanola'	RCA (Spain)	LSC 16359

Philharmonic Society of Guitarists, London, 1947, Julian Bream is third from right in front row. On his right Dr. Boris Perott.

Andres Segovia (right) and Vladimir Bobri (left) at the Guitar Review celebration honoring Segovia's 80th birthday, 21 February, 1973.

VLADAMIR BOBRI

Born – Kharkov, Ukraine

13th May, 1898

Vladamir Bobri was brought up in a family atmosphere of culture and scholarship, and he acquired an adventuresome attitude toward life and art. He is a graduate of the Imperial Art School of Kharkov, where he became interested in the theatre and in early Ikon painting. He studied scenic design by apprenticeship at the State Dramatic Theatre. Because of the turbulent events of the Revolution, Bobri fled from Russia in 1917, leaving his homeland forever.

In Constantinople (Istanbul), Vladamir Bobri designed sets and costumes for the Russian ballet, produced movie posters, and painted Ikons in a monastery; in Anatolia (Turkey), he engaged in archeological work. Then, in 1921, he went to the USA and settled in New York, where he has become known for his imaginative murals, advertising art, and book illustrations.

Although Bobri is a painter, he has a secondary, almost equal love for music, especially for the music of the guitar. In 1936 he was a founding member of the Society of the Classic Guitar, an organisation that was to have far-reaching influences on the growth of interest in the guitar in this country. Since 1948, he has been editor and art director of 'The Guitar Review'. He is the author of many essays on subjects related to the classic guitar and has composed a number of works for the instrument.

On 31st August 1972, Vladamir Bobri was named 'Puntius Counselor at Large Efficientior' to 'Musica en Compostela', that unique organisation devoted to the study and interpretation of the music of Spain, located in Santiago de Compostela. The honour, in the form of a beautifully illuminated parchment, was given in consideration of his outstanding contribution to the appreciation of the classical guitar through his Presidency of The Society of the Classic Guitar and his work as editor of 'The Guitar Review'.

On 10th January, 1973, Vladamir Bobri was decorated with the Cross of Isabel la Catolica with the rank of Knight-Commander (Comendador). This important decoration was bestowed in recognition of his lifelong achievements as a designer, painter, art director, composer and writer, and for his utilization of these talents to make others more keenly aware of the richness of Spanish culture. Presentation of the cross was made by H. E. Alberto Lopez Herce, Consul General of Spain in New York, at a ceremony attended by Spanish dignitaries, including Andres Segovia.

Vladamir Bobri is without doubt one of the most important guitar personalities of the twentieth century.

SELECTED READING
'Guitar Review' – Regular contributor and editor

SELECTED MUSIC

Very Easy Pieces	FC
Complete Study of Tremelo	FC 3046
Eight Melodic Exercises	NY 2604
130 Daily Studies for the Classical Guitar	FCS 2605

PHILIP JAMES BONE

**Born – Luton, England
29th January, 1873**

**Died – Luton, England
17th June 1964**

Philip Bone

One of the leading personalities on the fretted instrument scene of Great Britain for many years, Philip James Bone, F.R.S.A., M.R.S.T., was born in Luton on 29th January 1873. Educated and trained for the Scholastic profession, it was during his early days as a teacher that Bone became attracted to the mandolin and guitar. At first he played as a pastime, with no serious intent, but his interest in these instruments developed into a passion and he came to London to study under G. B. Marchisio, Professor of Mandolin and Guitar at the Trinity College of Music.

His progress was phenomenal and he was chosen to give the first performance in England of two of Beethoven's compositions for mandolin and piano 'Sonata' and 'Adagio' at Trinity College in London.

He was awarded the Medal of the Royal Society of Arts for mandolin playing, and then followed one of the longest and most distinguished careers in the history of fretted instruments.

He was Founder and Conductor of the Luton Mandolin Orchestra for forty years. Under his direction the orchestra gained high honours in the international sphere and was probably the first British mandolin orchestra to play on the Continent. He conducted 'The Trocadero' by request before the President of France in Paris in 1909.

His publications 'The Guitar and Mandolin' and 'Biographies of Celebrated Composers and Players' are world renowned and he made contributions to 'Cadenza', 'Keynotes', 'B.M.G.' and other musical journals. The numerous honours conferred on him included election to Fellowship of the Royal Society of Arts and membership of the Royal Society of Teachers.

In 1951 the British Federation of Banjoists, Mandolinists and Guitarists, then in its 22nd year, elected him its President – an office he held for 13 years.

SELECTED READING
'The Guitar and Mandolin   Philip J. Bone   Schott (1914 and 1954 revised)

Niibori Guitar Orchestra

Carlos Bonell

CARLOS BONELL

Born – CARLOS ANTONIO BONELL

23rd July 1949

Carlos Bonell was born in London of Spanish parents in 1949. At the age of five he began to play the guitar: his first interest was Spanish folk music, but by the age of seven he had already decided firmly on the classical repertoire – by studying both guitar and violin. Carlos' first teacher was his father, a keen amateur guitarist. His first public appearance was as a guitarist at the age of 10, and from the age of 13 he dedicated himself exclusively to the guitar. He continued his studies at the Royal College of Music in London where he was invited to teach immediately upon completing his studies there in 1972.

The first major break-through in his career came with his nomination as a 'Young Musician '73' by the Arts Council Arts Association. This led to many concerts throughout the United Kingdon including appearance at the Camden, City of London, Brighton and Harrogate festivals. After his first concert appearance with the Royal Philharmonic Orchestra in the Royal Festival Hall came invitations from many great orchestras including the London Symphony, the Halle, the Amsterdam Chamber Orchestra and the Philharmonia. And in 1975 came the first of many hundreds of concerts in Europe and America, including the New York 'Mostly Mozart', the Flanders' and the Israel Festivals.

Apart from his recital and concerto work Carlos Bonell's enthusiasm for chamber music has led to many memorable performances with such artists as Pinchas Zuckerman, John Williams, Teresa Berganza and Lynn Harrel.

His recent record releases include a recital disc for Decca (with the first recording of Tarrega's unpublished 'Traviata' fantasia), and the first Digital recording of Rodrigo's Aranjuez concerto.

SELECTED RECORDS

'Guitar Music of Spain'	Enigma	VAR 1015
'Guitar Music of the Baroque'	Enigma	VAR 1050
'Guitar Showpieces'	Decca	SXL 6950
'Rodrigo's Aranjuez/Fantasia'	Decca	SXDL 7523

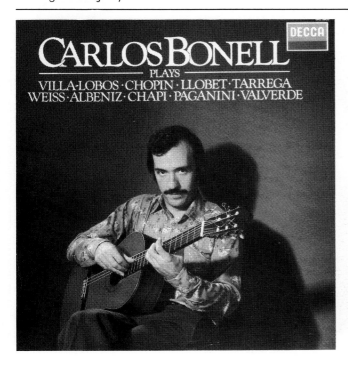

Liona Boyd

LIONA BOYD

Born – London, England

1952

Born in London, England, Liona Boyd is now a Canadian citizen. Her father, a psychologist/sculptor first moved to Canada in 1958, but returned to England for a short while, finally settling in Canada in 1962.

The young guitarist first took a serious interest in the instrument at the age of 14, after hearing a concert given by Julian Bream. Liona Boyd then began to take lessons with the noted Toronto teacher Eli Kassner and soon showed remarkable progress. At the age of 17 she was accepted into a master class given by Julian Bream in Stratford, Ontario.

In 1968 Liona Boyd attended the University of Toronto, and in 1972 graduated with a Bachelor's degree in music and performance. A little later she won the Canadian National Music Competition Award for the guitar. Following on this achievement Liona Boyd became a pupil of Alexandre Lagoya, both in Canada and later in Paris, France. She stayed in Europe for a year and a half and on her return to Canada, in 1974, signed a recording contract with Boot Records. Her first release for this label was highly successful. A concert tour of Canada followed with the popular artist Gordon Lightfoot. This exposed Miss Boyd's classical guitar ability to a much wider audience, and since that time she has been one of the busiest guitarists in North America.

In the last few years Liona Boyd has become a major recording artist for the CBS label. She has appeared in concerts throughout North America both as a soloist, and also with the legendary Nashville guitarist, Chet Atkins.

SELECTED RECORDS

'Guitar Artistry of Liona Boyd'	London	CS 7068
'Liona Boyd'	CBS	73879
'Spanish Fantasy'	CBS	M36675
'Miniatures for Guitar'	CBS	M36732

SELECTED READING

Liona Boyd	Article – 'Guitar Player' – October 1978
Liona Boyd	Article – 'Frets' – December 1980
Liona Boyd	Article – 'Guitarra' – March 1980

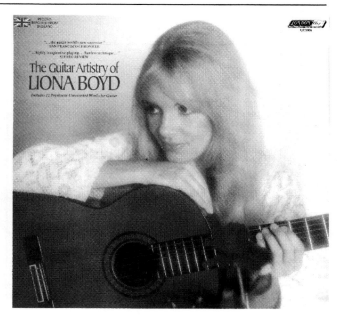

FREDERICK BRAND

Born – Regensburg, Germany 1806

Died – Wurzburg, Germany 1874

Frederick Brand

Regarded by many as one of the great guitar virtuosi of the nineteenth century, Frederick Brand was known mainly in his native land, Germany.

He was originally a teacher in Mannheim, but after his marriage he moved to Wurzburg. Here he met the guitar virtuoso Adam Darr, and together these two great guitarists obtained a lot of engagements as a guitar duo and also as soloists. Both guitarists received high critical acclaim wherever they went.

Frederick Brand, as well as being a highly talented player, was a most respected teacher of the instrument. He wrote many original compositions for the guitar, and these were published by Pacini of Paris and Schott of Mayence.

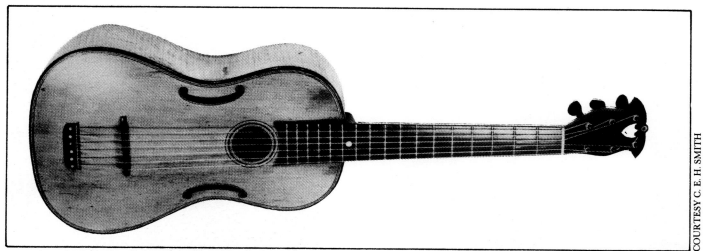

An unusual 19th century guitar made by the Mauchant Brothers, Mirecourt, France. Now on display at the Gemeentemeseum – Gravenhage, The Hague, Netherlands.

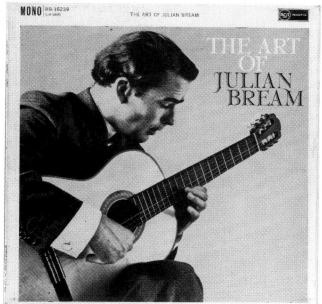

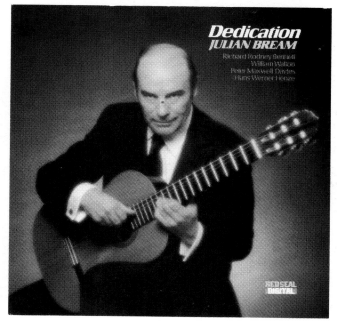

A selection of Julian Bream records.

Julian Bream

JULIAN BREAM

Born – Battersea, London, England

15th July 1933

Julian Bream is one of the greatest guitarists the world has known. By the time he was seventeen, although he had not played outside Great Britain, he was already known by reputation to guitarists all over the world.

Julian Bream was brought up in a musical environment. His father, a commercial artist and book illustrator, also ran a small dance band in which he played jazz guitar. Bream was very attracted to the jazz guitar style of Django Reinhardt, the legendary gypsy guitarist, that he heard on his father's records. His father had encouraged his son to play the piano, but also taught him to play the plectrum guitar. In 1944, on his eleventh birthday, Julian Bream was given a classical guitar by his father. In 1945 he won a junior exhibition award for his piano playing. This entitled him to study the piano and the cello at the Royal College of Music in London. In the same year his father took him to play at an evening held by the London Philharmonic Society of Guitarists. Dr. Boris Perott, the Society's president, was so impressed with Bream's obvious musical talent, that he offered to teach him the classical guitar. This he did for one year. It was Dr. Perott, and also Wilfred Appleby, who introduced Julian Bream to Andres Segovia. On hearing the youth play, Segovia was so impressed that he offered to give the thirteen year old some lessons. Julian Bream then made his professional debut in Cheltenham in 1947.

Encouraged by his father, Julian Bream decided to make his career in music and the guitar. At the age of fifteen he was awarded a full scholarship at the Royal College of Music and for three years studied piano, harmony and composition there.

Julian Bream made his Wigmore Hall, London, debut to great critical acclaim, in 1951. Despite three years in the British Army (1952-55), he continued to appear frequently on radio and television programmes as well as at public concerts. Bream's first European tours took place in 1954 and 1955. He then performed extensively in North America (beginning in 1958), the Far East, India, Australia, Pacific Islands, and other parts of the world. In addition to master classes given in Canada, and the USA, Bream has also conducted an International Summer School in Wiltshire, England. His many recordings for RCA have made him well known to a large worldwide audience and have won for him some of the highest awards in the recording industry. Included are the Award of the National Academy of Recording Arts and Sciences, two Grammy awards (1963 and 1966), and an Edison Award (1968). Since 1952 when he played part of his Wigmore Hall Recital on the Lute, Julian Bream has also been noted for his lute playing and is responsible for bringing to light much music for that instrument which had lain dormant for over three hundred years. Bream has also done much to broaden the contemporary guitar repertoire by commissioning works from such famous composers as Benjamin Britten, William Walton, Hans Werner Henze, Peter Fricker, Richard Rodney Bennett, Malcolm Arnold, and Lennox Berkley.

In the last few years Julian Bream has also appeared in concert and on three recordings with fellow guitarist John Williams. This association has been an enormous success. BBC Television have presented a special programme about Julian Bream's life as a concert guitarist, and also a series of four master classes presented by Julian Bream for guitarists.

SELECTED RECORDS

'The Art of Julian Bream'	RCA	RB 16239
'Popular Classics for Spanish Guitar'	RCA	RB 6593
'Guitar Music of Villa Lobos & Torroba'	HMV	CLP 1763
'Bach Recital for Guitar'	HMV	CLP 1929
'Julian Bream Plays Bach'	RCA	RL 42378
'Rodrigo Concerto/Vivaldi Concerto/Britten Dances'	RCA	SB 6635
'Baroque Guitar'	RCA	SB 6673
'Twentieth Century Guitar'	RCA	SB 6723

JULIAN BREAM – Selected Records (continued)

'Julian Bream & Friends – Boccherini Quintet/Haydn Quartet	RCA	SB 6772
'Classic Guitar – Giuliani/Diabelli/Mozart/Sor'	RCA	SB 6796
'Guitar Concertos – Giuliani/Arnold'	RCA	SB 6826
'Julian Bream Plays Villa Lobos'	RCA	SB 6852
'Romantic Guitar'	RCA	SB 6844
'Julian Bream 70s'	RCA	SB 6876
'Giuliani/Sor'	RCA	ARL 1-0711
'Rodrigo/Berkeley Guitar Concertos'	RCA	ARL 1-1181
'Julian Bream Plays Villa Lobos'	RCA	RL 12499
'Music of Spain – Sor/Aguado'	RCA	RL 14033
Duo with John Williams		
'Together'	RCA	SB 6862
'Together Again'	RCA	ARL 1-0456
'Live (2 lps)'	RCA	SB 6862

SELECTED READING

Julian Bream	Article – 'Guitar' – January 1973
Julian Bream	Article – 'Guitar' – October 1973
Julian Bream	Article – 'Guitar' – March 1974
Julian Bream	Article – 'Guitar' – August 1973
Julian Bream	Article – 'Guitar' – March 1977
Julian Bream	Article – 'Guitar' – February 1980
Julian Bream	Article – 'Frets' – June 1981
Julian Bream	Article – 'Guitar Player' – October 1971
Julian Bream	Article – 'Guitarra' – July 1981
Julian Bream	Article – 'Guitarra' – September 1981

Julian Bream
—playing music by Mudarra on the guitar

Hundreds of eyes with eagerness impel
The Wizard-Medium towards his simple throne,
A crackle of applauding palms,
Welcoming, anticipating—
Then noiselessness.

From the tense silence the Six-voiced Oracle
Melodiously declaims, reincarnating
Alonso de Mudarra of Seville
Whose music was conceived
Four Spanish centuries ago.

Hundreds of ears miraculously
Hear, nay, **SEE**
Liquids sounds transformed into a stream
Dancing and sparkling—
And Spanish children singing.

The magic wanes, the sunlit music fades,
A silent mistiness pervades—
Or is it moistening of eyes
Brimming with wonder?

Wilfrid M. Appleby

REGINALD SMITH BRINDLE

guitar & lute

ISSUE NO. 15 – OCTOBER 1980

Born – Preston, England

5th January 1917

Reginald Smith Brindle studied at the Bangor College of the University of Wales under D. E. Parry Williams and was awarded the Gwynnedon Scholarship.

His first interest in the guitar began before World War II when he used to play in jazz bands. His main instruments were the saxophone, the clarinet, the guitar, and the double bass. Brindle realized the full potential of the guitar when he heard some records by the gypsy jazz guitarist, Django Reinhardt. In 1939 he joined the army and during his military service (until 1946) Brindle took the guitar with him everywhere to continue his music studies. He became aware of the classical guitar in early 1946 when he went to Florence and met Professor Gullino. Gullino introduced him to the classical literature of the guitar and played him many records of Segovia which greatly impressed Brindle.

A university fellowship had enabled Smith Brindle to continue his studies under Pizzetti at the

Reginald Smith Brindle

Academia di Santa Cecilia in Rome. Here he received a diploma for advanced composition and also the Luigi Sturo Prize. He then studied twelve note technique with Dellapicolo for a period of two years.

Since that time Reginald Smith Brindle has lived for much of the time in Italy, writing music for documentary films, conducting British music and acting as a music critic. He has composed over sixty original works for guitar which have made him one of the most important composers for the classical guitar in the twentieth century.

SELECTED READING

Reginald Smith Brindle	Article – 'Guitar' – June 1973
Reginald Smith Brindle	Article – 'Guitar & Lute' – October 1980

SELECTED MUSIC

Danza Pagana	Schott
Do Not Go Gentle	Zerboni
El Polifemo de Oro	Bruzz
Etruscan Preludes	Schott
Four Poems of Garcia Lorca	Schott
Fuego Fatuo	Schott
Guitar Cosmos – Progressive Pieces for Guitar	Schott
Memento in Two Movements	Bèrben
Nocturne	Schott
November Memories	Zerboni
Sonata – El Verbo	G 121
Sonatina Fiorentina	Schott
Ten Simple Preludes, ed. Duarte	UE 29162
Variants on Two Themes of J. S. Bach	Peters
Vita Senese	Schott

Leo Brouwer

LEO BROUWER

Born – Havana, Cuba

1939

Generally regarded throughout the world as one of today's most outstanding guitarists, Leo Brouwer first studied the guitar with I. Nicola, a pupil of the great Pujol. He specialised in composition, completing his studies at The Juilliard School and in the Music Department of Hartford University.

In 1961 he was named Director of the Music Department of the Cinema Institute of Cuba, Professor of Composition in the Music Conservatory and musical advisor to the National Radio and Television Chain of Havana.

He is currently Director of the experimental department of the Cuban Institute of Cinema Arts and Industry where he continues his work as a composer.

Leo Brouwer is the first Cuban composer to use aleatory and 'open' forms, and has written more than 70 compositions that include several works for guitar, percussion, prepared and non-prepared pianos, a Cantata for Two Percussionists and Pianist, a contemporary ballet, a chorus of twelve members, three children and a harp, and a series of orchestral works.

Leo Brouwer has been heard as a guitarist and as a composer at the Festivals of Aldeburgh, Avignon, Edinburgh, Spoleto, Berlin (Festwochen), Toronto, Arles, Martinique and Rome, as well as in the most important European musical centres.

As well as being an outstanding guitarist, Leo Brouwer is also a talented conductor and composer. His compositions have been performed in Japan, Australia and Central and South America. Brouwer has conducted master classes for guitarists in France, Canada, Martinique, Cuba and Finland, and was a member of the jury in competitions in Munich, Caracas, Paris, among other cities.

Leo Brouwer conducted the Philharmonic Orchestra of Berlin (FRG) and the National Orchestra of Scotland. He also conducted the Manson Ensemble in London and the Theatre Orchestra of Rome for the World Premiere of his music for 'Julius Caesar' (1971). Brouwer was also guest composer to the Deutsche Akademische Austausdienst in Berlin (1972) along with Morton Feldman, Earle Brown and St. Bussot.

SELECTED RECORDS

'Les Classiques De Cuba'	Erato	STV 70669
'Scarlatti – Twelve Sonatas'	Erato	STV 70870
'Leo Brouwer'	Deutsche Gramaphon	2555 01
'Rara'	Deutsche Gramaphon	2530 307

SELECTED READING

Leo Brouwer	Article – 'Guitar' – June 1976
Leo Brouwer	Article – 'Guitar' – April 1977
Leo Brouwer	Article – 'Guitar and Lute' – January 1982

SELECTED MUSIC

Canticum	GA 424
Danza Característica	GA 422
Elogio de la Danza	GA 425
Fuga No. 1	ESC
La Espiral Eterna	GA 423
Parábola (modern)	ESC
Piece Without Title	ESC
Preludio	ESC
Tarantos (modern)	ESC
Tres Apuntes (3 Sketches)	GA 426
Two Popular Cuban Airs: Guajira Criolla, Zapateo	ESC
Two Popular Cuban Themes	ESC

JULIAN BYZANTINE

Born – London, England

11th June 1945

Julian Byzantine

Julian Byzantine commenced his advanced musical studies with John Williams at the Royal College of Music where he was awarded the first ARCM for guitar. During this period he won scholarships to further his studies with Julian Bream in England and Andres Segovia in Siena, where he was selected by the maestro to give a solo recital. After terminating these studies he taught on the staff of the Royal Academy of Music in London for two years.

Besides his work as a recitalist Byzantine makes frequent concerto appearances and has performed with some of the leading orchestras in Great Britain including the Royal Philharmonic Orchestra, The City of Birmingham Symphony Orchestra and the Scottish Chamber Orchestra and with many national orchestras abroad. In the field of contemporary music he has worked with Pierre Boulez and Peter Maxwell Davies and on numerous occa-sions the Arts Council of Great Britain have had works commissioned for him.

Julian Byzantine's reputation as a leading soloist has been extended by his broadcasts for radio and television, and these have included a special television feature of a documentary on the life and guitar music of Villa Lobos.

A particular interest in the manuscripts of the early guitarists and lutenists had led Julian Byzantine to become one of the rare exponents of the Baroque Guitar.

Julian Byzantine has become one of Great Britain's most established and widely travelled international concert artists. He has made extensive tours in Australia, Scandanavia, Latin America and the USA over the past few years.

SELECTED RECORDS

'Julian Byzantine Plays Villa Lobos etc'	Classics for Pleasure	CFP 40209
'Masterpieces for Classical Guitar'	Classics for Pleasure	CFP 40362

SELECTED READING

Julian Byzantine	Article – 'Guitar' – December 1980

OSCAR CACERES

Born – Montevideo, Uruguay

4th April 1928

Oscar Caceres

Oscar Caceres began his serious study of the guitar under the guidance of guitarists Ramon Ayestaran, Marin Sanchez and Atilio Rapat.

As a child he made such good progress on the instrument that Caceres gave his first public recital at the age of thirteen. It was in 1957, at the age of twenty-nine, that Oscar Caceres was to make his first European recital tour. He played with great success in Paris, Madrid, Valencia and Barcelona. On his return to South America he was to give the first live performance on this continent of Rodrigo's 'Concerto de Aranjuez'.

Caceres continued to play on extensive concert tours of South America, devoting at the same time a large part of his work to musical research. He has a special love of Rennaisance music, but at the same time retains a keen interest in twentieth century music. On a recent record release he has even included a section of Lennon and McCartney tunes arranged for classical guitar.

In 1967 Oscar Caceres decided to settle in Paris, France. He has, since that time, continued to give recitals and also to teach the guitar in most of the major cities of Europe.

SELECTED RECORDS

'Les Grandes Etudes Pour Guitare' Volume One	Erato	STV 70614
'Plays Leo Brouwer'	Erato	STV 70734
'Musique Pour Deux Guitares' Volume One (With Turibio Santos)	Erato	STV 70794
'Les Grandes Etudes Pour Guitare' Volume Two	Erato	ATV 70904
'Tresors D'Amerique Latine'	Erato	STV 70988
'Musique Pour Deux Guitares' Volume Two (With Turibio Santos)	Erato	STV 71092
'Oscar Caceres Plays Takemitsu/Brouwer'	Pavanne	ADW 7037
'Oscar Caceres Plays Bach/Weiss'	Pavanne	ADW 7040

Bartolome Calatayud

BARTOLOME CALATAYUD

Born – Palma De Mallorca, Spain
1882

Died – Palma De Mallorca, Spain
1973

Bartolome Calatayud's first teacher was Antonio Mestres, Professor and Director of the 'Instituto de Bachillerato' and also a guitarist. To Mestro is owed the formation of an excellent group of guitarists like Calatayud and the brothers Bernat.

Calatayud's progress with his teacher Mestro was such that soon he gave guitar concerts in Mallorca. The eminent Catalan guitarist and composer, Emilio Pujol was present at one of these concerts at the 'Circulo Mallorquin' and invited Calatayud to give a concert in Barcelona. A great friendship between the two musicians developed after this meeting.

Calatayud's first concert outside Spain was given in Toulouse, France. Other concerts soon took place in different countries of Europe. Calatayud learnt from Mestro the special harmony adapted for the guitar and from his youth felt more inclined towards composing. He wrote many compositions for the guitar including 'Una Lagrima', 'Danza Mora', 'Alegre Primavera', 'Gaviotas', 'Suite Antigua'. There are over 50 'Alegre Primavera', 'Gaviotas, 'Suite Antigua'. There are over 50 of Calatayud's compositions currently listed in the Publisher's Union Musical's catalogue.

Calatayud did a great deal of work in the spreading and correct interpretation of Mallorquin Folk music. In 1940 he was appointed director of 'Coros y Danzas' of the Seccion Femenina de Palma. With this organisation he toured South American countries with great success and made several records which have carried Palma's folk music to all parts of the world.

Calatayud had a special ability as a teacher and as a result had many pupils. Such was his reputation that many guitarists came to study with him from other countries than Spain.

SELECTED RECORD

'Inolvidable Guitarra'	Impacto	EL 225
'Gabriel Estarellas interprets Bartolome Calatayud'	Maller	API-86

SELECTED MUSIC

Alegre, campina, vals	20978 UME
Alegre, primavera	20434 UME
Boceto andaluz	20003 UME
Cuatro divertimientos	20557 UME
Cuatro Juguetes	21719 UME
Cuatro Piezas Para Guitarra	19675 UME
Cubanita, Habanera	21718 UME
Danza Espanola	20212 UME
Danza Mora	21780 UME
Danza Popular de Campdevanol	21266 UME
Dos Piezas Para Guitarra	19674 UME
Dos Piezas Para Guitarra	20004 UME
Estampa Gitana	20217 UME
Estudio Melodico	21091 UME
Galop	21781 UME

Matteo Carcassi

MATTEO CARCASSI

Born – Florence, Italy
1792

Died – Paris, France
16th January 1853

Thousands of student guitarists in countries throughout the world today know the name Carcassi as the author of their guitar method and composer of many attractive compositions and studies. There is no doubt he is most well known for these works, but Carcassi was also one of the great guitarists of the nineteenth century.

Matteo Carcassi studied the guitar from an early age in his native Italy. Before he was twenty he already had a reputation in Italy as a virtuoso of the guitar. In 1820 he decided to move to Paris, France, which at that time was regarded as the musical centre of Europe. During a concert tour of Germany in 1819 he had made friends with the French guitarist Meissonier. Meissonier a little later opened a publishing house in Paris. He was to become the publisher of most of Carcassi's works as the two guitarists had become firm friends.

In 1822 Carcassi established himself in London, after only a few concerts, as an exceptional guitar soloist and teacher. He soon returned to Paris, but was able to make an annual trip to London where his guitar talents were much in demand.

When he first arrived in Paris in 1820 Carcassi's talents had been somewhat shadowed by the older Italian virtuoso guitarist, Ferdinand Carulli, but, after a few years, Carcassi attained very great success. He gave annual concerts in most of the major cities of Europe, including London, but, despite a brief return to Italy in 1836, Paris was to become his permanent residence. He died there in 1853.

SELECTED MUSIC

Andantino & Romanze, from op. 60	GA 305
Fifty-four Selected Pieces: Book I (Easy)	GA 4A
Book II (Medium)	GA 4B
Book III (Difficult)	GA 4C
My First Carcassi, ed. Skiera (Selection of easy guitar solos)	Ricordi
Rondoletto, op. 41, ed. Danner (Fac. No. 8)	Belwin
Selected Works (Facsimiles), ed. Noad	Hansen
Six Caprices, op. 26	GA 72
Six Easy Caprices, op. 26, ed. Schwarz-Reiflingen	Sik.
Six Easy Variations, op. 18	Vieweg
Three Sonatinas, op. 1, & Six Caprices, op. 26	GA 5
Twelve Easy Pieces, op. 10	GA 73
Twenty Selected Waltzes	GA 3
Twenty-four Little Pieces, op. 21	GA 6
Two Waltzes from op. 4	GA 309
Variations on the Dream of Rousseau, op. 17	Kalmus

JORGE CARDOSO

Born: JORGE RUBEN CARDOSO KRIEGER
Posadas, Misiones Province, Argentina

26th January 1949

Jorge Cardoso, although still widely unknown to guitar audiences in the USA and western Europe, is without doubt one of the great guitarists/composers to emerge on the scene in the last twenty years.

Originally Cardoso studied the guitar with Lucas B. Areco and Luis J. Cassinelli. On gaining a scholarship from the National Fund in Arts in Argentina, he was able to study with Maria Hermini A. De Gomez Crespo. Later he studied harmony with Mario Perini, and later composition at the National University of Cordoba in Argentina. While studying composition at this university he also studied medicine. He eventually qualified in both, which porbably a first for any leading classical guitarist.

Jorge Cardoso, since the age of fourteen, won first prize at several important Argentinian competitions. In 1963, he won the solo instrumental class at the Festival of Music of the Littoral, at Posadas. In 1967 the National Folklore Festival at Cosquin. In 1971 the National Composition Competition at Salta, and in 1973 the International Concourse of the Classical Guitar at Moron (Buenos Aires).

Cardoso has appeared in many recitals and concerts throughout Argentina, Spain and France, but as yet received little or no exposure in other countries. He has several records to his name and

Jorge Cardoso

COURTESY JORGE CARDOSO

over 100 musical works published, including two concertos for guitar and orchestra.

Now resident in Madrid, Spain, Jorge Cardoso founded and directs the Ibero American Guitar Orchestra of Madrid. He spends most of his year in Spain, and also sometime in Japan, where he is very popular. He has established himself not only as a guitarist of outstanding ability, but also as a fine composer and teacher.

SELECTED RECORDS

'Clasicos Del Folklore SudAmericano'	DPM	PM 2040
'Suite SudAmericana'	Dial Discos	ND 5019
'Autores SudAmericanos'	Diapason	Dial Discos 52-5038
'Lamento Caingua'	Diapason	52-5054
'Cardosa and the Niibori Guitar Orchestra'	APAc	8009
'Suite Litoralena'	Diapason	52-5067

SELECTED READING

'Ciencia y Metodo En La Tecnica Guitaristica'	Capsa De Los Americas (Cuba)

SELECTED MUSIC

'Suite SudAmericana'	UME
'24 Pieces SudAmericana'	UME
'Gavota Del Crepusculo'	UME
'Mitosis'	Guitar Music, Tokyo
'Suite Portena'	Guitar Music, Tokyo
'Preludes by Bach'	UME

ABEL CARLEVARO

Born – Montevideo, Uruguay

16th December 1918

Abel Carlevaro

Abel Carlevaro began his study of musical theory under Tomas Mujica and Pablo Kimlos. He was originally self-taught on the guitar, using the printed methods that were available in Uruguay at that time. He later studied harmony, instrumentation and orchestration, applying his knowledge of these subjects to his guitar studies. Carlevaro originally decided to make his career in agriculture, but his love for the guitar eventually made him choose the field of music.

Abel Carlevaro met Andres Segovia in 1937 and following this meeting he was able to study with the maestro for a period of nine years. In 1942 Segovia presented him at the official music centre of the Republic of Uruguay. This recital established Carlevaro as a concert artist. In 1939, during the World Fair in New York, USA, Carlevaro broadcast several recitals for local radio stations. He received high critical praise for his playing, following which the Uruguayian Government gave him a special grant to enable him to travel.

Since the end of World War II Abel Carlevaro has given concerts in most countries of the world. He still appears regularly at major International guitar festivals both in a playing and teaching capacity, including the Recontres de la Guitarre organised by Radio France under the direction of Robert Vidal.

SELECTED RECORD

'Recital De Guitarra'	Antar	Telefunken ALP 1002

SELECTED READING

Cronomias I – Sonata for Guitar	Barry
Preludios Americanos	Barry
Suite of Ancient Spanish Dances (on text & themes of Sanz)	Barry

Ferdinando Carulli

FERDINANDO CARULLI

Born – Naples, Italy
10th February 1770

Died – Paris, France
17th February 1841

Ferdinando Carulli was the son of a distinguished writer, who was secretary to the Neopolitan Jurisdiction Delegate. Carulli's first musical instrument was the cello, but he became attracted to the guitar at an early age. Although the guitar was extremely popular in Italy at that time, there were very few serious teachers of the instrument.

Carulli's musical genius became evident whilst he was still a young man. He developed a series of studies and exercises, that were revolutionary in their concept, to help improve his technique on the instrument. With these studies any dedicated guitarist could achieve excellent standards of musicianship on the guitar.

In 1797, already a highly respected teacher and player, Carulli moved to Leghorn. In 1808 he again moved, this time to Paris, France. Here he was to remain for the rest of his life.

In 1810 Carulli wrote his comprehensive method for guitar (opus 241). Originally published in two volumes by Carli of Paris, this method became one of the standard instruction books for guitar. Its success was so great that five editions were printed in a relatively short period of time. A sixth edition was then printed. This was an enlarged version of the original containing an appendix of forty-four progressive pieces and six studies.

In 1825, Carulli wrote his 'L'Harmonie Applique A La Guitarre', a skilful work on the art of accompaniment, which was the first of its kind. Carulli published more than four hundred compositions for the guitar, which included studies, concerti, several trios for guitar, flute and violin, trios for three guitars, and many compositions for two guitars and guitar and piano. All these compositions are characterized by their richness of harmony and elegance of form.

Carulli's original method and much of his music is still available today, and is widely used by teachers and students. Without doubt this is positive proof of Carulli's musical genius.

SELECTED MUSIC

Allegretto	Bèrben
Best of Carulli, ed. J. Castle (11 selections)	MB
Capriccio	GA 310
Eighteen Little Pieces, op. 211, ed. Carfagna	Bèrben
Eighteen Very Easy Pieces, op. 333	GA 67
Nice und Fileno – Sonata, op. 2	ZM
Overture, op. 6, No. 1	N 3168
Preludes for Guitar, ed. Schwarz-Reiflingen, op. 114	N 3211
Six Andantes, op. 320, ed. Chiesa	GA 313
Solo, op. 76, No. 2	Zerboni
Three Sonatas	GA 40
Twenty-four Preludes, op. 114, ed. Balestra	Ricordi
Two Minuets from op. 270	GA 311
Variations on a Theme of Beethoven	Bèrben
Variations on the Italian Aria 'Sul Margine d'un Rio', op. 142	Zerboni

GEORGE CLINTON

Born – London, England

6th May 1931

George Clinton

George Clinton is today one of Great Britain's leading guitar personalities. He is the editor of 'Guitar', an excellent monthly magazine devoted to the guitar in all its forms. He also owns a publishing company, Musical New Services, which has many important classical guitar publications and recordings in its catalogue.

Clinton's first instrument was the violin. His father was a professional violinist and started his son on the instrument at the age of ten. At the age of twelve George Clinton changed to clarinet, an instrument to which he devoted his musical studies until he finished his army service years later. It was then he chose to study the classical guitar. He progressed quickly on the instrument and in 1959 gave his first public performance, a lunchtime recital at the Holborn Town Hall in London. Following this concert Clinton made several radio broadcasts for the popular BBC radio programme 'Guitar Club'.

For many years George Clinton maintained a busy life as a teacher, and also as a writer. He was a regular contributor to the long established 'BMG' magazine. In August 1972 the first issue of 'Guitar' magazine under his editorship was published. Since that time the magazine has gone from strength to strength. With the passing of 'BMG' and 'Guitar News', 'Guitar' is the most important magazine for classical guitarists in the United Kingdom today. George Clinton's love and deep interest of the guitar led him to develop the publishing side of Musical New Services. Included in this company's extensive range are books and records by Alice Artzt, John Mills, Forbes Henderson, and Paco Pena amongst others. There is also a well illustrated book on Andres Segovia, written and compiled by George Clinton himself, including many of his own photographs.

SELECTED READING
Various Articles   'Guitar' Magazine – 1972 to 1982

SELECTED MUSIC
An Anthology of Vihuela Music' – Arranged for Guitar   Musical New Services
Exercises for the Development of Left and Right Hands   Musical New Services

---

OLGA COELHO

Born – Manaus, Amazonas, Brazil

1909

Olga Coelho

COURTESY C.E.H. SMITH

Olga Coelho is one of the finest singer/guitarists the world has known.

Olga Coelho's musical instruction began at the age of six with piano studies which she continued for more than ten years. She then studied harmony with O. Lorenzo Fernandez and received her diploma from the National Institute of Music in Rio de Janeiro, where her family made their home. One of Coelho's voice teachers was the world famous Italian contralto, Gabriella Besanzoni Lage.

Olga Coelho became intensely interested in Brazilian folklore at an early age. Through her love of this folklore she was attracted to the guitar. Olga Coelho has concertized in South America, the United States, Canada, Europe, Australia, New Zealand, South America, the United States, Canada, Europe, Australia, New Zealand, South Africa, and the Extreme Orient. She has also recorded in the United States, London, Sweden, Brazil, and in Chile and Argentina. Olga Coelho has also written many articles on music and folklore for magazines in South America and the United

States. She speaks six languages (Portuguese, Spanish, French, Italian, German, English) and sings in several more including Russian, Swedish, Polish, Maori and Malay. Her talent is such that songs have been composed for her by many outstanding contemporary composers, including Villa-Lobos, Castelnuovo-Tedesco, J. Rodriguez, Andres Segovia, O. Lorenzo Fernandez, M. Carmargo Guarnieri, Terry Usher and Hans Haug.

She has been honoured by many Brazilian cities; and in Rio de Janeiro there is a permanent exhibition at the Museu do Teatro Municipal of her programmes, photographs and other memorabilia. In Buenos Aires she has been honoured by membership in the Republica de la Boca. She also has the distinction of being one of the few artists honoured by the New York Society of the Classic Guitar with honorary membership.

For many years Olga Coelho has been a close friend of Andres Segovia. He has made for her many transcriptions. She was the first singer/guitarist for whom Segovia wrote accompaniments.

SELECTED RECORD
'Chants and Folk Ballads of Latin America'   Decca   DL 10018

IRMA COSTANZO

Born – Buenos Aires, Argentina

1937

Irma Costanzo

COURTESY EMI RECORDS

Highly regarded throughout the guitar world as one of Argentina's finest classical guitarists, Irma Costanzo studied the guitar with Abel Carlevaro in Montevideo. Later she studied under Narciso Yepes both in Buenos Aires and Paris. For a time she also studied chamber music with Lyenko Spiller.

Irma Costanzo at the age of sixteen, in 1953, won the prize for the best performance in a competition held by the Association of Chamber Music. In 1961 she won first prize in the competion Juventudes Musicales of Argentina and also in 1962 the Grand Prix of the Fondo De Las Artes.

Since that time Irma Costanzo has established herself as a leading guitar soloist, appearing in concert in most countries of the world including North and South America, Europe, United Kingdom and also Japan.

SELECTED RECORDS

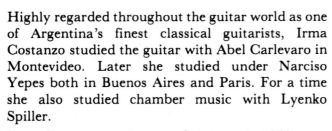

'La Maya De Goya'	EMI (Spain)	J063-21010
'Villa Lobos & Turina for Guitar'	EMI (VIC)	30215
'Plays Villa Lobos/Carlevao'	Qualiton	Q1 4000

NAPOLEON COSTÉ

**Born – Daubs, France
28th June 1806**

**Died – Paris, France
17th February 1883**

Napoleon Coste

Napoleon Costé started to play the guitar at the age of six. By the time he was eighteen he was not only teaching the guitar, but appearing regularly as a guitar soloist for the Philharmonic Society of Valencienne, France. For a period of four years, between 1824 and 1828, Costé took part in several concerts with the guitar virtuoso Luigi Sagrion.

He decided to move to Paris, France in 1830. Here Costé soon made a name for himself as a guitarist and teacher. His concert performances were attended by the elite of Parisian society, and he received high critical acclaim from the press.

Whilst living in Paris Napoleon Costé was able to meet other great masters of the guitar. He developed a personal and intimate friendship with Aguado, Carulli, Carcassi and Sor. So impressed was he by these great musicians that he decided to make an even more serious study of the guitar in music. Costé spent the next ten years studying harmony and counterpoint.

In 1840 he first published some of his original compositions for the guitar. Costé submitted four compositions into an International music contest in 1856 organised by M. Makaroff, a Russian nobleman. His grand serenade won second prize, first going to J. K. Mertz for his 'Concertino'.

Following his success in the competition, Napoleon Costé was to have over sixty of his compositions published. He wrote a second guitar part, in substitution of the orchestra, to Giuliani's 'Concerto for Guitar' opus 36. This made it a duo for two guitars. He also revised the original edition of Fernando Sor's guitar method for Lemoine, the Parisian publisher.

Around 1860 Costé fell after a concert and broke his right arm. After this accident he was never able to perform again in public. This was a great tragedy for there is little doubt that Costé was one of the greatest guitar virtuosi and composers France has produced. His guitar was eventually bequeathed to the Museum of the National Conservatoire of Music in Paris. This instrument was quite unique being of Costé's own design. It was of much larger dimensions than usual, and was tuned a fifth lower than the ordinary guitar. It also had a finger plate raised from the table of the guitar, not unlike those seen on twentieth century jazz guitars.

SELECTED RECORD

'Napoleon Costé – Music for Guitar and Oboe'	Simon Wynberg	Chandos ABR 1031

SELECTED MUSIC

Autumn Leaves – 12 Waltzes, op. 41	GA 12
Barcarole, Rondoletto, Marsch	GA 315
Rêverie	Ricordi
Rondeau	EMT 1406
Rondo, op. 51, no. 11	Berben
Zur Erholung (The Guitarist's Recreation), op. 41 (14 pieces)	GA 13

COSTAS COTSIOLIS

Born – CONSTANTINE COTSIOLIS
Athens, Greece

23rd July 1957

Costas Cotsiolis is now regarded as one of the foremost classical guitarists in Greece. He began to play the guitar at the age of six studying with Professor Ecmectsoglou at the Conservatoire Hellenique in Athens. He gave his first public recital in 1968 at the age of eleven in the Parnassos Room, Athens.

Between 1970 and 1973 he took part in several international concourses for guitar in France, Italy and in Spain. He also studied at various international seminars with Andres Segovia, Alirio Diaz and José Tomas. Cotsiolis eventually won a total of fifteen international prizes and diplomas for his guitar playing. In 1972 he completed his studies at the Conservatoire Hellenique in Athens. In November of the same year, at the age of fifteen, he performed the 'Concierto de Aranjuez' by Joaquin Rodrigo in Athens with the Orchestra Symphonique d'Etat.

Since 1972 Costas Cotsiolis has continued an active career as a classical guitarist and has given concerts and recitals in the principle cities of Greece. He has appeared with the symphony orchestra of Athens and Thessalonique, and also broadcast several times on Greek radio and television.

In 1976 he became head of the department for classical guitar in the Conservatoire in Athens. In the same year he was appointed the Artistic Director of the International Festival for the classical guitar in Volos, Greece.

Since 1978 Costas Cotsiolis has appeared all over Europe and also in Russia and Cuba. He has been active in annual guitar seminars at the Festivals of Esztergom in Hungary, Dubrovnik in Yugoslavia, and also Donietsk in USSR. 1978 saw the publica-

Costas Cotsiolis

tion in Greek of his book entitled 'Guitar Technique'. Cotsiolis has also recorded for the record companies 'Electrecord' in Romania and 'Melodia' in the USSR.

In 1981 he was the featured soloist with the orchestra 'Pro Musica' of Oxford, England at the Festival of Athens in Greece.

SELECTED RECORD
'Constantine Cotsiolis'   Melodiya   S 10-16481-2

SELECTED READING
'Costas Cotsiolis'   Article – 'Guitar' – May 1976

BETHO DAVEZAC

Born – in Uruguay

1938

Betho Davezac

Betho Davezac was first taught the guitar at the age of six by his father, a conservatory professor. He soon showed great promise and later studied harmony and counterpoint with Guido Santorsola, who was living in Montevideo, Uruguay at that time.

Davezac later attended master classes by Andres Segovia and Alirio Diaz. Achieving high regard from fellow musicians in Uruguay the young guitarist continued to lead a very active musical life. He was one of the founders of 'Grupo Artemus' who won the prize given by the Uruguayan Critic Society in 1965 for the best Chamber ensemble.

In 1966 Davezac decided to leave Uruguay and went to live in Paris, France. He first established himself as a teacher of the classical guitar. Davezac then entered the eighth ORTF guitar competition and was a prize winner. He later won first prize in both the 1967 Ville De Liege competition, and the 1969 Citta Di Allesandria competition.

Since then the talented Uruguayan guitarist has become a frequent recitalist in Europe, South America and Japan. His 1974 recording of Elizabethan music (Erato STU 70830) was awarded the 'Grand Prix International Du Disc' by the Academy Charles Cros.

SELECTED RECORDS

'Musique Elizabethaine'	Erato	STU 70830
'Variations Sur La Guitare'	Erato	STU 70926
'Guitare Francaise du XV Siecle' (with Jean Claude Orliac)	Erato	STU 71334

REY DE LA TORRE

Born – JOSÉ REY DE LA TORRE
Gibara, Cuba

9th December 1917

Rey De La Torre

Rey De La Torre began studying music and the guitar as a child in Havana, Cuba. His first teacher was Severino Lopez. After five years of study he astounded audiences with his ability after he had given several public recitals, and also some radio broadcasts.

Such was his success that the young guitarist travelled to Spain. Here he continued his studies with Miguel Llobet in Barcelona. In 1933 he appeared in concert with great success at the Granados Academy.

In 1939 De La Torre moved to New York, USA and established himself there as a leading recitalist and teacher of the guitar. His Town Hall concert in 1941 was highly acclaimed. Since that time De La Torre has made the USA his home, although he has appeared in concerts all over the world. He has appeared on numerous occasions on both radio and television, and premiered Rodrigo's 'Concerto de Aranjuez' with the Cleveland Symphony Orchestra. He has had several pieces specially written for him by important contemporary composers including Julian Orbon, José Ardevol and Joaquin Nin-Culmell.

SELECTED RECORDS

'20th Century Music for the Guitar'	Elektra	EKL 244
'Plays Classical Guitar'	Rpic	LC 3418
'Virtuoso Guitar'	Epic	LC 3479
'Romantic Guitar'	Epic	LC 3564
'Music for One and Two Guitars'	Epic	LC 3674
'Spanish Music for the Classical Guitar'	Nonesuch	2590-001

SELECTED READING

Rey De La Torre	Article – 'Guitar Player' – October 1975

ANTON DIABELLI

Born – Mattsee, Near Salzburg, Austria
6th September 1781

Died – Vienna, Austria
7th April 1858

Anton Diabelli was not only one of the finest guitarists of the early part of the nineteenth century, but an excellent pianist and composer. He was also a highly respected publisher of music for both the piano and the guitar, as well as church music. Diabelli received his first musical education as a choruster in the Monastery of Michaelbearn, and then at the Cathedral of Saltzburg. His parents originally had hoped he would enter the priesthood, and in 1800 he entered the Monastery of Reichenhaslach.

Before he was twenty years old Diabelli's talents as a composer were already recognised through his many compositions for one or more voices. The guitar was already Diabelli's main instrument and most of his vocal arrangements had guitar accompaniment. In 1803 the young guitarist decided to make music his career, and abandoned his original idea to take holy orders. He left for Vienna where his talents were immediately recognised by many of the musicians living there, including Joseph Haydn whose brother Michael had supervised Diabelli's musical training.

In 1807 Diabelli struck up a friendship with guitar virtuoso Mauro Giuliani. There is no doubt that Giuliani was technically the greater guitarist, but the two appeared often in concert either as a guitar duo, or piano and guitar duo. Giuliani found Diabelli's musicianship very stimulating. The guitar had achieved enormous popularity at that time in most of Europe, and especially in Vienna, and the two guitarists achieved success after success.

As a foremost teacher and recitalist of both the guitar and the piano, Diabelli earned a lot of money. He became a partner with the musical

Anton Diabelli

publishing firm of Peter Cappi in 1818. Six years later, in 1824, Diabelli bought out his partner and changed the name of the company to Diabelli and Company. Diabelli became Schubert's main publishers, and the company prospered under the talented musician's excellent management. He also published the music of Czerny and Strauss and became a close friend of Beethoven and Schubert. Beethoven used a Diabelli composition as the theme for his famous Piano Variations, op. 102.

In 1853 Diabelli sold his copyrights (at that time he had printed over 25,000 works), and business to C. A. Spira. Anton Diabelli died in Vienna in 1858 at the age of seventy-six. During his highly successful career as both a musician and businessman, Diabelli had earned enormous respect from his many friends and admirers, and has gone down in history as one of the most important guitar personalities of the nineteenth century.

SELECTED RECORD

'Music for Guitar and Piano' – Romulo Lazarde	Harmonia Mundi	HM 435

SELECTED MUSIC

Due Fughe, op. 46, ed. Ablóniz	Bèrben	Praludium & Andante Cantabile, from op. 39, ed. Teuchert	SY 2248
Five Easy Recital Pieces, op. 39	GA 322	Praludium, from op. 103	GA 321
Five Viennese Dances	UE 14463	Sonata in A Major, ed. Bream	Faber
Four Little Rondos, ed. Schindler	N 1516	Sonata for Guitar, op. 29/1, in C Major	UE 14472
Little Pieces for Beginners, op. 39	UE 14464	Sonatina in A Major, ed. Nagel, arr. Meunier	Breitkopf
Minuetto, from the Sonata in C	Bèrben	Three Sonatas	Kalmus
		Twenty-four Easy Old Viennese Landler, op. 121	GA 85
		Two Fugues, op. 46: no. 1 in Am, no. 2 in A	Ric. 132512

Alirio Diaz

ALIRIO DIAZ

Born – Caserio La Candelaria, Near Carora, Venezuela

12th November 1933

Alirio Diaz's first guitar teacher was his uncle who taught him to play the guitar by ear. At the age of ten Alirio Diaz had already written several interpretations of popular Venezuelan airs. When he was fifteen years old he was taken by Cecilio Zubbilaga to Trujilla to receive his first lessons in theory and solfeggio with Laudelino Mejias.

Diaz soon achieved great success in his musical studies, but earned his living as a proof reader. He also wrote articles for a weekly music paper 'The Crescent'. In 1945 he went to Caracas and advanced his guitar studies together with Raoul Borges at the Higher School of Music under the tuition of Clement Pimentel. Alirio Diaz was able to pay for his music education by money earned playing both in military bands and dance orchestras. After his graduation he gave his first recital at the National Library and received high critical acclaim. Subsequent recitals were so successful that in 1958 he was given a grant by the Ministry of Education to help him travel to Europe to further his guitar and music studies.

After studying with Regina Sainz De La Maza for one year, Diaz was awarded the first prize at the Royal Conservatory of Music in Madrid. The young guitarist left Madrid for Siena and for four years attended special courses given by Andres Segovia at the Musical Academy of Chigiana. He earned the high distinction of being the assistant professor of guitar on two of these courses.

Alirio Diaz then embarked on a strenuous concert tour of most countries of Europe and the Americas achieving enormous success. Diaz has made a particularly strong impression amongst guitatists, not only with his enormous guitar technique, but because of the introduction of his many interpretations of the music of his fellow countrymen. His rendition of compositions of Antonio Lauro (and those of other South American composers) have established Alirio Diaz as one of the most important guitarists of the twentieth century.

SELECTED RECORDS

'Masters of the Guitar' Volume Two	RCA	RB 6599
'400 Years of Classical Guitar'	Everest	3155
'Virtuoso Guitar'	Vanguard	HM 32SD
'Four Centuries of Classical Guitar'	Vanguard	VSD 71135
'The Classical Spanish Guitar' (2 LPs)	Vanguard	VPD 20002
'Guitar Music of Spain and Latin America'	EMI/HMV	HQS 1175
'Diaz Plays Bach'	EMI/HMV	HQS 1145
'Diaz Plays C. Tedesco-Quintet/Ponce-Sonata'	EMI/HMV	HQS 1250

SELECTED READING

Alirio Diaz	Article – 'Guitar' – August 1974
Alirio Diaz	Article – 'Guitar' – November 1979

MICHEL DINTRICH

Born – Bar Sur Aube, France

10th June 1933

Michel Dintrich

Michel Dintrich is one of the most influential and popular guitarists in France today. He first studied the guitar with Ida Presti at the Schola Cantorum in Paris, France. Later he participated in Andres Segovia's Master Classes at the Academy Chigiana in Siena, Italy.

Established as a major guitarist, Dintrich has concertized throughout Europe and North Africa. He has made many transcriptions for the guitar of original baroque music. In recent years he has changed to a ten string guitar, similar to the one developed and used by Narciso Yepes.

As well as teaching and playing the guitar Michel Dintrich has made several important recordings. He also broadcasts regularly on French radio and television. Dintrich has written and played the soundtrack music of several French films including 'Madagascar Au Bout De Monde'. He also owns a very fine collection of rare antique guitars.

SELECTED RECORDS

'Recital De Guitarre' (2 LPs)	Musidisc	16030
'Les Immortels'	Barclay	920 104
'With Duo Patrice Fontanarosa'	Classic	991 025

A selection of B.M.G. magazines, a guitar magazine of the past.

John W. Duarte

JOHN W. DUARTE

Born – JOHN WILLIAM DUARTE
Sheffield, England

2nd October 1919

John Duarte is not only one of the foremost twentieth century composers for the guitar, but is also regarded as a world authority on matters relating to the guitar and its music.

He started playing the ukulele at the age of fourteen, and a year later he was introduced to the plectrum guitar by a local dance band guitarist. Soon after he began to take lessons from Terry Usher in Manchester. Six years later, in 1940, John Duarte began to take an active interest in the classical guitar, an instrument on which he was self taught.

At that time John Duarte decided that the concert platform was not his metier. He embarked upon an intensive study of the classical guitar as a musical instrument and its relationship to the world of music as a whole. His understanding and panoramic view of the guitar have been invariably assisted by friendships with many of the world's greatest players, including Andres Segovia and the late Ida Presti.

As a composer and arranger, John Duarte has had more than one hundred works published in six countries. Many of these have been recorded by the major guitarists of the age. In 1958 his composition, based on the American folk song, 'The Colorado Trail', won first prize in a worldwide competition arranged by the Classical Guitar Society of New York. Duarte currently resides in London, England, and teaches in all aspects of guitar playing, at all levels. He is the author of several didactic works including a comprehensive book written specifically for teaching the guitar to children. He has also published a book of technical studies endorsed by Segovia.

Over the last 30 years, through hundreds of his published articles in the most prestigeous international guitar magazines, John W. Duarte has become one of the most influential guitar personalities of the twentieth century. His special talents are continuously called upon not only to write important articles on the guitar, but also to write sleeve notes for guitar records for most of the major record companies. He has also been an adjudicator in several international guitar contests.

SELECTED READING

John Duarte	Article – 'Guitar' – February 1974
John Duarte	Article – 'Guitar' – March 1975
John Duarte	Complete list of works – 'Guitar & Lute' – October 1979

SELECTED MUSIC

All in a Row, op. 51	Bèrben	Simple Variations on 'Las Folías'	CO 152
Birds, op. 66 (Swallows, The Swan, Sparrows)	Zanibon	Six Easy Pictures, op. 57	Novello
A Delight of English Lute Music	GA 224	Sixteen English Folk Songs	Novello
English Suite	Novello	Some of Noah's Ark, op. 55 – 6 Sketches for Guitar	LD 583
Etude Diabolique, op. 49	Bèrben	Sonatina Lirica, op. 48 – Homage to	Bèrben
Fantasia & Fugue on 'Torre Bermeja', op. 30	Bèrben	Mario Castelnuovo-Tedesco	
A Flight of Fugues, op. 44, for 1 or 2 guitars	Broek	Sonatinette	Novello
For My Friends	CO 183	Sua Cosa, op. 52	Bèrben
A Grace of Minuets	Schott	Suite Ancienne, op. 47	Bèrben
Meditation on a Ground Bass, op. 5	Schott	Suite Piemontese	Bèrben
Miniature Suite, op. 6	Schott	Three English Folk Songs	Novello
Mutations on the 'Dies Irae', op. 58	Bèrben	Three Modern Miniatures	Schott
My Fair Ladies	Faber	Tout en Ronde, op. 57: Ritual Dance,	UE 29153
Night Music	G 124	Waltz, Spring Dance	
Nocturne & Toccata, op. 18	Broek	Two Pieces: Prelude, op. 3; Larghetto, op. 4	CO 153
Partita	CO 215	Variations on a Catalan Folk Song, op. 25	Novello
Petite Suite Française, op. 60	ESC		
Playford Tunes	Broek		
Prelude, Canto, and Toccata	Bèrben		
Prélude en arpèges	ESC		

HERBERT J. ELLIS

Born – Dulwich, London, England
4th July 1865

Died – London, England
13th October 1903

Herbert J. Ellis

Herbert Ellis was the son of a licensed victualler. His first instrument was the piano, but he became fascinated by the banjo. Although Ellis had no true academic music education, his natural musical talent enabled him to write a highly successful tutor 'Through School for the Banjo'.

In 1888, with the rising popularity of the guitar and mandolin, Ellis decided to study and master these other fretted instruments. He had soon written the 'Through School for Mandolin'. This publication was also highly successful and several editions had to be printed. He then completed his trio of best selling fretted instrument tutors with the publica-

tion of his 'Through School for Guitar'. This guitar method, with its unique and simple manner, became the most popular method of its type for many years. It is in fact still used today (a revised edition by Bernard Sheaff of 1948) almost one hundred years after it was first published.

Herbert J. Ellis proved to be one of the most important and lasting guitar personalities on the English scene. In all over one thousand of his original compositions for guitar and mandolin were published. Although these were very popular in the latter part of the nineteenth century, they are seldom played today.

GABRIEL ESTARELLAS

Born – Palma De Mallorca, Spain

14th October 1952

Gabriel Estrellas

COURTESY GABRIEL ESTRELLAS

Little known outside his native country, Gabriel Estarellas is one of the finest guitarists to have emerged from Spain in recent years.

Estarellas began his music and guitar studies at an early age. By the time he was twelve he had given his first public recital. This performance was received with great enthusiasm. Estarellas crossed to the main land of Spain to study with José Tomas, and later completed his musical studies with Gerardo Perez Busquier.

In 1970 Estarellas was awarded the first prize at the 'Concurso International Ramirez' in Santiago De Compostella. In the same year he also won first prize at the 'Concurso International De Viotti'.

An intensive concert tour of Europe was made in 1972, during which Gabriel Estarellas performed the world premiere of 'Tansman's Musique De Cour', a concerto for guitar and orcjestra. Over the next few years the young guitarist was much in demand for concerts, and also radio and television broadcasts throughout Europe. In 1975 he won the 'Francisco Tarrega' competition in Benicasim, Spain. He also performed in that same year the world premiere of A. Blanquer's 'Concertino for Guitar and Orchestra'. Over the past few years many contemporary composers, including Richard Stoker, Angelo Gilardino and Bernardo Julia have dedicated works to him. In 1978 Estarellas was nominated to be the conductor of the Manacor's Chamber Orchestra, and in the same year he performed the world premiere of Barnardo Julia's 'Concerto Juglar' for guitar and orchestra.

Gabriel Estarellas currently spends much of his year in Spain where he holds the post of Director and Professor of Guitar at the Academia de Auditorium, Palma De Mallorca.

SELECTED RECORD

'Estarellas Interprets'	Fonal	MM-S 56
'Estarellas Interprets Calatayud'	Maller	API-86

DIMITRI FAMPAS

Born – Melina, Near Volos, Greece

22nd December 1921

Dimitri Fampas

Dimitri Fampas is one of the most important guitar personalities in Greece today. He showed that he had musical talent at an early age. At the age of twenty he studied the guitar under Niko Ioannou, at the same time studying theory and harmony at the Athens Conservatory. In 1953 he graduated winning not only the first prize of the year, but a special award for his musical ability.

An active concert career followed for Fampas in the major recital halls of Greece. In 1955-56 he won scholarships to study under Andres Segovia and Emilio Pujol at the Academy of Chigiana in Sienna.

In 1959 he again studied with Segovia at Santiago De Compostella.

Since that time Fampas has continued a busy career as a concert artist and teacher. He has played in nearly every major European city, and has made several radio broadcasts. He has also written several original compsotions for the guitar which he has also recorded. Fampas has been involved in teaching, not only at his home in Athens where he is the Professor of Guitar at the National Conservatory, but also abroad.

SELECTED RECORDS

'Greek Music for Guitar'	Polydor	Greece 45-96
'Dimitri Fampas Plays'	Odeon EMI	Greece OMGC 67

SELECTED MUSIC

Bolero	CO 154
Greek Dance No. 1	Ric. 129953
Greek Suite No. 4	BR 3221

EDUARDO FERNANDEZ

Born – Montevideo, Uruguay

1952

Eduardo Fernandez

Eduardo Fernandez began his study of the guitar at the age of seven with Raul Sanchez, a former pupil of Andres Segovia. Further studies included work with composer Guido Santorsola in interpretation, harmony, counterpoint and fugue. His study of the guitar continued with Abel Carlevaro the famous Uruguyan guitarist.

Fernandez began concertizing in 1963 as part of a duo guitar team with his brother but since 1971, he has pursued a career as soloist. He won first prize in both the Uruguayan Guitar Society Competition and the International Competition of Porto Alegre, Brazil. In both of these competitions, the judges were unanimous in their choice of Fernandez as first prize winner. In 1975, he was chosen as one of four finalists in the Radio-France Competition and in that same year he was a prize winner in the 'Andres Segovia Competition' in Palma De Mallorca, Spain.

In 1977 Eduardo Fernandez gave a highly acclaimed performance at his United States debut in New York City. Since that time he has maintained a very active concert career in both North and South America. Eduardo Fernandez has also taught at several international guitar seminars including those held in Sao Paulo and Buenos Aires.

ZANI DE FERRANTI

Born – MARC AURELIO DE FERRANTI,
Bologna, Italy 6th July 1802

Died – Pisa, Italy
28th November 1878

Zani De Ferranti

Zani De Ferranti was, at the age of twelve, recognised to be a child prodigy, not only as a violinist but also as a poet and linguist.

In 1818 he made a highly successful concert tour of Europe on the violin. Everywhere he played, Ferranti's virtuoso performances were received with high acclaim. In 1820 he went to Russia and gained the position of librarian to Senator Miatleff in St. Petersburg. A little later he was appointed Court Musician to Narischkin, a Russian price. It was during his stay in Russia that Ferranti became attracted to the guitar, and within a relatively short period of time he became a virtuoso guitarist. Ferranti gave his first public recital as a guitarist in Hamburg, Germany in 1824. He later played in Brussels, Belgium in 1821, Paris, France in 1826, and in London, England in 1827.

Ferranti toured the United States of America in 1845 with the famous violinist Sivori. On his return to Europe in 1846 Ferranti was appointed Court Guitarist to King Leopold of Belgium. In 1854 Ferranti once again made a concert tour of France and Italy. At the end of this tour he decided to remain in Bologna, his native town. Ferranti continued to devote his life to the guitar, both playing and composing, until his death in Pisa, in 1878, at the age of seventy-six.

SELECTED MUSIC

Triois Mélodies Nocturnes et une Etude	Leduc
The Selected Works	ECH 416

ELIOT FISK

Born – Philadelphia, USA

10th August 1954

Eliot Fisk

COURTESY KAZUKO HILLYER   PHOTO PETER SHAAF

Eliot Fisk began to study the guitar at the age of seven. His father was a professor of marketing at the Wharton School of the University of Pennyslavania. He studied first with William Viola of Philadelphia and performed his first solo recital at the age of thirteen. In 1970 he won a full scholarship to the Aspen Music School where he studied with Oscar Ghiglia before joinging the Aspen faculty as Ghiglia's assistant at the age of eighteen. In the same year Fisk received a grant to study at the Banff School of Fine Arts with Alirio Diaz.

Eliot Fisk graduated *summa cum laude* from Yale College in 1976. His studies there with Ralph Kirkpatrick, the noted harpsichordist and Scarlatti scholar, inspired Fisk to continue his interest in expanding the guitar repertoire through transcriptions of works by Scarlatti, Haydn, Mozart,

Beethoven and Paganini, amongst others. In 1977 Fisk received his MA degree from the Yale School of Music, and that autumn he founded the school's guitar department. In addition to teaching at Yale, Eliot Fisk serves on the faculty of the Aspen School of Music and frequently gives master classes at universities throughout the country. While keeping a demanding solo concert schedule, he has performed in duo recitals with the renowned soprano Victoria de los Angeles. He is also a co-founder of the Concerto Soloists of Philadelphia, with whom he has appeared as a soloist at the Wolf Trap and in the group's Carnegie Hall debut in 1979.

Eliot Fisk is without doubt, as his recent record releases and concert performances have established, one of the finest American classical guitarists to have emerged in recent years.

SELECTED RECORDS

'Plays Scarlatti and Bach'	MLAR	C45 000 006
'Latin American Guitar'	Music Masters	MM 20008
'American Virtuoso'	Music Masters	MM 20032

SELECTED READING

Eliot Fisk	Article – 'Guitar & Lute' – July 1981
Eliot Fisk	Article – 'Guitar Player' – June 1980

WILLIAM FODEN

Born – St. Louis, USA
23rd March 1860

Died – St. Louis, USA
9th April 1947

William Foden

William Foden was of English ancestry. His father was the owner of a music store in St. Louis. Foden's first instrument was the violin, and he began his musical studies at the age of seven. By the time he was sixteen he had already become the leader of a local orchestra. One of his school friends played the guitar and Foden, at the age of sixteen, became attracted to the fretted instrument.

In 1887 he became a member of a professional trio comprised of violin, flute and guitar. In the same year he organized a Beethoven mandolin and guitar orchestra. The name of this group eventually became to be known as Foden Mandolin and Guitar Orchestra.

Foden's first concert as a guitar soloist was on 29th January 1904, when he appeared at the Carnegie Hall in New York city. By that time he was accepted as a virtuoso of guitar and his frequent public performances were highly acclaimed by both the critics and audiences alike.

In 1921 William Foden published in two volumes his famous Guitar School (William J. Smith & Company, Publishers of New York). The work proved very practical in its development of technique through easy compositions to more difficult pieces. He also published a graded series of guitar lessons as a correspondence course, as well as two books of guitar chords and chord progressions. His most important work, begun in 1904 and completed in 1941, was his 'Grand Sonata for Guitar'.

William Foden spent many years as a leading teacher and recitalist in New York City. In his latter years he returned to St. Louis continuing to devote his life to teaching and playing the guitar. An outstanding musician William Foden was one of the foremost guitar personalities and players the United States has produced.

SELECTED MUSIC
Six Short Preludes   CO 159

DANIEL FORTEA

Born – DANIEL FORTEA GUIRMERA,
Bennloch, Castellon De La Plana, Spain
28th April 1878

Died – Castellon, Spain
5th March 1953

Daniel Fortea

COURTESY C. E. H. SMITH

Daniel Fortea is regarded by many as one of the most important guitarists and teachers that Spain has produced.

He began to study the guitar at an early age using the methods of Aguado and Tarrega. At the age of twenty he began to take lessons with Francisco Tarrega in Castellon. He made such good progress that on several occasions Tarrega devoted part of his concert programme to guitar duos with Fortea.

In 1909, after Tarrega's death, Daniel Fortea moved to Madrid where he became a popular and successful concert artist. It was in Madrid that he founded the Academia De Guitarra and also the Biblioteca Fortea, which eventually became a world famous publisher of guitar music.

Fortea also edited and published a regular news sheet, 'Boletin Revista De La Bibliotera Fortea' which first appeared in 1935 and which, apart from its news items, contained a regular music supplement.

Daniel Fortea was a prolific composer for the guitar. He also made hundreds of transcriptions from classical and modern composers, as well as a 'Method for Guitar' (based on the studies of Sor and Aguado), which was published in 1921. A second edition, in two volumes, was published in 1930.

Daniel Fortea continued to devote his life to the guitar, right up to his death, following a heart attack at the age of 75, in 1953.

SEATTLE CLASSIC GUITAR SOCIETY

GUITAR NEWS

The Official Organ of the

INTERNATIONAL CLASSIC GUITAR ASSOCIATION

No. 65   Single copy price 1/8 (U.S.A. 35c.)   MAY/JUNE, 1962

After the Concert

*The Presti-Lagoya Duo with Segovia
after the Duo's recital,
New York 1961.*

GUITAR NEWS

The Official Organ of the

INTERNATIONAL CLASSIC GUITAR ASSOCIATION

No. 87   Single copy price 2/- (U.S.A. 45c.)   JAN./FEB., 1966

AT COMPOSTELA

ROBERT J. VIDAL INTERVIEWS
ANDRES SEGOVIA

GUITAR NEWS

The Official Organ of the

INTERNATIONAL CLASSIC GUITAR ASSOCIATION

No. 94   Single copy price 2/6 (U.S.A. 50c.)   JUNE/AUG., 1967

GOLDEN JUBILEE

THE PRESENTATION TO
MARIA LUISA ANIDO

GUITAR NEWS

The Official Organ of the

INTERNATIONAL CLASSIC GUITAR ASSOCIATION

No. 112   Single copy price 15p (U.S.A. 50c.)   APRIL/JUNE, 1971

THOMAS F. HECK

GUITAR NEWS

The Official Organ of the

INTERNATIONAL CLASSIC GUITAR ASSOCIATION

No. 107   Single copy price 2/6 (U.S.A. 50c.)   JAN./MARCH, 1970

FREDERICK NOAD

GUITAR NEWS

The Official Organ of the

INTERNATIONAL CLASSIC GUITAR ASSOCIATION

No. 81   Single copy price 1/8 (U.S.A. 35c.)   JAN./FEB., 1965

MATHANYA OPHEE

A selection of 'Guitar News' which ceased publication in 1973.

104

HECTOR GARCIA

Born – Havana, Cuba

19th November 1930

Hector Garcia

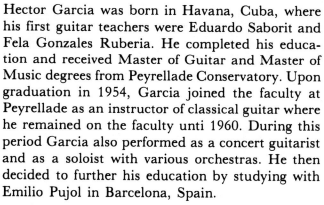

Hector Garcia was born in Havana, Cuba, where his first guitar teachers were Eduardo Saborit and Fela Gonzales Ruberia. He completed his education and received Master of Guitar and Master of Music degrees from Peyrellade Conservatory. Upon graduation in 1954, Garcia joined the faculty at Peyrellade as an instructor of classical guitar where he remained on the faculty unti 1960. During this period Garcia also performed as a concert guitarist and as a soloist with various orchestras. He then decided to further his education by studying with Emilio Pujol in Barcelona, Spain.

In 1960 Garcia left Cuba but was taken prisoner after the 'Bay of Pigs' invasion. Although he had no musical instrument in prison he did continue to compose a lot of music for the guitar. He was released on 24th December 1962 and went to the United States of America. Garcia moved to Albuquerque, New Mexico in 1963, and resumed his career as a concert guitarist. He gave concerts on the West Coast and also performed as soloist with the Los Angeles Symphonette. He also performed in New York's famed Town Hall, the Smithsonsian Institution in Washington, D.C., and other principal cities in the east. An extensive concert tour of major European cities included Madrid, Barcelona, Bilbao, Paris, London, Stockholm, The Hague, Amsterdam, Brussels and the Canary Islands.

Hector Garcia was honoured by the outstanding contemporary composer, Mario Castelnuovo-Tedesco, who wrote a guitar composition on the name of Hector Garcia. Garcia was appointed in 1967 to the faculty of the University of New Mexico when the chair in classical guitar was established. Garcia has generated a high degree of interest there in the classical guitar, drawing students from throughout the United States. The programme includes intensive study and research in the history of the guitar and its literature.

In 1969 Garcia was appointed as assistant to Emilio Pujol in the master classes held for guitarists annually in Cervera (Lerida), Spain.

SELECTED READING
Hector Garcia

Article – 'Guitar Player' – June 1975

Oscar Ghiglia

OSCAR GHIGLIA

Born – Livorno, Italy

13th August 1938

Oscar Ghiglia grew up in an artistic atmosphere, his mother was a pianist, his father a painter. Initially it was thought he would become a painter. His father wanted to paint a family portrait one day, and to entice his son to remain still during the long sittings put a guitar into his hands, teaching him each session a bit more of the rudiments of playing. When the painting was done, Oscar Ghiglia had decided to become a professional guitarist and not a painter.

Ghilgia enrolled in Rome's Santa Cecilia Conservatory and graduated with honours in 1961. From the conservatory Ghiglia was admitted to Andres Segovia's master classes in Siena, and made his professional debut at the Festival of Two Worlds in Spoleto the following year. In 1963 he was the judges' unanimous choice for First Prize at the International Guitar Competition in Paris, and he then won First Prize at the Guitar Competition in Santiago de Compostela, Spain. Then came an invitation from Segovia to be his assistant for two years at the University of California at Berkeley. With this rare honour, Oscar Ghiglia's career took on great momentum, and numerous recitals and concerts worldwide soon followed. In addition to appearing extensively in all parts of North and South America and Europe, Oscar Ghiglia is a frequent performer in the Far East, Israel, Australia, New Zealand and the South Pacific.

Oscar Ghiglia is very much in demand as a teacher all over the world. In North America he has given master classes in, among others, Chicago, Detroit, Los Angeles, Salt Lake City, and Toronto. He has also taught at the University of Missouri, Southern Methodist University, Florida State University, the San Francisco and Cincinnati Conservatories, and the Juilliard School and Mannes College. Since 1969 he has been Artist-in-Residence at the Aspen Festival, and from 1976 he has taught annually in Siena.

SELECTED RECORDS

'Schubert & Carulli For Guitar'	World Record Club	ST 1040
'Paganini For Guitar & Violin'	EMI/HMV	CSD 3511
'Guitar Music of Four Centuries'	Angel	S 36282
'The Guitar in Spain'	Angel	S 36508
'Spanish Guitar'	Angle	S 36849
'Ghiglia Plays Baroque Masters'	Angel	S 39715

SELECTED READING

Oscar Ghiglia	Article – 'Guitar Player' – March 1972
Oscar Ghiglia	Article – 'Guitar' – August 1974

Mauro Giuliani

MAURO GIULIANI

**Born – Bisceglie, near Bari, Italy
27th July 1781**

**Died – Vienna, Austria
8th May 1829**

Mauro Giuliani was one of the most famous nineteenth century guitarists, and probably one of the most brilliant guitar virtuosi the world has known.

As a young boy Giuliani could play the violin, flute and guitar well, but by his teens the young musician had decided to devote his life to the guitar. A self-taught player, Giuliani was not only a great guitarist, but also became one of the greatest composers for the guitar the world has known.

By the time he was twenty years old, Giuliani was already regarded as a virtuoso in his native country, Italy. A European concert tour in 1800 established his reputation throughout the continent. For the next seven years he continued to give recitals in the major cities of Europe. In 1807 he decided to settle in Vienna, Austria, which was at that time one of the great musical centres of Europe.

In Vienna Giuliani led a highly successful career as a teacher and recitalist. He was appointed Chamber Musician and Teacher to the Archduchess Marie Louise. Many members of the Austrian Royal family and nobility studied the guitar under him.

Giuliani's musicianship and guitar artistry inspired Beethoven to say that 'The guitar is a miniature orchesta in itself' (a comment used by Berlioz years later). The guitarist developed a close friendship with Moscheles, Hummel and Diabelli. All were fine guitarists, and they often appeared in concert with Giuliani.

Giuliani was a prolific composer for the guitar. Over three hundred of his compositions were published and these range from very simple exercises and studies to works demanding virtuoso ability on the guitar. Amongst these are several concerti with orchestral accompaniment, duets for violin and guitar, and duets for flute and guitar. The first guitar magazine ever published, the 'Giulianad', was named in his honour. This magazine was first published in London in 1833. Mauro Giuliani died in Vienna, Austria, at the age of 48. He remains to this day on of the greatest guitarists the world has ever known.

SELECTED RECORDS

'Handel Variations/Grand Sonata (Pepe Romero)	Philips	9500 513
'Guitar Concertos OP36/OP70' (with Pepe Romero)	Philips	9500 320
'Le Rossiniane' (with Angel Romero)	Angel	SZ 37326
'Guitar Concertos' (with Julian Bream)	RCA	SB 6826
'Le Rossiniane' (with Julian Bream)	RCA	ARLI 0711

SELECTED READING

'The Birth of the Classic Guitar' Dissertation, Yale University (1970)	Thomas F. Heck
'Guitar Concertos of Giuliani'	Article – 'Guitar' – November 1976
Mauro Giuliani	Article – 'Guitar Review' No. 18 – 1955
Mauro Giuliani	Article – 'Guitar Review' No. 37 – 1972

SELECTED MUSIC

Six Variations, op. 2, ed. Chiesa	Zerboni
Variations from 'La Molinara', op. 4	Zerboni
Variations on a Ballet Theme, op.7	Zerboni
Rondo, op. 8, no. 2	GA 410
Twelve Monferrine, op. 12	Zerboni
Rondo, op. 14, no. 5	Bèrben
Sonata in C, op. 15	SY 460
Rondo, op. 17, no. 1	GA 411
Variations on an Original Theme, op. 20	Zerboni
Twelve Waltzes for Guitar, op. 21, facsimile of 1st edition of 1808	Schroth
Twelve Ecossaises, op. 33	Zerboni
Divertimenti, op. 37	GA 414
Variations on an Aria, op. 38	Zerboni

MAURIO GIULIANI – Selected Music (continued)

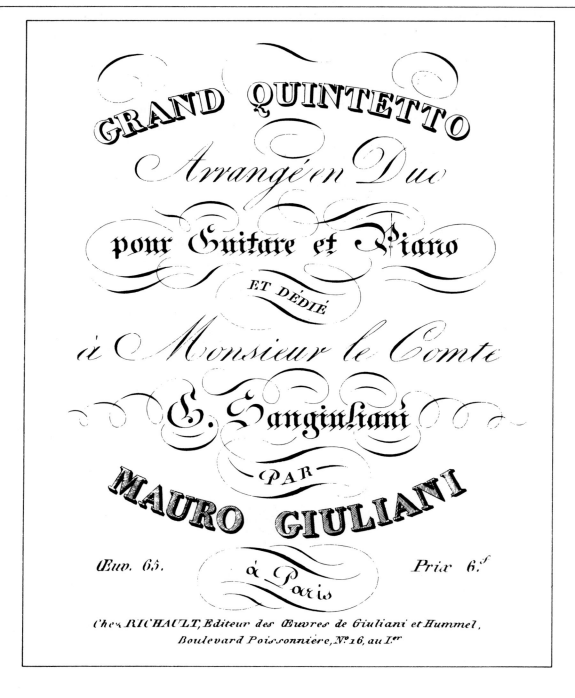

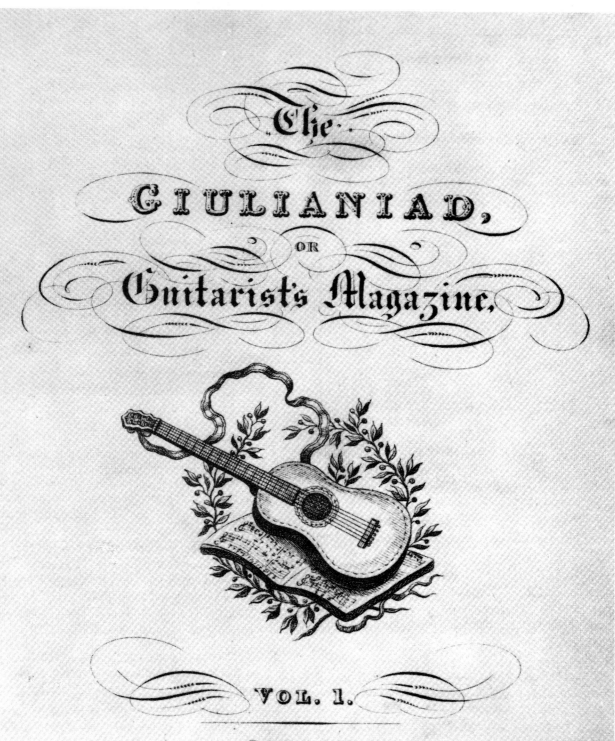

The.

GIULIANIAD,

OR

Guitarist's Magazine,

VOL. 1.

LONDON,

Published for the Proprietor by Sherwood & C.° 23, Paternoster Row,
Chappell, Music Seller to the King 50, New Bond Street,
and Duff, 65, Oxford Street.

Price Bound. (1.ˢᵗ Vol.) ⎰ in Numbers, each   2/6
also of Johanning & C.° 6, John Street, Oxford Street.
Hutchison Jun.ʳ

Cover of first English guitar magazine, 'The Giulianiad'.

VICENTE GOMEZ

Born – Madrid, Spain

8th July 1911

Vicente Gomez

COURTESY VICENTE GOMEZ

Vicente Gomez began to play the guitar when he was seven years old. His father owned a tavern, and by the time he was eight years old Gomez was already entertaining customers with flamenco music on his guitar. His obvious talents on the instrument were quickly recognised and he was encouraged by his schoolteacher to take private lessons in Solfeggio.

Gomez turned to the classical guitar after he became a pupil of Don Quintin Esquembre, a former pupil of Tarrega. He made rapid progress and furthered his classical training when he entered the Madrid Conservatoire.

Vicente Gomez made his first public appearance at the age of thirteen at the Teatro Espanol. A highly successful concert tour of Spain soon followed, and in 1932-33 he toured France and North Africa. An extensive tour of Russia and Poland was made in 1936, and later in the same year Gomez gave recital in Cuba, Mexico and the United States of America.

For the next twenty years Vicente Gomez enjoyed enormous success both in Spain and in the United States of America. As well as numerous public recitals and radio broadcasts his guitar playing and original music was featured in several Spanish and Hollwood films. In 1948 he opend a nightclub 'La Zambra' in New York City, and late in 1953 he established a school in Los Angeles entitled 'The Academy of Spanish Arts'.

Since 1958 Vicente Gomez has dedicated most of his time to teaching and the writing of music. Most of his original records are now out of print but it is hoped that several new recordings will be released in the very near future.

SELECTED RECORDS

'Guitar Recital'	Decca	DL 8018
'Guitar Extraordinary'	Decca	DL 4312
'Blood Wedding Suite'	Decca	DL 78918
'Artistry of Vicente Gomez'	Decca	DL 78965

SELECTED READING

Vicente Gomez	Article – 'Guitar Player' – December 1977
Vicente Gomez	Article – 'Guitar & Lute' – July 1979

SELECTED MUSIC

Vicente Gomez Guitar Album	Belwin

JOSÉ LUIS GONZALEZ

Born – Alcoy, Spain

2nd July 1932

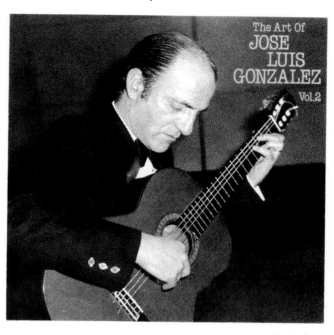

José Luis Gonzalez gave his first public guitar recital at the age of sixteen in Madrid's Realto theatre. In 1957 he graduated from the Valencia Conservatory. His talents were recognised very early on his his career, and the young guitarist became a scholarship pupil of Regina Sainz De La Maza in Madrid. Later he studied several times with Andres Segovia at Santiago De Compostela.

In 1961 he won the Margarita Pastor prize in a competition organised by the Orense Conservatory which was being held in conjunction with the music at Compostela Festival. Now established as one of the most important classical guitarists to have merged since the end of World War II, José Luis Gonzalez gave many highly successful concerts in Europe and North Africa.

In 1962 Gonzalez decided to move to Australia. There he settled in Sydney and soon established himself as a busy recitalist and teacher. Gonzalez continues to give many guitar concerts in major countries throughout the world, having achieved great success recently in Japan. He now has once again resettled in Spain.

SELECTED RECORDS

'El Arté de la Guitarra Espanola'	CBS	S 73656
'Portrait of the Guitar'	CBS	61654
'Art of José Luis Gonzalez' – Vol. One	CBS/Sony	28AC 1184
'Art of Jose Luis Gonzalez' – Vol. Two	CBS/Sony	28AC 1239

JOSEF HOLECEK

Born– Prague, Czechoslovakia

1939

Josef Holecek

Josef Holecek showed obvious talent on the guitar at an early age. After examinations he entered the guitar class of the Prague Conservatory. He finished his studies there under Professor Sadlik receiving his diploma in 1956.

In that same year Holecek was one of the five finalists of the International Guitar Competition in Paris, organised by the ORTF (French radio and television). He was awarded a scholarship to study under Professor Karl Scheit at the Academy of Music in Vienna, Austria. There he completed his studies receiving an honours dilpoma after only one year in 1967.

Back in Czechoslovakia Josef Holecek started and developed his activities as a pupil of the Prague Conservatory. There he was engaged as a guitarist in the National Theatre of Prague from 1960 to 1967. As well as teaching the guitar at the Theatre Academy of Prague from 1962 to 1967, he also lead a guitar class at the Conservatory of Pilsen during his last year in Prague.

After Holecek finished his studies with Karl Scheit in Vienna he went to Sweden and was engaged as a teacher of the guitar at the Framnas Folkhogskola. He also directed several summer guitar courses with international participation in both Sweden and Finland. Since the autumn of 1970 he has been a guitar teacher at the Gothenburg Conservatory. Josef Holecek has given concerts throughout Czechoslovakia, and also in the major cities of Austria, Sweden and Finland.

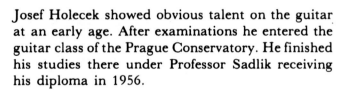

SELECTED RECORD

'With Marta Schele'	BIS	LP-31

SELECTED MUSIC

Guitar Jokes – Parodies & Transcriptions	CG 5946
Guitar Moods	CG 5915
Mini Studies	CG 5914

MIKIO HOSHIDO

Born – Tokyo, Japan

19th September 1947

Mikio Hoshido

Mikio Hoshido is one of Japan's leading young classical guitarists.

He first appeared as a guitar soloist at a concert in Tokyo at the age of nineteen in 1966. Two years later in 1968 he gave his first solo guitar concert, also in Tokyo. Since that time Mikio Hoshido has given concerts throughout Japan and has appeared on radio and television. From 1968 to 1970 he studied guitar with José Tomas, Andres Segovia and Alirio Diaz.

In 1972, at the regular concert of the Japan Philhar-monic Symphony Orchestra, he performed the Japanese première of the work by Albert Pizzini, 'Concierto para Tres Hermanas'. In 1976 he held a joint recital for contemporary works in Tokyo with German guitarist Siegfried Behrend.

From 1977 to 1978 Hoshido went to Spain where he studied guitar with Narciso Yepes at the invitation of the Spanish government. In 1978 Hoshido gave a recital at the Chateau de Sorbonne, Paris, and following this played in the major cities of Spain and Belgium.

SELECTED RECORDS

'Hoshido Recital'	Audio Lab	ALC-1044
'Favourite Show Pieces of Guitar'	CBS/Sony	25AG-628
'M. Carcassi 25 Studies'	CBS/Sony	20AG-680
'Method of the Guitar I'	CBS/Sony	20AG-354
'Method of the Guitar II'	CBS/Sony	20AG-541

SELECTED MUSIC

Method of Guitar	Zen-On ◊240190
'Las Cantigas de Santa Maria' para Guitarra	Zen-On, ZG-33

DON A. F. HUERTA

**Born – Orihuela, Valencia, Spain
6th June 1804**

**Died – Paris, France
1875**

Don Huerta

Don A. F. Huerta was one of the great guitar virtuosi of the nineteenth century.

As a child Huerta showed a strong inclination for music and from the age of fourteen studied music at the San Pablo College in Salamanca. His special subjects were singing and guitar playing and he achieved distinction in both. His most important guitar teacher was the renowned Manuel Garcia.

During the period of the Peninsular War in Spain, Huerta was enlisted into the army. He fought on the side of General Riego who eventually lost the war. Huerta was forced to seek refuge in France and settled in Paris. There he devoted himself entirely to music, in particular to the guitar and singing.

Very impulsive by nature, Huerta suddenly decided to cross the Atlantic to go to the United States of America. There he was to make his living singing and playing the guitar. After a visit to Martinique and Cuba, Huerta lost his voice and was forced to devote himself to the guitar. He began an intense study of the instrument and he was soon giving solo guitar recitals throughout the United States. He became generally regarded as the greatest guitarist on the North American Continent of the period.

Huerta returned to Europe in 1826 and settled in London, England. There he became associated with many distinguished musicians including La Pasta, Moscheles, Donizelli and La Blache. Huerta was to live in London until 1830. During this period he married one of the daughters of guitar maker Louis Panormo and also enjoyed enormous success as a guitarist.

In 1830 Huerta returned to France and once again decided to live in Paris. As in England, Huerta enjoyed great popularity and success in France and Europe as a whole. Over the next few years he toured throughout Europe and the Middle East dazzling audiences with his guitar virtuosity. He was made a Knight of the Order of Gregory the Great, an honour of which he was particularly proud. Whilst he was in Spain he declined an offer from Queen Isabelle II to become her permanent court guitarist. He preferred to continue living in Paris, and it was there that he died in 1875 at the age of 71.

A typical Mozzani nine string concert guitar played by Mario Maccaferri during the nineteen twenties.

Sharon Isbin

SHARON ISBIN

Born – Minniapolis, Minnesota, USA

7th August 1956

Sharon Isbin began to play the guitar at the age of nine. Her first serious study of the instrument was with Aldo Minella in Italy. Her father, a professor at the University of Minnesota, had taken the family with him to Italy for a year's sabbatical.

On her return to Minniapolis Sharon Isbin continued her studies with Jeffrey Van, and later with Sophocles Papas. She made rapid progress and attended master classes given by Oscar Ghiglia and Alirio Diaz.

In 1979 Isbin received her master's degree in music from Yale University where she had conducted weekly master classes for three years. She also studied with the renowned Bach interpreter and scholar, Rosalyn Tureck, in Oxford, England.

Since 1974, when she gave her first European tour at the age of seventeen, Sharon Isbin has been acclaimed by guitar enthusiasts and critics alike all over the world. In 1975 she was awarded the first prize in the international competition 'Guitar 75' held in Toronto, Canada. The following year she again won the top prize in the guitar division of the Munich International Competition. Her performances for this event were televised and broadcast throughout the world. As a winner of the Queen Sofia 1979 International Competition in Madrid, Sharon Isbin performed Rodrigo's 'Concierto de Aranjuez' in a nationwide broadcast with the Spanish National Radio Orchestra.

In May, 1977 Sharon Isbin made a highly acclaimed debut at London's Wigmore Hall, followed by the first of several BBC appearances. Her March 1979 New York debut at the Lincoln Centre's Alice Tully Hall was again well received. The previous year she performed as a guest soloist with the Minnesota Orchestra, premièring 'Concerto for Guitar', a work written for her by the Israeli composer Ami Maayani. In June 1978, she made her first solo tour of Japan and later that summer gave master classes and performances for the Rubin Academy Summer Festival in Jerusalem. Sharon Isbin has also appeared as a guest artist at the Grand Teton Music Festival in Wyoming, the Festival Les Arcs in Bourg Saint Maurice, and the Strasbourg International Music Festival, France.

Sharon Isbin has proved herself to be one of the foremost guitarists on today's music scene in the United States of America. She now lives in New York City, and as well as leading a busy life as a recitalist, is currently a member of the guitar department of the faculty of the Manhattan School of Music.

SELECTED RECORDS

'Bach, Britten, Brouwer'	Sound Environment	TR 1013
'Concierto de Aranjuez'	Denon/PCM	OX 7210 ND
'Guitar Recital'	Denon/PCM	OX 7224 ND
'Spanish Works for Guitar'	Denon/PCN	OF 7012

SELECTED READING

Sharon Isbin	Article – 'Guitar' – September 1977
Sharon Isbin & Rosalyn Tureck	Article – 'Guitar' – September 1980
Sharon Isbin	Article – 'Guitar & Lute' – April 1981
Sharon Isbin	Article – 'Guitarra' – September 1980
Sharon Isbin	Article – 'Guitar Player' – May 1980

ALEXANDER IVANOV-KRAMSKOY

Born – Moscow, Russia
1912

Died – Minsk, Russia
11th April 1973

Alexander Ivanov-Kramskoy

Alexander Ivanov-Kramskoy was one of the best known contemporary Russian guitarists.

He devoted himself to the classical guitar rather than to the seven-string instrument which since Andrei Sychra (1773-1850) dominated, until recently, the Russian guitar world.

Ivanov-Kramskoy published a method for six-string guitar which, although specially adapted for self study, is still widely used in schools of the Soviet Union. He gave many concerts and radio performances of this own compositions and those of other Russian composers as well as music from the standard concert repertoire.

Ivanov-Kramskoy was a very capable musician and wrote a large number of original pieces for the guitar. He also transcribed for the guitar all kinds of interesting music by Soviet and other composers. He was also a most talented and respected chamber music players. He made a recording of his own variations on Russian themes for guitar and orchestra, now out of print, on the Monitor label. This record confirms the fine technical ability of Ivanov-Kramskoy.

SELECTED RECORD
'Concerto for Guitar and Strings'   Monitor   MG 2024

RICARDO FERNANDEZ IZNAOLA

Born – Havana, Cuba

21st February 1949

COURTESY IZNAOLA

Ricardo Fernandez Iznaola

Ricardo Fernandez Iznaola was born in Cuba but his parents moved to Venezuela shortly after the revolution in Cuba. Iznaola's family had first settled in Columbia and it was there that Iznaola began to play the guitar.

After his family had settled in Caracas, Venezuela, the young guitarist continued to teach himself for four years using the available written methods and also listing to records. He then entered the Escuala Superior De Musica in Caracas and studied under Professor Manuel Perez Diaz. Iznaola soon showed remarkable progress and in 1968 won third prize in the Manuel Leoncio Porras competition in Caracas. In the same year he went to Madrid, Spain to study with Regino Sainz De La Maza.

Iznaola was to study with Sainz De La Maza until 1973. In 1968 he won the first prize at the Francisco Tarrega competition in Benicassum. In 1969 and 1971 he also won prizes in competitions held in Munich, Granada, Madrid and Caracas.

Ricardo Fernandez Iznaola has since 1970 been a naturalized Venezuelan, yet he has made his home in Madrid, Spain where he teaches at the Music Conservatory. In recent years Iznaola has concertized throughout Europe and the USA often featuring twentieth century Latin American music in his programme. He is also a regular contributor to the magazine 'Guitar and Lute'.

SELECTED RECORDS

'Original Guitar Music'	Belter	70.912
'Venezuelan Music for Guitar', Vol. 1	Promus	LPP 2048
'Venezuelan Music for Guitar', Vol. 2	Promus	LPPS 20154
'La Guitarra en Latino America'	Promus	LPPS 20238

SELECTED READING

Ricardo Fernandez Iznaola	Article – 'Guitar' – December 1975
Ricardo Fernandez Iznaola	Article – 'Guitar' – April 1980
Ricardo Fernandez Iznaola	Article – 'Guitar & Lute' – March 1977

JEAN PIERRE JUMEZ

Born – Hesdin, Pas De Calais, France

9th February 1943

Jean Pierre Jumez

Jean Pierre Jumez, one of the leading classical guitarists in France today, came from a family of pianists and organists. He first studied the guitar in Paris with Jean Lafon, 1959-61. From 1962-63 Jumez studied under José Sierra at the Music Conservatory at Saint Germain en Laye, near Paris. The following year the young guitarist studied the art of flamenco with Pedro Soler, and in 1966 he moved to the USA to study jazz with Charlie Byrd in Washington.

Returning to Europe, Jumez completed his music studies at the Santa Cecilia Academy in Rome, Italy, with the conductor Gianluigi Gelmetti and Professor Nataletti. The latter is a specialist in the study of popular music around the world.

In 1972 Jumez made his United Stated debut at the Carnegie Recital Hall in New York City. Since that time he has become one of the most travelled of contemporary classical guitarists. He has appeared in over one hundred countries, including concert tours of the Soviet Union. In 1977 he became the first classical guitarist to perform in Peking, China.

Many works have been dedicated to him. Among them the 'Petite Suite Francaise' by John Duarte and 'Pictures of an Exhibition' by Soviet composer Piotr Panin. Jumez has premièred a great amount of compositions, particularly in the French repertoire, included are: 'Concerto for Guitar and Symphony Orchestra' (Jacques Casterede, 1978); 'Swing Nr 2' by Jacques Bondon; 'Deux Etudes De Concert' by Andre Jolivet 'Soliloque En Souvenir De Manuel De Falla' by Henri Sauguet; and 'Hommage a Alonso Mudarra' by Georges Auric.

Jean Pierre Jumez is the founder of the Martinique International Guitar Festival and is a permanent member of the Yehudi Menuhin Foundation jury (France). He is also President of the International Guitar Information and Documentation Centre ('Guitharotheque', in Saint Germain en Laye). He has conducted various master classes around the world.

Aside from the classical field, Jumez has constructed a unique repertoire of works inspired by folk music discovered through his many travels, these include pieces from Africa, Asia, Russia, South America, as well as Eskimo and Arab music.

SELECTED RECORDS

'Les Couleurs De La Guitare No. 1'	Festival	FLD
'Les Couleurs De La Guitare No. 2'	Festival	FLD 700
'Les Couleurs De La Guitare No. 4'	Festival	FLD 709
'Nimble Fingers of Jean Pierre Jumez'	Westminster	WGS 8240

SELECTED READING

Jean Pierre Jumez	Article – 'Guitar' – May 1977
Jean Pierre Jumez	Article – 'Guitar Player' – November 1974
Jean Pierre Jumez	Article – 'Guitar & Lute' – March 1982

HIROTSUGU KAKINUMA

Born – Tokyo, Japan

5th Setpember 1944

Hirotsugu Kakinuma

COURTESY ZENON CO.

Hirotsugu Kakinuma is one of the foremost classical guitarists to have emerged from Japan in recent years.

After winning awards in the 9th and 10th Tokyo International Guitar Competition in 1966 and 1967, Kakinuma went to Spain where he studied guitar with Regina Sainz de la Maza and José Tomas. In 1971, he participated in a seminar given by Andres Segovia in Santiago de Compostella. After studying with Narciso Yepes, he was invited to Italy by Renato Fazano, conductor of the Virtuosi di Roma. In 1972 Kakinuma won the contest. 'Rassegna Giovani Interpreti' held by the Radio Televisione Italiana. Since 1974, he has taught at the National College of Music and from September, 1980, has directed the Avigliana Conservatoire.

Over the past few years Kakinuma has held advanced courses in Japan since 1976 in Italy at Spotorno and also at the Pamparato 'Festival dei Saraceni'. He does guitar revisions and transcriptions and has recently published a guitar method. Kakinuma has carried out an intense concert schedule both as a soloist and in chamber groups and orchestras. He has also taken part in international festivals in Japan and in various European cities.

JOHN KNEUBUHL

Born – Boulder, Colorado, USA

1943

John Kneubuhl

John Kneubuhl began his guitar studies at the age of twelve. He had no formal education on the instrument and is largely self taught.

Kneubuhl studied literature at Yale University. Whilst he was there he began performing in the coffee houses of New York's Greenwich Village. Here his technical ability on the guitar, fine musical sense and wide repertoire won him a high reputation.

His formal debut took place in 1970. Since that time Kneubuhl has played throughout the United States of America both as a solo recitalist and also with various musical groups including the Baltimore Symphony Orchestra.

Kneubuhl currently resides in Santa Barbara, California. His record release 'American Guitar', recorded under the auspices of the Yehudi Menuhin foundation, received high critical acclaim. As well as being a fine performer of the guitar's standard repertoire, Kneubuhl is an outstanding interpreter of contemporary music for the instrument.

John Kneubuhl has also several television, radio and film appearances to his credit, and is highly regarded as one of the most important young classical guitarists in the United States today.

SELECTED RECORD
'American Guitar'   Orion   ORS 78323

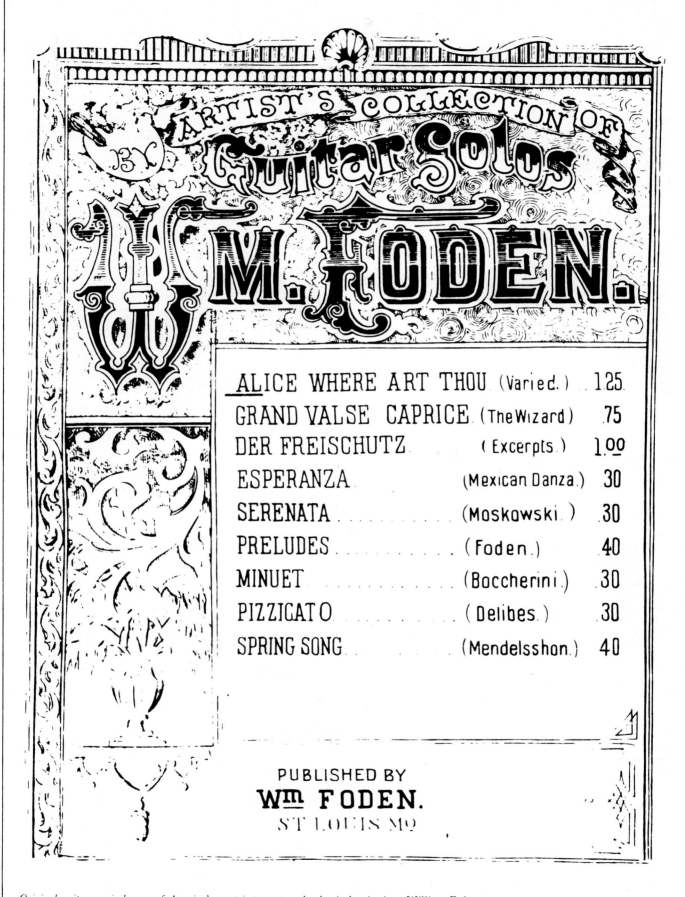

ARTIST'S COLLECTION OF
Guitar Solos
BY WM. FODEN.

ALICE WHERE ART THOU	(Varied.)	1.25.
GRAND VALSE CAPRICE	(The Wizard)	.75
DER FREISCHUTZ	(Excerpts.)	1.00
ESPERANZA	(Mexican Danza.)	.30
SERENATA	(Moskowski.)	.30
PRELUDES	(Foden.)	.40
MINUET	(Boccherini.)	.30
PIZZICATO	(Delibes.)	.30
SPRING SONG	(Mendelsshon.)	.40

PUBLISHED BY
WM FODEN.
ST LOUIS MO

Original guitar music by one of America's most important early classical guitarists, William Foden.

Alexandre Lagoya

ALEXANDRE LAGOYA

Born – Alexandria, Egypt

21st June 1929

Alexandre Lagoya is without doubt one of the foremost guitarists of the twentieth century. Born in Alexandria, Egypt, the son of an Italian mother and Greek father, Lagoya began to play the guitar at the age of eight.

He gave his first concert at the age of thirteen, and despite some objections from his parents, decided to make the guitar his career. He gave many recitals in the villages of Egypt and toured other parts of the Middle East and Europe. At the age of eighteen he moved to Paris, France, and further his musical education at the Ecole Normale De Musique. By the time he was nineteen Lagoya had given more than five hundred concerts, and his career as a professional guitarist was assured. It was in Paris that Lagoya was able to perfect his technique, studying harmony and counterpoint with the famed teachers, Maestro Saudry. He also met other musicians – among them Darius Milhaud, Francis Poulenc, Henri Dutilleux, Olivier Messiaen, Joaquin Rodrigo and Heitor Villa-Lobos.

In 1950 he visited Siena to study with Andres Segovia. In the same year he met Ide Presti, a guitarist he much admired. They met in the home of André Verdier and a mutual love for the instrument developed into a love for each other. They married in 1952 and not only joined lives but musical forces as well to become the legendary concert duo – Presti-Lagoya. Though they had made formidable reputations as solo performers, their work together brought them even more fame. They founded a guitar class at the Schola Cantorum in Paris and also made regular world tours. In fifteen years they played 2,000 concerts and also worked out many brilliant new techniques for the guitar.

In 1967 the Presti-Lagoya duo was at the height of its fame; when Ida Presti whilst preparing for a concert in New York city suddenly fell ill and died. Lagoya, grief stricken, continued teaching but did not perform in concert. Emotionally, he had been devastated, and it took him a year and a half to re-study his repertoire. After a break of five years he began a new careeer as a solo guitar recitalist.

Alexandre Lagoya, is now one of the world's busiest concert guitarists, and plays at least 100 concerts a year. He is also Professor at the Paris National Conservatory, a position he has held since 1969, when he created a guitar class for the institution. In the summer, Lagoya teaches at the International Academy of Music in Nice, a position he has held since 1960, as well as in other parts of the world.

SELECTED RECORDS

'L'Extrordinaire Alexandre Lagoya'	Philips	6521 013
'La Guitare Est Mon Maitre'	Philips	6504 041
'Lagoya'	Philips	6504 120
'Lagoya Plays Sor and Villa Lobos'	Philips	6504 131
'Concerto for Classical Guitar and Jazz Piano' (Bolling)	RCA	CY 3007
'Rampal and Lagoya in Concert' (2 LPs)	RCA	ARL 2-2631
'The Spanish Guitar'	CBS	M35857

WITH IDA PRESTI

'Music for the Classical Guitar'	Nonesuch	H 71161
'Musique Baraque Pour Deux Guitares'	Philips	6504 003
'Concertos Pour Deux Guitares'	Philips	6504 018
'Musique Espagnole Pour Deux Guitares'	Philips	6504 020
'Presti – Lagoya – Ouevres Pour Deux Guitares'	Philips	6504 049
'Masters of the Guitar' – Volume One	RCA	RB 6589

SELECTED READING

Alexandre Lagoya	Article – 'Guitarra' – May 1980
Alexandre Lagoya	Article – 'Guitar Player' – February 1982

SELECTED MUSIC

Caprice	Ric. R1608
Rêverie	Ric. R1607

ROBERTO LARA

Born – Tres Arroyos, Argentina

23rd May 1927

Roberto Lara is one of Argentina's foremost guitarists.

He completed his musical studies at the Music Conservatory in Buenos Aires. Since then he has made several concert tours of South America and Europe, and although very famous in South America is little known to guitarists in the rest of the world.

Lara currently spends much of his year teaching, and he also records for the Qualiton record company in Argentina. Several of his recordings have been released by Lyrichord Disc Incorporated in the United States of America. Lara has also made many transcriptions for the guitar, including a vast amount of traditional Argentinian melodies.

SELECTED RECORDS

'The Guitar of the Pampas'	Lyrichord	LLST 7253
'The Classic Guitar'	Lyrichord	LLST 7299

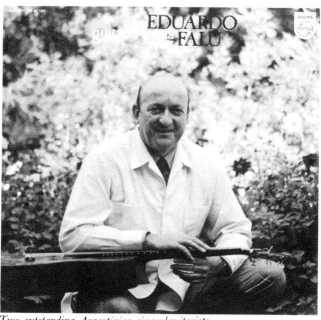

Two outstanding Argentinian singer/guitarists.

ANTONIO LAURO

Born – Ciudad Bolivar, Venezuela

3rd August 1917

The popularity of the music of Antonio Lauro has grown enormously over the past few years throughout the world. Lauro, born in Ciudad Bolivar, Venezuela in 1917, has made a great contribution to the library of contemporary classical guitar music. Not only through his own compositions, but also through his many arrangements for the guitar of the music of fellow Venezuelan composers, Sojo, Borges, Cisneros, Ramon y Rivera, Landaeta and others.

Antonio Lauro has an academic musical background. He studied at the Academy of Music in Caracas under Vincente Emilio Sojo and Juan Bautista Plasis. His original instrument was the piano, but on hearing the Paraguayan guitar virtuoso Agustin Barrios Mangore in concert, Lauro decided to devote his musical study to the guitar.

A prolific composer and arrange, Lauro has written and arranged many works, the bulk of which are as yet unpublished. Most of these are for the guitar but he has also composed works for a Cappela Choral Group, Orchestra, Orchestra and Choir, Piano, Piano and Voice, Organ and Voice, String Quartet, Wind Quartet, and other instrumental combinations. The inspiration for his compositions is, more often than not, derived from the Folklore,

Antonio Lauro

PHOTO GEORGE CLINTON   COURTESY GUITAR MAGAZINE

Instruments, and Regional Dance Rhythms of Venezuela.

It was the Venezuelan virtuoso guitarist, Alirio Diaz, who really first drew the guitar world's attention to the genius of his countryman. Originally a student of Lauro, Diaz became a close friend of the composer. He revised and fingered many of Lauro's original compositions and arrangements for the guitar. Diaz has for the last few years often included a selection of these in many of his concert programmes, as he has toured the world annually. As a result the music of Antonio Lauro has now become the feature of many other leading guitarists' concert repertoires. Lauro is without doubt one of the instruments most popular original composers.

SELECTED RECORDS

'David Russell Plays Antonio Lauro'	Guitar Masters	GMR 1001
'Guitar Music of Spain and Latin America' – Alirio Diaz	EMI/HMV	HQS 1175

SELECTED READING

Antonio Lauro	Article – 'Guitar' – October 1980
Antonio Lauro	Article – 'Guitar & Lute' – January 1980
Antonio Lauro	Complete List of works – 'Guitar & Lute' – January 1980

SELECTED MUSIC

Angostura – Valse Venezolano, ed. Díaz	B 901
Carora – Valse Venezolano, ed. Díaz	B 903
El Marabino – Valse Venezolano, ed. Díaz	B 904
Four Venezuelan Waltzes, ed. Díaz	B 794
María Luisa – Valse Venezolano, ed. Díaz	B 905
Sonata	ZA 5539
Suite Venezolano, ed. Díaz	B 793
Two Venezuelan Pieces: Valse Criollo & Pavana, ed. Papas	CO 166A
Variations on a Venezuelan Children's Song, ed. Díz	B 940
Air De Jaropo	B 902

Two nineteenth century guitars. Typical French guitar (left), rare Gennaro Fabricatore, 1831, Naples, Italy (right).

LUIGI LEGNANI

Born – LUIGI RINALDO LEGNANI,
Ferrara, Italy 7th November 1790

Died – Ravenna, Italy
5th August 1877

Luigi Legnani began his musical education at the age of eight when his parents moved to Ravenna. As a singer and guitarist he soon showed immense talent and by the time he was seventeen he was taking a prominent part in the opera at the Ravenna Theatre.

Legnani's first public recital as a guitar virtuoso was in Milan in 1819. From that time he was regarded as one of the foremost guitarists in Europe. He toured Europe extensively from 1922, appearing in Austria, Italy, Switzerland and Russia where he played before the Grand Duke Nicolas.

In 1836 Legnani befriended the violinist/guitarist Nicolo Paganini. The two lived together on Paganini's estate the Villa Cajona near Palma. The two great musicians performed many recitals together, and in fact Paganini's last concert was given in association with Legnani.

Legnani became very interested in the actual construction of the guitar. When he visited the leading guitar makers in Vienna, Austria, – Staufer and Ries – he left them with designs of several new models including a terz guitar. Both these makers produced guitars bearing Legnani's name. In 1850 Legnani decided to give up his career as a concert recitalist. He returned to Ravenna and devoted his life to the construction of guitars.

Legnani was not only a talented luthier and virtuoso guitarist, but also a prolific composer for the guitar. He wrote over two hundred and fifty compositions for the instrument, including a 'Method for Guitar' (opus 25) which was published by Ricordi of Milan. The bulk of Legnani's compositions were published in Vienna, Austria, by the publishing house of Leidesdorf.

Luigi Legnani, an honorary member of the Philharmonic Societies of Rome, Florence, Ferrara and Munich, and one of the greatest classical guitarists of the nineteenth century died in Ravenna, at the age of eighty-seven, in 1877.

SELECTED MUSIC

Caprices in All Major & Minor Keys, op. 20, no.s 1-18 and Nos. 19-36	Kalmus
Caprices in All Keys, op. 20, Books 1 & 2	GA 35/GA 36
Introduction, Theme, Variation, & Finale, op. 64, ed. Chiesa	Zerboni
Introduction, Theme, & Variations, op. 224	GA 74
Introduction & Theme, op. 237	Kalmus
Six Little Caprices, op. 250, ed. Pomilio	BA 11240
Six Caprices, op. 250	Bèrben
Ten Selected Caprices, ed. Storti	Bèrben
Twelve Selected Caprices, ed. Savio	BA 11363
Variations on the duet 'Nel cor piu non mi sento', from 'la Molinara' ed. Chiesa	Zerboni

DAVID LEISNER

Born – Los Angeles, California, USA

22nd December 1953

David Leisner

Since his success as a prize winner in the 1975 International Guitar competition in Toronto, Canada, David Leisner has become regarded as one of the best classical guitarists in the United States of America. His recent concert performances, and his record release on the Titanic label, confirm this opinion. He also won the Silver Medal at the 1981 International Guitar competition held in Geneva, Switzerland.

Although born in California, Leisner is a graduate of Wesleyan University in Connecticut and is now a resident of New York City. Over the years he has studied the guitar and music with several important teachers, both in the United States of America and Europe. He has studied guitar with John Duarte, Angelo Gilardino, Theodore Norman, and David Starobin; interpretation with Karen Tuttle and John Kirkpatrick; and composition with Richard K. Winslow.

David Leisner recently made an important contribution to the repertoire of guitar music by his rediscovery of many of the work of Johann Kaspar Mertz, a contemporary of Schubert and Mendelssohn. The young guitarist is also a talented composer and singer. He has had two works commissioned by a London choral group and a New York theatre company. His Suite Op. 1 has recently been published by the Bèrben Company in Italy. Leisner has appeared several times on National Radio in the USA and also in concert with the world famous hamonica player, Larry Adler.

David Leisner was recently appointed to the faculty of the New England Conservatory of Music in Boston and also to the roster of Affiliate Artist Incorporated, an organisation which establishes corporate sponsorships for extended artist residencies in communities throughout the United States.

SELECTED RECORD
'The Viennese Guitar'   Titanic   TI-46

DAGOBERTO LINHARES

Born – San Paulo, Brazil

1953

Dagoberto Linhares

Dagoberto Linhares started his guitar studies with Manuel Sao Marcos at the age of nine. At fourteen he won first prize at the Sao Paulo City Competition as well as the "Young Instrumentalists' award. In 1971 he played solo guitar in the South American première of Castelnuovo Tedesco's 'Romancero Gitano' (based on Garcia Lorca) for chorus and guitar.

Linhares moved to Europe in 1972 and was appointed professor at the Fribourg Conservatory in Switzerland. Subsequently he attended Master Classes given by Turibio Santos and Julian Bream. Dagoberto Linhares continued his success in international competitions when he won first prize in the Geneva Conservatory 'Virtuosité' examination in 1973. He was also granted the Swiss Musician

Association Award. The following year he was laureate at the Maria Canals competition in Barcelona and, in 1975, at Concours International d'Execution Musicale in Geneva.

Since his debut at the Wigmore Hall, London, in 1974, Linhares has given numerous concerts throughout Europe, the United States and Latin America. He has made several broadcasts for continental radio stations.

His 1977 engagements included tours of Italy and appearances at Bratislawa Festival (Rodrigo's Concierto de Aranjuez'), Tibor Varga Festival (Villa Lobos Concerto), and the Festival Estival in Paris, France.

Dagoberto Linhares currently lives in Geneva, Switerland.

MIGUEL LLOBET

Born – Barcelona, Spain
17th October 1878

Died – Barcelona, Spain
22nd February 1938

Miguel Llobet

Miguel Llobet's father was a noted wood carver of religious images. As a result Llobet was raised in an artistic atmosphere, as many distinguished artists and musicians used his father's studio as a meeting place. His father had hoped that Llobet would follow in his footsteps and also become an artist. Llobet was in fact a skillful artist as can be seen by the excellent sketches he made throughout his life.

Llobet's uncle gave him his first guitar when he was eleven years old, and he began to study the instrument with Macan Alegre at the Municipal School of Barcelona. Alegre immediately recognised Llobet's special musical talent and introduced him to the leading guitarist in Spain at that time, Francisco Tarrega. Llobet soon made great progress under Tarrega's tutelage, and in 1900 he made his recital debut in Malaga. This concert was a resounding success and as a result Llobet was invited to play for the Spanish Royal family in Madrid.

True international fame came to Llobet after his first concert in Paris, France, at the Salon Washington-Palace on 26th January 1905. A series of highly acclaimed concerts followed. Llobet's reputation had been established in Paris with the help of his friend, pianist Ricardo Vines. With his infleunce great musicians including Debussy, Ravel, Fauré, Dukas and Stravinsky, were often members of Llobet's audience. Miguel Llobet continued a highly successful career as a recitalist. He toured throughout Europe, South America and the United States of America. There is no doubt that Llobet was one of the most influential guitarists of the era. He was probably the first guitarist to make a recording with a microphone. These first records were made by Parlophon Electra in Barcelona in 1926. He was also to make several duo recordings with the Argentinian guitarist Maria Luisa Anido.

Llobet was not only a great guitar virtuoso, but also a fine transcriber and arranger for the instrument. It was as a result of Llobet's repeated requests that Manuel De Falla wrote 'Homenaje Pour Le Tombeau De Claude Debussy' (1920) for the guitar.

Despite rumours that Llobet died during a bombing raid in Barcelona during the Spanish civil war, there is now positive proof he died of natural causes, after a bout of pleurisy, on 22nd February 1938 at the age of 59.

SELECTED RECORD

'The Recordings of Miguel Llobet' (2 LPs)	El Maestro	EM 8003

SELECTED READING

'Miguel Llobet, Chitarrista Dell Impressionismo'	Bruno Tonazzi – Bèrben, Milan (1966)

SELECTED MUSIC

El Mestre – Catalan Folk Song	BA 12124
Estilo Popular Argentino, No. 1	UME
Estilo Popular Argentino, No. 2	UME
Five Catalan Folk Melodies, ed. Papas	CO 232
La Filla del Marxant	BA 12123
Leonesa	UME
Respuesta	UME
Romanza (in C minor)	UME 21695
Scherzo – Waltz	UME 20371
Ten Popular Catalan Songs	UME

MICHAEL LORIMER

Born – Chicago, USA

13th January 1946

Michael Lorimer

Michael Lorimer, although born in Chicago, was raised in Los Angeles, California. He first became interested in the classical guitar at the age of ten when he heard one of his father's records of Andres Segovia. Lorimer's first teacher was Los Angeles guitarist Guy Horn, and he studied with him until he was fourteen years old.

Dorothy De Goede, a former pupil of Segovia, introduced Lorimer to Segovia in 1962. The master guitarist was so impressed by the young player that he suggested Lorimer come to Siena to study with him. This he did after he had graduated from High School at the age of seventeen. Lorimer continued his guitar studies under Segovia at Santiago De Compostela, Spain.

Michael Lorimer returned to the United States and for the past few years has led a busy career as a concert recitalist and teacher. He now plays a minimum of thirty recitals a year. He teaches on a regular basis at Berkeley, California, and also at the San Francisco Conservatory of Music. In 1980 he was the visiting professor of guitar at the University of Carolina, at Wilmington, USA. Lorimer has for the past five years written a column on the classical guitar for the prestigious magazine, 'Guitar Player'

For the last six years Michael Lorimer has played and made a serious study of the Baroque guitar. He has included this instrument into most of his recent concert recitals.

Michael Lorimer has without doubt established himself as one of the most important guitarists in the United States in recent years, not only as a recitalist and teacher, but also as a transcriber of several excellent books of transcriptions for guitar (published by Charles Hansen Music, USA).

SELECTED READING

Michael Lorimer   Article – 'Guitar Player' – October 1973
Michael Lorimer   Article – 'Guitar Player' – December 1975
Michael Lorimer   Article – 'Frets' – September 1980
Michael Lorimer   Article – 'Guitar & Lute' – July 1980

VINCENZO MACALUSO

Born – Milwaukee, Wisconsin, USA

9th January 1941

Vincenzo Macaluso began his studies on the guitar at the age of ten with his father. His first interest was jazz and he eventually studied with jazz guitarist, Barney Kessel. Macaluso made great progress and soon established himself as a prominent jazz/studio guitarist in the Los Angeles area.

It was during his late teens that Macaluso began a serious study of classical music. Within a few years he developed a fine technique on the classical instrument and became generally accepted as one of the leading classical guitarists on the West Coast of America. Macaluso became one of the few American guitarists to change over to the ten string guitar originally designed by Narciso Yepes. He played this instrument exclusively for several years and recorded four albums with the ten-string guitar for the Klavier label. For the last few years Macaluso has returned to playing the six-string guitar exclusively as he felt the sonority of this instrument could not be duplicated on the ten-string instrument.

Vincenzo Macaluso is currently Artist in Residence and Professor of Guitar at Whittier College in California.

Vincenzo Macaluso

SELECTED RECORDS

'10-String Guitar Interprets the Classics'	Klavier	KS 508
'10-String Guitar Interprets the French Classics'	Klavier	KS 523
'10-String Guitar Interprets the Spanish Classics'	Klavier	KS 552

An interesting nineteenth century music cover.

Mario Maccaferri

STUDIO RAWDIN

MARIO MACCAFERRI

Born – Cento, Bologna, Italy

20th May 1900

Mario Maccaferri gained his diploma and left school at the age of nine. He began to work as a dish washer and then later as an apprentice carpenter. After a while he heard of a vacancy in the workshops of the famous Italian luthier Luigi Mozzani, which he was to fill in 1911.

It was during his apprenticeship with Mozzani that he took an interest in the playing of the classical guitar and by the age of sixteen Maccaferri had gained a high reputation as a concert guitarist. He undertook serious study of music at the Academy in Siena from 1916 and during the period 1920-1923 he gave many guitar recitals. Throughout this period he maintained his interest in the technical side of guitar making and engineering as a whole, as a technical advisor in the Mozzani workshops. In 1926 Maccaferri was to receive the highest possible diploma for music and guitar playing from the Academy in Siena.

In 1923 Maccaferri left Mozzani and embarked on a European concert tour including Italy, Switzerland, France and Germany. In the eyes of some press reviewers he was an artist of the highest calibre, equal both in artistry and interpretation to the then young Andres Segovia. During this period he advertised as a maker of all fretted instruments and violins, violas and cellos and in 1926-1927 he won top prizes for the violin and cello making contests held in Rome, Fiume and Monte Catini. In 1926 Maccaferri visited London appearing in concert at the Wigmore Hall. He decided to stay there for a while to try and earn a living as a guitar teacher. It was in London that he developed the first prototypes of the distinctive and famous Maccaferri guitars to be built later in Paris. These were to be used by top European jazz guitarists, including the legendary Django Reinhardt.

In 1933 Maccaferri continued his career as a concert artist playing in Berlin, Hamburg, Cologne, Brussels and Antwerp. This suddenly came to a halt when he broke his hand in a swimming pool accident. Whilst in Paris, Maccaferri had studied the manufacture of saxophone reeds. With the oncoming German invasion Maccaferri left for the United States in 1939 where he set up a saxophone reed business. Within a short period of time his company, the French/American Reed Mfg Company, became the leading supplier in the United States of clarinet and saxophone reeds.

Maccaferri then went into plastics and his company, Mastro Industries, developed a line of best selling plastic guitars and ukuleles. There is no doubt that Maccaferri's engineering genius helped millions of children throughout the world buy a playable guitar at a price they could afford.

In 1981 Mario Maccaferri finally closed Mastro Industries. At the age of 81 he is still a guitarist, luthier and innovator, first and foremost. He has recently designed some new guitars for the Ibanez company in Japan. Maccaferri counts amongst his friends, artists such as Andres Segovia and amongst his earlier pupils the late Ida Presti and also Len Williams, the father of John Williams.

SELECTED READING

Mario Maccaferri   Article – 'Guitar' – May 1975
Mario Maccaferri   Article – Guitar' – January 1976
Mario Maccaferri   Article – 'Guitar' – August 1977
Mario Maccaferri   Article – 'Guitar Player' – April 1974
Mario Maccaferri   Article – 'Guitar Player' – November 1976
'The Rebirth of Django's Guitar'' – M. J. Summerfield   CSL Booklet 1974

IVOR MAIRANTS

Born – Rypin, Poland

18th July 1908

Ivor Mairants

Ivor Mairants is well known throughout the world to guitarists of all styles. In recent years he has devoted more of his time to the classical guitar, and has composed several original works for the instrument, made many transcriptions of classical melodies, and has also written a best selling flamenco guitar method.

Ivor Mairants became a professional guitarist at the age of twenty. Over the past fifty years he has gradually become regarded throughout the world as one of the leading authorities on the guitar in all its forms. Although not strictly a classical guitarists, his contribution to the promotion of the classical guitar in Britain over the years has been enormous.

Ivor Mairants was a featured member of many of Britain's leading dance bands in the nineteen thirties and forties, including those of Ambrose, Roy Fox, Lew Stone, Geraldo and Ted Heath. He is still regularly featured on many radio, television and record dates. In the last few years he was often heard with the very popular Mantovani orchestra, and more recently with Manuel and his Music of the Mountains.

Of particular importance to guitarists is the fact that Ivor Mairants has devoted so much of his time to writing music and methods for the guitar. He established a school of music in London from 1950-60 and amongst his many pupils were several players who are today some of Britain's top guitarists. Recently he has devoted a lot of his energies to developing his fine music stoe in the west end of London. This store offers one of the world's finest selection of classical guitars.

Ivor Mairants still spends every spare moment writing for the guitar – jazz, classical and flamenco, and many of his methods and solos, old and new, are used by thousands of guitarists throughout the world.

SELECTED READING
'My Fifty Fretting Years' – An Autobiography – Ivor Mairants   Ashley Mark (1980)

SELECTED MUSIC

6 Solos for Classic Guitar	EMI	6 Part Suites	Breitkopf & Hartel
6 Bagatelles	EMI	Sonata (to a Sonic Age)	Brons/Hansen
A Bundle of Blues	Chappells/Hansen	Meditation	Chappells/Hansen
6 Progressive Pieces for Solo Guitar	EMI	The Spirit of New Orleans	Chappells/Hansen
6 Easy Pieces	EMI	Travel Suite	EMI
6 Lute Pieces	EMI	3 Rhythmic Dances	EMI

CARMEN MARINA

Born – MARIA DEL CARMEN MANTEGA PASCUAL
Santander, Spain

17th July 1936

Carmen Marina showed a natural ability for music at an early age. When she was sixteen she won a scholarship to the Royal Conservatory of Music in Madrid. From this prestigious Conservatory she graduated in the classical guitar and composition. She also won an honorary award for her opera 'The Old Man and The Sea' based on the Ernest Hemmingway novel of the same name.

At the age of eighteen Carmen Marina made a highly successful concert tour of North Africa and France. For several years she attended Segovia's annual master classes in Siena, Italy and Santiago De Compostela in Spain. As well as a hectic concert schedule, Marina made several European television and radio broadcasts.

In 1971 Carmen Marina went to the United States of America and has lived there since. She made a very successful concert debut at the Carnegie Hall, New York City. Marina currently divides her time teaching at the Institute of Guitar Music, New York (an institute which she established with her husband in 1976), and a busy schedule of concerts, recording and broadcasting on both radio and television.

In 1979 a grant from the US-Spanish Joint Committee for Educational and Cultural Affairs, allowed Carmen Marina to write a series of song cycle based on the poetry of Miguel de Unamuno, Gerado Diego, Rafael Alberti, Garcia Lorca and others, which later, were performed in the United States and Spain. In 1981, Carmen Marina premièred on the Spanish-American television in

Carmen Marina

PHOTO J. ABELES

COURTESY CARMEN MARINA

New York, Channel 47, a cycle of songs based on Rafael Albertis' 'Poems of Parana'.

Carmen Marina is not only a fine guitarist and composer, but also a talented singer as can be heard on her recordings on the IGM label.

SELECTED RECORDS

'Recordando A Espana'	SMC 1121
'Nineteenth Century Guitarists'	SMC 1122
'Albeniz for Guitar'	SMC 1123
'Bach for Guitar'	SMC 1124
'Spanish Gold' – Guitar and Voice	IGM 333-01

Akinobu Matsuda

AKINOBU MATSUDA

Born – AKINOBU JIRO MATSUDA
Himeji, Japan

28th June 1933

Akinobu Matsuda graduated at Kobe University in 1957, where he read Economics. He had begun to play the guitar at the age of fourteen and had immediately showed great promise.

He gave his first public recital in Kobe, Japan in 1958 and this was a great success for the young guitarist.

In 1959 his playing was commended by Andres Segovia, who was principal artist at the Osaka International Festival in Japan that year. In 1960 Matsuda travelled to Europe where for two years he studied with Segovia and Alirio Diaz. During this time he also studied with John Williams who was the Profesor of Guitar at the Royal College of Music in London.

In 1962, Akinobu Matsuda made the first of three concert tours in the United States. He then made his debut in Singapore and Hong Kong in 1964. His debut at Carnegie Hall, New York took place in 1969. In the same year he also appeared for the first time at Wigmore Hall, London.

In 1973 Matsuda undertook a successful concert tour of Great Britain and broadcast on the radio in both Dublin and Paris. He also gave a recital in Bergen, Noway. The following year he performed at the Hong Kong Arts Festival as a solo guitarist.

Akinobu Matsuda has been awarded many prizes, including the Papas-Puyana Prize at the International Guitar Competition under the auspices of Andres Segovia and sponsored by the Conservatory of Music at Orense, Spain. In 1963 he received the Japan Critic Club Prize of the Year and in 1979 he became a Honorary Member of the Board of Directors of the International Castelnuovo-Tedesco Society. In the same year he was given the ward of the Cultural Services from Himeji City.

At present Matsuda concertizes widely in addition to recording and teaching.

SELECTED RECORDS

'The Classic Sound of the Guitar'	Argo	ZDA 205
'Sound of the Guitar'	ARM	ARM 3001

SELECTED READING

Jiro Matsuda	Article – 'Guitar' – March 1973

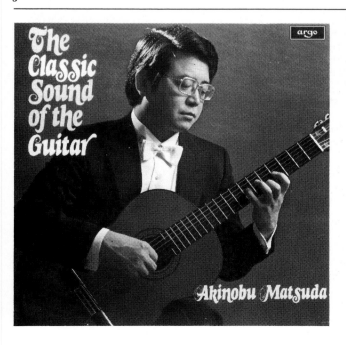

JOHANN KASPAR MERTZ

Born – Pressburg, Hungary
17th August 1806

Died – Vienaa, Austria
14th October 1856

Johann Kaspar Mertz commenced his study of music, on both the guitar and flute, at an early age. A child prodigy, he was able at the age of twelve to support his parents from the income he earned as a teacher.

In 1840 he left Hungary for Vienna, Austria. On 29th November 1840 he made his concert debut in front of the Empress Carolina Agusta at the Court Theatre, Vienna. This recital was a great success and Mertz embarked on a concert tour of several European countries. Whilst living in Vienna, Mertz met and married Josephine Plantin. She was also a guitar virtuoso and they appeared often together in concert. The two guitarists enjoyed great success and popularity, and as a result were much in demand as teachers, especially to the society elite of Vienna.

Johann Kaspar Mertz was not only a virtuoso guitarist, but a prolific composer. He composed, arranged and transcribed over one hundred works for the guitar. Mertz, who suffered from a heart complaint for many years, died on 14th October 1856 at the age of fifty in Vienna.

Johann Kaspar Mertz

COURTESY C. E. H. SMITH

SELECTED MUSIC

Capriccio, op. 13, no. 3	Bèrben
Kindermärchen (Children-s Fairytale), ed. Leisner	Presser
Polacca, ed. Leisner	Presser
Romanze	Presser
Tarantelle	Presser
Three Nocturnes, op. 4	N 3326
The Selected Works – 4 volumes	ECH 417/420

SELECTED READING

'Mertz's Last Compositions'	Article – 'Soundboard' – Spring 1982

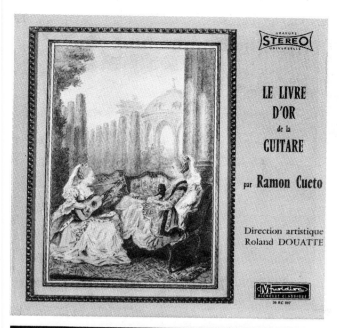

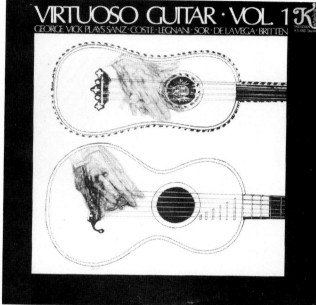

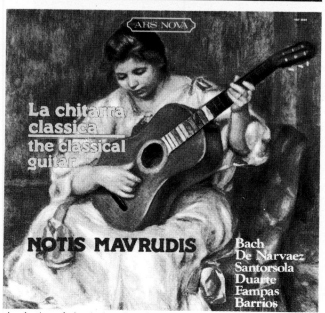

A selection of classical and modern guitar art on record sleeves.

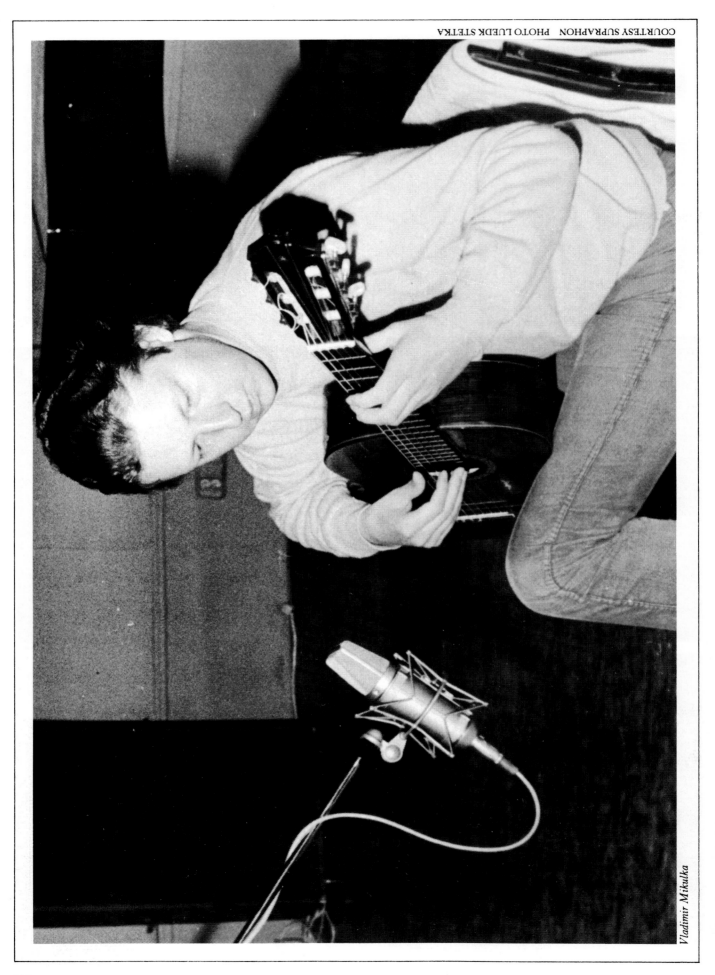

Vladimir Mikulka

VLADIMIR MIKULKA

Born – Prague, Czechoslovakia

11 December 1950

Vladimir Mikulka started playing the classical guitar at the age of thirteen. Within two years he was already a student of the foremost Czech guitarist Jiri Jirmal at the State Conservatory in Prague. At the age of nineteen, Vladimir Mikulka proved to the world his outstanding ability on his chosen instrument by winning the international competition for guitar in Paris, organized by the French radio and television organisation, ORTF.

Mikulka's victory in this competition led to many concert bookings throughout the world. He played to enthusiastic audiences in most countries in Europe, Scandanavia, the Soviet Union, Cuba and Australia.

There is no doubt that Vladimir Mikulka is one of the finest guitarists to have emerged on the scene in the last ten years. Not only a great player, Mikulka is also a talented teacher and as a result has been called upon to conduct several International Master Classes for guitarists.

In a relatively short period of time Vladimir Mikulka has established himself amongst the elite of today's classical guitarists. He has participated in many International Music Festivals including those held at Helsinki, Paris, Rome and Amsterdam. His recent tour of Japan was highly successful, and his first recordings are quite outstanding.

SELECTED RECORDS

'Plays Bach'	Supraphon	1-11-1585
'Guitar Recital'	Denon (Japan)	OX 7164 ND
'Rodrigo/Tedesco' Concertos	Panton	11-0608 G
'Haydn Quartet/Giuliani – Opus 30'	Supraphon	1100-2700

SELECTED READING

Vladimir Mikulka   Article – 'Guitar' – September 1978

John Mills

JOHN MILLS

Born – Kingston Upon Thames, England

13th September 1947

John Mills was initially a self-taught player from the age of nine. After making exceptional progress as a pupil of the Spanish Guitar Centre in London he studied in 1966-69 at the Royal College of Music, London with John Williams. During his three year course of study there, he also went to Spain in 1968 to take part in Master Classes given by Andres Segovia, at Santiago De Compostela.

John Mills has now been giving recitals regularly throughout the British Isles for several years, performing a number of times at the Wigmore Hall, Purcell Room, and Queen Elizabeth Hall in London. In 1972 he made his international debut with a concert tour of Eastern Canada, and has since returned many times to perform throughout Canada and the United States. In the summer of 1975 he was chosen to play one of the major evening recitals at the 'Guitar 75' Festival in Toronto. John Mills has also made concert tours of Australia, Sweden, Japan, South Africa, and Brazil. In little more than ten years John Mills has given over two thousand recitals.

John Mills is not only recognised worldwide as being one of Britain's finest guitarists, but also for his excellent teaching ability. His new guitar method, 'The John Mills Guitar Tutor', has recently been published by Musical New Services of Great Britain. He has also given many master classes both at home and abroad and has several records to his credit. Mills has appeared several times on the BBC Radio programme 'The Classical Guitar' and has also been featured on television and in recitals on many local radio stations throughout Great Britain. In recent years he has appeared quite regularly as part of a guitar duo with the Canadian guitarist Lynn Gangbar.

SELECTED RECORDS

'Five Centuries of Classical Guitar'	Discources	ABK 10
'Student Repertoire' – Volume One	Guitar	G 101
'Student Repertoire' – Volume Two	Guitar	G 102
'20th Century Guitar' Music	Guitar	G 105

SELECTED READING

John Mills	Article – 'Guitar' – December 1973
John Mills	Article – 'Guitar' – June 1978

Jorge Morel

JORGE MOREL

Born – JORGE SCIBONA
Buenos Aires, Argentina

9th May 1931

Jorge Morel showed a musical aptitude at a very early age. His father, an actor and also an accomplished guitarist, began teaching his talented son the rudiments of the instrument when Jorge was only eleven years of age. It soon became apparent that the youngster was destined for a career in music. He entered the University of Musical Studies in Buenos Aires where he learned all the basic music subjects, and majored in guitar under the guidance and inspiration of the renowned South American guitarist and composer, Pablo Escobar. It was Escobar who gave Morel his professional debut at age sixteen on a radio programme featuring both teacher and pupil. The young guitarist was immediately recognised as a major talent and from that time began his concert career while still a student at University.

Not until receiving his degree at the age of eighteen did Jorge Morel begin to experiment and develop the unique style and brilliant technique that today are so much a part of his artistic identity. As is the case with all great virtuosi, his own arrangements and compositions are the most tangible examples of his aims, standards and ideals as a creative and performing musician. Jorge Morel's prime calling is based in contemporary modes of expression. Morel's compositions abound in bracingly modern rhythms and harmonies, naturally leaning toward the melodies and idioms of South America. A fine interpreter of the standard classical repertoire, Morel has also dazzled audiences throughout the world with his exciting transcriptions for guitar of the music of Gershwin, Bernstein, Lennon & McCartney amongst other modern composers.

Jorge Morel first went to the United States in 1961 making a highly successful debut at Carnegie Hall. Since that time he has toured throughout North America and in Hawaii and Puerto Rico, but remained virtually unknown to British and European audiences until his Wigmore Hall, London debut in October 1979. This debut was a great success, and since that time Jorge Morel has concertized annually in Great Britain and Europe, as well as in North America.

SELECTED RECORDS

'The Warm Guitar'	Decca	DL 4167
'Artistry of Jorge Morel'	RCA	LSP 3953
'Guitar Moods'	SMC	1110-2
'Magnificent Guitar'	Decca	DL 4966
'The Fabulous Jorge Morel'	Village Gate	VGLP 2001
'Virtuoso South American Guitar'	Guitar Masters	GMR 1002
'Jorge Morel Plays Broadway'	Guitar Masters	GMR 1004

SELECTED READING

Jorge Morel	Article – 'Guitar' – December 1979
Jorge Morel	Article – 'Frets' – Setpember 1979
Jorge Morel	Article – 'Guitar Player' – March 1970

LUIGI MOZZANI

Born – Faenza, Italy
9th March 1869

Died – Rovereto, Italy
12th August 1943

Luigi Mozzani

COURTESY MARIO MACCAFERRI

Luigi Mozzani showed a great interest in music at an early age, and dedicated every free moment he had to the study of the guitar.

He later studied the oboe and also composition at the Conservatory of Music in Bologna under Professor Castelli. There Mozzani earned his diploma at the age of eighteen. For two years he was the first oboeist at the San Carlo Theatre in Naples. He then travelled throughout Europe and Asia and at the age of twenty went to North America with a symphony orchestra.

This concert tour was to prove a financial disaster for the organisers, following which Mozzani decided to make the guitar his career rather than the oboe.

Mozzani's first public recitals on the guitar met with great success and he was regarded as a virtuoso. He returned to Europe and lived in Paris where at the age of twenty-five he became one of the most sought after teachers of the guitar by Parisian high society. Mozzani continued to give many highly acclaimed recitals in France, Austria and

Germany. During these years as a guitar recitalist, Mozzani became frustrated with some of the limitations of the guitar as it was constructed at that time. He decided to return to Italy to study guitar construction in depth. He eventually founded important schools for luthiers in Cento, Bologna and Rovereto. One of his most famous pupils was Mario Maccaferri. Mozzani continued to study the construction of the guitar right up to his death. His workshops produced a large amount of instruments, and among his many patents was the well-known guitar-lyre, an instrument with an adjustable neck.

Although latterly much of his time was devoted to instrument construction, Mozzani was also a talented composer and transcriber of guitar music. Quite a lot of his works were published, but there still remains many of his compositions unedited and unpublished. A distinctive feature of Mozzani's guitar technique was the use of a metal thumb pick on the right hand. This technique was also used by Mario Maccaferri throughout his concert career, during the nineteen twenties.

SANTIAGO NAVASCUES

Born – Madrid, Spain

23rd July 1933

Santiago Navascues

COURTESY GENDAI GUITAR   PHOTO KIICHI ARAKAWA

Santiago Navascues is a graduate of the Real Conservatorio in Madrid, and also of the Music Academy in Munich, Germany.

Navascues is highly regarded as one of Europe's finest guitar teachers. Although he does give frequent recitals, and also has made several recordings for the German company Arcola Eurodisc, Navascues spends most of his years as a teacher.

He is currently professor of the guitar at the Richard Strauss Conservatory in Munich, Germany, where he has been teaching since 1972. He conducts the 'International Guitar Seminar' annually in Reisbach and is editor of guitar works for the publishing house 'Biblioteca de la Guitarra'.

SELECTED RECORDS

'Music for the Spanish Guitar'	Vanguard	10137
'Santiago Navascues'	Eurodisc	86852
'Santiago Navascues'	Eurodisc	86853
'Santiago Navascues'	Eurodisc	88597
'Santiago Navascues'	Eurodisc	89247
'Santiago Navascues'	Eurodisc	28902

MICHAEL NEWMAN

Born – New York City, USA

21st December 1957

COURTESY JOSEPH AASTORE JNR.   PHOTO DON HUNSTEIN

Michael Newman

Since his Carnegie Hall debut in March 1974, Michael Newman has established himself as one of the United States' finest classical guitarist.

Michael Newman was brought up in a musical environment as his father worked for the Guild Guitar Company in New York City. His father was also keen on music and had a large record collection in which many classical guitar records were included. These were to influence the young musician to study the guitar. At the age of seven Newman studied the piano. He lost interest in this instrument and the took up the guitar studying with a local teacher, Thomas Anthony, for three years. Newman made such good progress in 1971 he began studying with Albert Valdes Blain at Mannes College of Music, New York. On the advice of Blain, he then enrolled full-time at Mannes College where he eventually earned his Bachelor of Music degree. Newman also studied

with Oscar Ghiglia at the Aspen Music Festival and the Accademia Musical Chigiana in Siena, Italy.

Michael Newman has served as a guest soloist with the Hartford and Rochester Chamber Orchestres, the Omaha Symphony, the Cleveland and Fort Wayne Philharmonics and also the renowned Atlanta Symphony. He has given solo guitar recitals throughout the United States, and was a recipient of the Concert Masters- 'Young Artist Award' 1973. More recently he was a prize winner at the International Guitar Competition of the Guitar '78 Festival held in Toronto, Canada.

Michael Newman is also highly regarded as a teacher and is currently on the faculty of both the Mannes College of Music and Rutgers University as instructor of guitar. In addition to this he has conducted several workshops and masters classes for guitar.

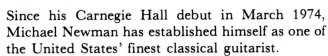

SELECTED RECORDS

'Michael Newman'	Sheffield Lab	SL 10
'Italian Pleasures'	Sheffield Lab	SL16

SELECTED READING

Michael Newman	Article – 'Guitar & Lute' – October 1981

Pablo Escobar, outstanding Argentinian guitarist/composer of the past.

Nicolo Paganini

NICOLO PAGANINI

Born – Genoa, Italy
27th October 1782

Died – Nice, France
27th May 1840

Until recently only a few music lovers realized that the nineteenth century virtuoso violinist, Nicolo Paganini, was also a great virtuoso guitarist. Ferdinand Carulli, a contemporary of Paganini, wrote in his guitar tutor, 'the fact may not be generally known that Paganini was a fine performer on the guitar, and that he composed most of his airs on this instrument, arranging and ampilfying them on the violin according to his fancy'.

Nicolo Paganini's first instrument was the mandolin. His father had a great love of music and from the day his son was able to hold the mandolin he ensured every spare moment was spent in practising. Paganini's musical talent was soon very obvious and he began to study the violin with the noted teachers Costa and Servetto.

It was in 1795, at the age of thirteen, that Paganini began to study the violin with Allesandro Rolli. Rolli was not only a violin virtuoso, but also a talented guitarist. It seems likely that Paganini also studied the guitar with this teacher. Nevertheless for the next few years Paganini devoted his talents entirely to the violin and his virtuoso performances excited audiences throughout Italy.

In 1801 Paganini became attached to an aristocratic lady whose favourtie instrument was the guitar. During the three years he lived in this lady's chateau, Paganini devoted himself to the guitar. His first composition for the guitar was written in 1801. In 1805 Paganini returned to touring the continent, his concerts once again devoted to his virtuoso violin playing.

Paganini became a close friend of the guitar virtuoso Luigi Legnani, and they toured and performed together on many occasions. Legnani, in fact, lived with Paganini at his villa near Palma. On 9th June 1837 Paganini was to give his last public concert. This concert was held in Turin, Italy, and Paganini shared the programme with Luigi Legnani.

Paganini's health began to deteriorate in 1838/39, and in 1840 he moved to Nice in the south of France to miss the winter and try to recuperate. Unfortunately his health deteriorated very rapidly and he finally died in Nice on 27th May 1840, at the age of fifty-eight.

Paganini, the legendary violinist, was not only a virtuoso guitarist but a prolific composer for the instrument. He composed at least a hundred and forty solos for the guitar, many duets for violin and guitar, also several trios and quartets which included a guitar part. His most outstanding composition for the guitar is probably his 'Grand Sonata in A', a piece he often publicly performed with Legnani.

SELECTED RECORDINGS

'John Williams Plays Paganini'	CBS	73745
'Paganini's Grand Sonata – Oscar Ghiglia'	EMI	CSD 3511

SELECTED READING

'Nicolo Paganini'	Article – 'Guitarra' – March 1979
'New Light on Paganini'	Articles – 'Guitar Review' – Nos. 2, 3, 5
'Paganini'	Sheppard/Axe/Rod – Paganini Publication 1979
'Nicolo Paganini'	John Sugden – Midas 1980

SELECTED MUSIC

Caprice No. 24, arr. John Williams	B & H	Romanze (from the Violin Sonata), ed. Scheit	UE 13068
Five Compositions for Solo Guitar, ed. Pilia	Ric. 132432	Six Original Compositions, ed. Scheit	UE 14465
Five Pieces for Guitar, ed. Behrend	EMT 1420	Sonatina, ed. Scheit	UE 14455
Grand Sonata, arr. Meyerriecks	CO 214	Twenty-six Original Compositions for Guitar	Z 11250
La Campanella, ed. Casuscelli	BA 8442		
Minuet & Sonatina, op. 25, tr. Prat	BA 9548		
Perpetual Motion, for 1 or 2 guitars, tr. Fleury	BA 11585		
Pièce Intime	ZM 1863		

SOPHOCLES PAPAS

Born – SOPHOCLES THOMAS PAPAS
Sopiki, Epirus, Greece

18th December 1893

Sophocles Papas

COURTESY C. E. H. SMITH

Sophocles Papas was born in a small Grecian town, and received his first musical instruction from his father, an amateur violinist. Later, whilst living in Cairo, Egypt, Papas took lessons on the mandolin but soon changed over to the guitar.

Papas went to the United States in 1914 to study argriculture in Massachusetts. With the onset of World War I Papas joined the American Army in which he served as a gunsmith. He took his guitar with him and his playing was much admired by other soliders. It was during his army service that Papas formulated the idea of becoming a guitar teacher.

On his return to the USA, at the end of the war, Papas established himself as a guitar teacher in Washington DC. In 1922 he founded his Columbia School of Music. Papas's talents as a solo guitarist and teacher were quickly recognized. His school of music was a great success, offering instruction in nearly all instruments, but specialising in the guitar. The school became the only such establishment in the United States where a student could work for a Bachelor's degree in music with the guitar as the principal instrument.

Sophocles Papas became a close friend of Andres Segovia and many of his teaching methods are based on the technique and musical approach of Segovia. Papas wrote a guitar method for the classical guitar which has proven over the years to be a worldwide best seller.

Sophocles Papas is a founder of the prestigeous Washington Guitar Society, and has also involved himself as a prominent publisher of guitar music. He is President of the Columbia Music Company.

SELECTED READING
Sophocles Papas   Article – 'Guitar Player' – February 1975

SELECTED MUSIC
Five Solos for Guitar   CO 102

A Grobert guitar originally owned by Paganini and then later by Berlioz. Now in the Paris Conservatoire museum.

A Staufer guitar owned by Franz Schubert. Now in the Vienna museum.

COURTESY C. E. H. SMITH

159

Christopher Parkening

CHRISTOPHER PARKENING

Born – Brentwood, California

1947

Christopher Parkening began to play the guitar at the age of eleven, after hearing his cousin the late Jack Marshall, who was a leading Californian studio guitarist.

Parkening's first teachers were Celedonio and Pepe Romero. They soon noticed the young guitarist's exceptional talent on the instrument and within one year Parkening gave his first public recital. At the age of fourteen he enerted the annual state-wide auditions of the Young Musicians Foundation. Judges included Jascha Heifetz, Gregor Piatigorsky, Mario Castelnuovo-Tesdesco and others. The Foundation at that time offered no category in which guitarists could compete; but so impressed were the judges with Parkening's virtuosity that he was scheduled as a special 'out-of-competition' performer.

After this competition Parkening developed a friendship with Mario Castelnuovo-Tedesco and a little later Parkening made his formal concert debut playing Tedesco's 'Concerto in D for Guitar and Orchestra' under the auspices of the Young Musicians Foundations of Los Angeles on 10th March 1963. This highly acclaimed performance led to further engagements with the Los Angeles Philharmonic Orchestra, the Pasadena Symphony Orchestra and numerous other orchestras in Souther California.

With letters of recommendation from Castelnuovo-Tedesco and cellist Joseph Schuster, Parkening was accepted as a scholarship student by Andres Segovia in a Master Class at the University of California at Berkley. Segovia chose him from three hundred students present to perform daily before the class, and later selected Parkening as a soloist when the Master Class was televised nationally.

In January 1966 Parkening gave the world premiere of the 'Second Concerto in C for Guitar and Orchestra' by Castelnuovo-Tedesco. In the same year Parkening took up academic and musical studies at the University of Southern California; and he again attended on full scholarship a Segovia Master Class held at the North Carolina School of Arts.

In July 1968 Parkening was named one of the outstanding young artists of the year by High Fidelity Magazine. The following September he made his first concert tour of the United States and Canada. In the same year began to make the first of several recording for Angel Records, several of these have been best sellers, his recording of the music of Bach reputably having sold over one hundred thousand copies.

In the autumn of 1968 Parkening was invited by Segovia to serve with him on the judges' panel at the International Guitar Competition in Santiago de Compostela, Spain. Parkening then became one of the United States busiest recitalists, making his New York debut at the Alice Tulley Hall in November 1972. In August and September 1972 Parkening had completed his first tour of Japan. Parkening was chosen to be the principal soloist at the country's first Rodrigo Festival during this tour.

Christopher Parkening is also the author of 'The Guitar Method' and also several books of classical transcriptions for the guitar.

For several years Parkening was Head of the Guitar Dept of the University of Southern California School of Music. He now lives in Montana where he holds a series of master classes for the guitar annually at the Montana State University.

SELECTED RECORDS

'In the Classic Style'	Angel	S-36019
'In the Spanish Style'	Angel	S-36020
'Romanza'	Angel	S-36021
'Parkening Plays Bach'	Angel	S-36041
'Parkening and the Guitar'	Angel	S-36053
'Christopher Parkening Album'	Angel	S-36069

SELECTED READING

Christopher Parkening	Article – 'Guitar' – July	Christopher Parkening	Article – 'Guitar Player' – June 1970
Christopher Parkening	Article – 'Frets' – June 1980	Christopher Parkening	Article – 'Guitar Player' – June 1972

MARIO PARODI

Born – Istanbul, Turkey

Died – Buenos Aires, Argentina

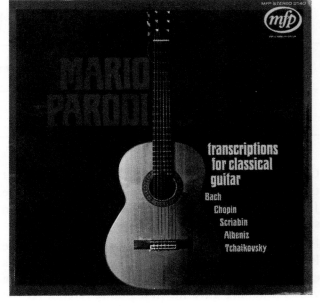

Mario Parodi was born in Istanbul, Turkey, of Italian parents. From an early age he was drawn to music, his first instrument being the piano. On hearing a concert given by an Argentinian orchestra, which included a number of guitarists, Parodi decided the guitar was to be his chosen instrument. As there were virtually no guitar teachers in Turkey at that time, Parodi was self-taught.

As a concert artist Parodi toured throughout Turkey, Greece, Italy, Switzerland, Germany and Argentina. He recorded in both Italy and Argentina and published numerous transcriptions and compositions of his own. Parodi had a unique and very individual style. He dedicated most of his concert programmes to his own transcriptions of the classical masters including Liszt, Schumann, Chopin, Debussy, Beethoven and Brahms.

SELECTED RECORDS

'The Classical Guitar'	Music for Pleasure	MFP 2094
'Transcriptions for Classical Guitar'	Music for Pleasure	MFP 2140

SELECTED MUSIC

Seis Instantaneas	BA 12564
Poema	BA 12565
Prelude No. 1	BA 10270
Three Preludes: Nos. 3, 4, 8	BA 11283

Two Brazilian guitarists of the past, Manuel Sao Marcos (left), Antonio Rebello (right).

BORIS A. PEROTT

**Born – St. Petersburg, Russia
1882**

**Died – London, England
12th March 1958**

Boris A. Perott

Boris Perott was for many years one of the most important guitar personalities in Great Britain. Perott, by profession a doctor of medicine, was born in Russia but became a naturalized British subject.

Boris Perott originally studied the piano at an early age and later progressed to the balalaika and mandolin.

Perott's first introduction to the guitar was at the age of eight. His first lessons (on the seven-string guitar) were with the famous guitar virtuoso J. Decker-Schenk. It was not long before Perott took up the six-string guitar under V. P. Lebedeff and made his first public appearance as a soloist in St. Petersburg in 1903. Perott received high critical acclaim for his performance by the press.

The following year Perott started a tour of Russia with V. Lebedeff and V. Ivanoff. This tour also took him to Siberia, Germany, and France. Perott appeared before the Imperial Court for which he was presented with a gold watch by the Emperor of Russia, Nicholas II. Boris Perott continued his career as a doctor of medicine, but gave many public and private performances on the guitar for a period of twelve years. After the death of Lebedeff, his widow chose Boris Perott to be her teacher and to guide her with her studies of the guitar, together with several of her husband's pupils.

Following the revolution in Russia Boris Perott came to Great Britain and set up in practice as a doctor in London where for many years he was regarded as one of the foremost teachers of the classical guitar in London.

Probably the most outstanding player who studied under Boris Perott was Julian Bream. It was Perott who introduced Julian Bream to Segovia, and he quickly recognised the young guitarist's enormous talent. It was the Philharmonic Society of Guitarists, which Perott founded in London in 1929, which was to help promote the young prodigy in his early years. In 1930 Boris Perott began to contribute a regular series to 'B.M.G.' magazine in London, proving himself to be an expert historian of the guitar.

Although Boris Perott's professional career was in medicine, he was an eminent heart specialist, his first love throughout his life was always the guitar.

RICHARD PICK

Born – St. Paul, Minnesota, USA

20th October 1915

Richard Pick

Richard Pick's first encounter with music was through his father who taught him the piano and violin at the age of five. On the death of his parents Pick became the foster son of Max Pick, who was the concert master of Minneapolis, Minnesota, and a professor of Musicology, violin and piano.

Living in such a musical environment, it was only natural that Pick developed a great love for music. The piano was his first instrument although Pick did play the guitar to accompany his singing. Pick them met Frank Lannom, a well known Chicago guitar teacher. For the next six or seven years Pick took guitar lessons from Lannom, and then he went to Urbana, Illinois, to enter the University of Illinois.

Needing money to finance his studies Pick worked in local dance bands, playing the plectrum guitar. A few opportunities arose for him to play the classical guitar on the radio. Pick suddenly realized that the classical guitar was the instrument for him to express his musical talent. Pick entered DePaul University of Chicago and earned his BSc degree. Soon after Pick gave his first public guitar recital, on 2nd March 1941. This concert was sponsored by the University of Chicago Musice Department.

Today, Richard Pick is known throuhgout the United States as a fine classical guitarist, and also as a composer of many pieces for the guitar. Over the years he has lectured on music and the guitar at many American Universities and still teachers the guitar for the Chicago School of Music.

SELECTED RECORD
'Guitar'   Music Library   MLR 7066

SELECTED MUSIC
Favourite Classic Guitar Solos   MB 93613

BARBARA POLASEK

Born – Reichenberg, Germany

8th March 1939

Barbara Polasek

Barbara Polasek was born into a family of Bohemian musicians. Her exceptional musical talents were obvious at an early age, and encouraged by her family she made great progress on the guitar.

At the age of twelve she gave her first public recital. Barbara Polasek then continued with her musical studies at the Weimar Academy and the Prague Music Conservatory. She then went to Spain and studied with Andres Segovia. In 1959 Polasek won the First International Prize of Vienna, and in 1964 she won the First Prize for Interpretation at the Concours de Guitare in Paris, awarded by the ORTF (French Radio and Television Service).

Since that time Barbara Polasek has continued an active career as a guitar recitalist and teacher. Her highly successful British debut was at the Wigmore Hall, London, on 25th October 1966. She also appeared at the Festival of Malais in Paris, and the Flanders Festival at Louvain in 1969. She is married to the prominent cellist Jan Polasek.

SELECTED RECORDS

'Anthology of the Guitar' – Volume One	RCA	VICS 1038
'Plays Bach'	Erato	STU 70573

SELECTED MUSIC

Gitarre im Gruppenunterricht	SY 2221

ALBERTO PONCE

Born – Madrid, Spain

13th March 1935

Alberto Ponse

Alberto Ponce's first guitar tutor was his father. He later went to the Barcelona Municipal Conservatory for seven years, where he completed his course with honours.

The young guitarist was introduced to Emilio Pujol, who invited him to study with him at the Lisbon Conservatory of Music. Ponce became very taken with Pujol's approach to music and the guitar. He studied with Pujol in Lisbon for three years, and then went to Chigiana to study further with Pujol. Whilst he was in Chigiana, Alberto Ponce specialized in the music of Spain's Golden age, in particular with the vihuela and its music. Ponce studied the vihuela as well as the guitar, and

in 1961 he was awarded First Prize for the vihuela by the Academy at Chigiana.

In 1962 Ponce won the First Prize for interpretation at Concours de Guitare in Paris, France. This prize was awarded by the presenters ORTF (French Radio and Television). In the same year Ponce began teaching at the Paris Ecole Normale Music which was under the directorship of Alfred Cortot.

Albert Ponce has since remained in this important teaching position, at the same time maintaining a busy concert schedule throughout Europe and Canada. He has also made several recordings for the French company, Arion.

SELECTED RECORDS

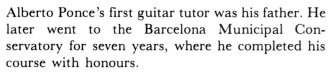

'Ohana – Oeuvres De Guitare'	Arion	ARN 38240
'La Guitare au 20th siecle	Arion	ARN 30S150
'Sourire De La Guitare'	Arion	ARN 36341

DOMINGO PRAT

Born – MARSAL DOMINGO PRAT,
Barcelona, Spain 17th March 1886

Died – Buenos Aires, Argentina
December 1944

Domingo Prat

COURTESY C. E. H. SMITH

Domingo Prat originally studied the guitar at the Municipal Music School of Barcelona, Spain. Later he was a pupil of the outstanding guitarist Miguel Llobet.

Prat established himself in Buenos Aires, Argentina where be became highly regarded as an authority and teacher of the classic guitar. He was the first exponent of the Tarrega method in South America and was a prolific writer of guitar methods, studies and transcriptions. His most lasting achievement is his 'Dictionary of Guitarists' published in Spanish in 1934 by Romero and Fernandez of Buenos Aires.

SELECTED READING

'Diccionario Guitarras, Guitarristas and Guitarreros'	Prat – Buenos Aires (1934)

SELECTED MUSIC

Bajor el Sauce – Milonga Criolla	BA 11675
Danza Española No. 1	BA 9579
El Escondido – Danza Argentina	BA 8989
El Palito – Danza Argentina	BA 8991
Gran Jota, Con Variaciones	BA 11549
Gueya (1 or 3 guitars)	BA 9501
La Firmeza – Danza Argentina	BA 8990
Pasionarias – Vidalitas	BA 11676
Recuerdos de Saldungaray – Triste Argentino	BA 9561
Recuerdos de Santiago del Estero – Triste	BA 9562

MADAME SIDNEY PRATTEN

Born – CATHERINE JOSEPHA PELZER
Muhlheim, Germany – 1821

Died – London, England
10th October 1895

Madame Sidney Pratten

Madame Sidney Pratten was one of the most important classical guitarists of the nineteenth century. Her first guitar teacher was her father, Ferdinand Pelzer. By the time she was seven years old she was already regarded as a highly accomplished guitarist.

In 1829 the Pelzer family moved to London, England. Here Catherine Pelzer dazzled British audiences with her appearances with the opera singer Madame Gringi, and also with another young guitar prodigy, Giulio Regondi.

In 1838 Catherine Pelzer moved to Exeter where she established herself as a teacher. One of her pupils, Lady John Somerset, persuaded her to return to London and teach members of the nobility. This she agreed to do and it was in London that she met the distinguished flautist Robert Sidney Pratten. They married in 1854.

In 1868 Robert Pratten died and the young guitarist was so distressed she gave up her public performances for three years. In 1871 she returned to the concert stage to perform Mauro Giuliani's 'Third Concerto'. Giuliani's niece played the piano part for this concert.

Madame Sidney Pratten's last public performance was at the age of 72 in 1893. There is no doubt that she was one of the outstanding figures of the nineteenth century guitar world. She also wrote several popular guitar methods and the prominent guitar makers, Panormo and Lacote, labelled hundreds of guitars with her name in order to promote sales of their instruments.

Ida Presti, 1947.

Ida Presti

IDA PRESTI

Born – YVETTE IDA MONTAGNON, Suresnes, France
31st May 1924

Died – New York City, USA
24th April 1967

Ida Presti's father, Claude Montagnon, was a French professional piano teacher. Her mother, Olga Lo-Presti, was of Italian birth. Ida Presti received her first music lessons on the piano at the age of five from her father. At the age of six she changed over to the guitar and soon showed that this was the instrument on which her extensive musical talents would be exposed. In 1932 Ida Presti studied the guitar for two years with Mario Maccaferri who was living in Paris at the time, and her father continued to teach her harmony and musical theory.

Ida Presti was to give her first public recital in 1932, at the age of eight, making her concert debut in Paris two years later. On 13th February 1938, she was given the honour of being the first guitarist to be invited to play at the Société des Concerts du Conservatoire de Paris. This Conservatoire was founded in 1828, and never before had a guitarist appeared who was considered good enough to play before this austere gathering of renowned virtuosi. On the occasion of the Centenary of Paganini's birth, in 1940, Ida Presti played his guitar in a com-memorative concert. All her performances were outstanding, and over the next twenty years she was to make extensive concert tours both in France and abroad. Ida Presti also appeared in a French film entitled 'La Petite Chose'.

In 1952 she met classical guitarist Alexandre Lagoya at the home of a mutual friend, André Verdier. A year later on 23rd May 1953 they were married. Two years later the Lagoya-Presti guitar duo made its first public appearance. Regarded as the finest classical duo the world has ever known, Presti and Lagoya were to perform two thousand concerts all over the world. Together they founded a prestigious guitar class at the Schola Cantorum in Paris, and made several magnificent recordings for the Philips Record Company, which bear testimony to their greatness.

Tragically, whilst preparing for a concert in New York City in 1967, Ida Presti, one of the finest classical guitarists of the twentieth century, suddenly fell ill and died shortly afterwards from an internal haemorrhage resulting from cancer of the lung.

SELECTED RECORDINGS
With Alexandre Lagoya

'Music for the Classical Guitar'	Nonesuch	H 71161
'Musique Baraque Pour Deux Guitares	Philips	6504 003
'Concertos Pour Deux Guitares'	Philips	6505 018
'Musique Espagnole Pour Deux Guitares'	Philips	6504 020
'Presti – Lagoya – Oeunces Pour Deux Guitares	Philips	6504 049
'Masters of the Guitar' – Volume One	RCA	RB 6589

SELECTED READING

Ida Presti	Memorial Issue – 'Guitar Review' No. 31 – 1969

Emilio Pujol

EMILIO PUJOL

Born – EMILIO VILLARUBY PUJOL, Granadella, Spain
7th April 1886

Died – Barcelona, Spain
15th November 1980

Emilio Pujol's first introduction to music was through singing and also as bandurria soloist with a mandolin and guitar orchestra. This orchestra appeared with enormous success at the Paris exhibition of 1900. It was in 1900 that Pujol changed to the guitar and became a pupil of Francisco Tarrega in Barcelona. In 1907 Pujol, who had already made a name for himself throughout Spain as a guitar virtuoso, left for a concert tour of Argentina, Uruguay and the United States.

Pujol married the talented flamenco guitarist Mathilde Cuervas. They appeared in concert together in many countries including a successful tour of Great Britain in 1923. In 1924 Pujol discovered in a Paris museum an ancient vihuela.

He became very interested in this instrument and over the years became one of the leading personalities behind its revival.

In 1947 Pujol was appointed professor of guitar at the National Conservatoire of Music in Lisbon, Portugal. He retained this position till his death in 1980.

Pujol was not only a fine guitarist and teacher, but one of the foremost musicologists of the twentieth century. He wrote several important books about the guitar including 'Rationale Method for the Guitar;, 'The Dilemna of Timbre on the Guitar', and a biography of his teacher Francisco Tarrega.

SELECTED READING

Emilio Pujol	Article – 'Guitar' – July 1977
Emilio Pujol	Article – 'Guitar Player' – April 1977
Emilio Pujol	Complete list of Works – 'GUitar & Lute' – May 1978
'Tarrega – Enasayo Biografico' – Emilio Pujol	Ramos and Alfonso (1960)
'Emilio Pujol' – Juan Riera	Lerida (1974)
'El Dilema Del Sonido En La Guitarra' – Emilio Pujol	Ricordi (1960)
Emilio Pujol	Article – 'Guitar Review' No. 5 – 1948

SELECTED MUSIC

Atardecer – Crepsucule	ESC
Bagatella	BA 11006
Becquerian (Endecha-Complainte)	ESC
Canción de Cuna – Berceuse	ESC
Canto de Otoño	ESC
Caprice Varié sur un thème d'Aguado	ESC
Cubana	Celesta
Deuxieme Triquilandia – 5 selections	ESC
El Abejorro	BA 11109
Els Tres Tambors – The Three Drums	BA 11111
Endecha a la amada ausente	ESC
Fantasía Breve	BA 11110
Festival – Danza Catalana	BA 12046
Four Short Pieces	Kalmus
Homenaje a Tárrega	GA 150
Manola del Avapies	BA 11448
Pequeña Romanza	ESC
Preludio Romantico	BA 11007
Rapsodia Valenciana	ESC
Salve	BA 1112
Seguidilla	BA 1113
Sevilla – Evocación	ESC
Tonadilla	ESC
Troisième Triquilandia – 3 Selections	ESC
Two Preludes	ESC
Variations sur un Thème Obsedant	ESC
Veneciana	ESC
Villanesca – Country Dances	BA 12342

Konrad Ragossnig

KONRAD RAGOSSNIG

Born – Klagenfurt, Austria

6th May 1932

Konrad Ragossnig received his first guitar lessons at the age of nine. In order to widen his musical studies Ragossnig also took lessons on the piano and cello at the Klagenfurt Conservatory of Music. He went on to complete his musical studies as a pupil of Karl Scheit, the professor of guitar at the Academy of Music and Performing Arts in Vienna.

In 1960 Konrad Ragossnig was appointed a professor of guitar at the same Academy, a position he held until 1964. In 1960 Ragossnig studied under Andres Segovia in Spain, and won first prize at the Cheltenham Festival in England in the same year. A year later, in 1961, Ragossnig won first prize for interpretation at the Concours International for Guitar in Paris, France. Following this Ragossnig made extensive concert tours of Europe as well as many appearances on Radio and Television.

About this time Konrad Ragossnig began to take an intense interest in the lute. He mastered this baroque instrument, and now often includes it with the guitar in his concert recitals. Numerous composers have written works especially for Konrad Ragossnig, including H. E. Apostel, J. Bondon, Mario Castelnuovo-Tedesco, H. Haug, J. Rodrigo and A. Schibler.

Konrad Ragossnig, one of the world's most outstanding classical guitarists, has lived in Switzerland since 1964 where he is professor of guitar at the Basle Music Academy. He also continues an active career as a recitalist and recording artist on both the guitar and the lute.

SELECTED RECORDS

'Master of the Guitar' – Volume Three	RCA	RB 6599
'Dances and Songs for Two Guitars' (with Walter Feybli)	Turnabout	TV 34605S
'Anthology of the Guitar' – Volume Two (with Werner Tripp – Flute)	RCA	VICS 1504
'Bandon Concerto De Mars'	RCA	VICS 1367
'The Spanish Guitar'	Turnabout	TV 34494S
'Guitar Recital'	Supraphon	1-11-1040
'Concertos Pour Guitare 18th Siecle'	VOX Musicalis	35050
'Spanische Guitarre – Musik'	Claves	P 806
'Duo with Hans-Martin Linde (Flute)	EMI	065-45 386

SELECTED READING

'Handbuch der Gitarre und Laute'	Konrad Ragossnig – B. Schott's – 1978

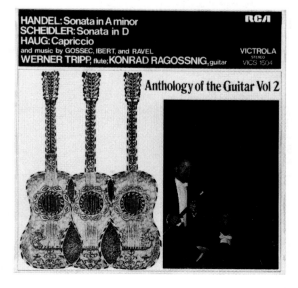

MANUEL LOPEZ RAMOS

Born – Buenos Aires, Argentina

1929

Manuel Lopez Ramos

Manuel Lopez Ramos studied guitar from an early age. His teacher was Miguel Michelone. At the age of nineteen Manuel Lopez Ramos was already regarded as one of Argentina's finest guitarist.

In 1948 he won the Argentine Chamber Music Associates first prize. In 1952 he embarked upon a highly successful international concert tour, appearing as solo artists and also with several leading symphony orchestras.

In 1952 he appeared in Mexico City. Soon afterwards he accepted the position as Professor of the Guitar at the Music School of the University of Mexico. In 1963 Manuel Lopez Ramos toured the USSR playing fourteen recitals.

Manuel Lopez Ramos continues a busy life as a recitalist and teacher. In recent years he has appeared at several international guitar Festivals, and has also directed special courses for guitarists at the University of Arizona, the National School of Music of the UNAM, and the Conservatoire of Guatemala.

SELECTED RECORDS

'Masters of the Guitar' – Volume Two	RCA	RB 6599
'Anthology of the Guitar' – Volume Three	RCA	VICS 1541
'Castelnuovo-Tedesco – Quintet for Guitar and String Quintet'	RCA	VICS 1367
'La Guitarra Clasica'	Boston	B-216

SELECTED READING

Manuel Lopez Ramos	Article – 'Guitarra' – September 1979

GIULIO REGONDI

Born – Lyons, France
1822

Died – London, England
6th May 1872

Giulio Regondi

COURTESY C. E. H. SMITH

Giulio Regondi, one of the great guitar virtuosi of the nineteenth century, was originally taught the guitar by this father.

By the time Regondi was seven he had already made his first public recital in Paris. He amazed his audience with his immense talents and the critics dubbed him 'The Infant Paganini'. His father took advantage of his son's unique talents by presenting him in concert in most of the major cities of Europe.

In 1831 Giulio Regondi, who was also a virtuoso performer on the concertina, gave concerts in several British provincial cities. At the end of his concert tour his family settled in London, and Regondi was to live there until his death in 1872.

Giulio Regondi continued an active career as a virtuoso of the guitar and the concertina. He was also a prolific composer. Much of his music has been out of print for most of the twentieth century, but there has been a recent revival of interest in Regondi's music, and several of his compositions have recently been republished.

SELECTED RECORD
'The Guitar Works of Regondi' – Leif Christensen   Paula 10

SELECTED MUSIC
Rêverie, Notturno per Chitarra op. 19, ed. Chiesa   Zerboni
The Guitar Works of Giulio Regondi   ECH 415

SELECTED READING
'Giulio Regondi'   Article – 'Guitar and Lute' – January 1982

CELEDONIO ROMERO

Born – Malaga, Spain

1917

Celedonio Romero was the youngest son of the Spanish architectural engineer who designed the harbour of Gibraltar. Introduced to the guitar when he was five years old, Romero's talent convinced his family that he should follow a career in music. As a result Celedonio Romero was enrolled and later graduated from the Conservatory of Madrid.

Celedonio Romero's first public recital was in Madrid when he was twenty years old. His performance was well received by the audience and critics alike. Soon after his Madrid debut, Celedonio Romero married a young actress at Malaga's Teatro Cervantes. During the Spanish Civil War he played the guitar many times for his fellow loyalists. When Malaga surrendered to General Franco's forces, Romero was imprisoned but later released. He then earned his living by entertaining the troops.

Romero's reputation as a fine classical guitarist continued to grow, but because he refused to commit himself to the opposition, the Franco regime denied him the right to concertize outside Spain. In 1957, after considerable pressure and governmental red tape, Romero and his family were granted a passport to visit Portugal. The following year, with the help of sympathetic American friends, they were able to emigrate to the United States.

Celedonio Romero, a fine classical guitarist in his own right, who now lives in the Los Angeles area of California, has made a unique contribution to the classical guitar in the fact that under his tuition, all his three sons have become highly talented

Celedonio Romero

guitarists. In particular Angel and Pepe have become two of the great guitar virtuosi of the twentieth century. For many years Celedonio Romero has appeared with great success in concert all over the world with his three sons as a guitar quartet, 'The Romeros'.

SELECTED RECORDS

'European Court Music'	Philips (Universo)	6582-001
'Compositions for Two Guitars'	Philips	9500-352
'Classical Music for Four Guitars'	Philips	9500 296
'Rodrigo Concertos Andaluz/Aranjuez	Mercury	75021
'An Evening With the Romeros'	Mercury	75022
'Royal Family of the Guitar'	Mercury	75027
'Vivaldi Concertos'	Mercury	75054

SELECTED READING

The Romeros	Article – 'Guitar Player' – April 1972
The Romeros	Article – 'Guitar & Lute' – September 1978

Romero Family Quartet

Angel Romero

ANGEL ROMERO

Born – Malaga, Spain

1946

Angel Romero, the younger son of guitarist Celedonio Romero, made his debut as a guitar soloist with the family quartet at the age of six. A year later Angel gave his first solo recital in Valencia, Spain.

In 1958 the Romero family emigrated to the United States and settled in the Los Angeles area. Celedonio founded a guitar school there, at the same time maintaining a concert career for himself and his three talented sons.

In 1964 Angel Romero became the first guitarist to appear at the famous Hollywood Bowl. He performed the Rodrigo 'Concierto De Aranjuez' with the Los Angeles Philharmonic Orchestra.

In 1970, together with his brother Pepe, Angel performed the wolrd première performance of Rodrigo's 'Concierto Madrigal' for two guitars and orchestra.

Angel Romero has developed into one of the world's most outstanding classical guitarists. He maintains a busy concert schedule throughout the United States and abroad. He currently has an exclusive recording contract with Angel Records in America, as well as appearing on Philips and Mercury recordings of the Romero Guitar Quartet.

SELECTED RECORDS

'Virtuoso Works for Guitar'	Angel	S 37312
'Rodrigo Concerto and Fantasia'	Angel	S 37440
'Classical Virtuoso'	Angel	S 36094
'Spanish Virtuoso'	Angel	S 36094
'Angel Romero – Rodrigo and Torroba'	Angel	S 37312
'The Divine Giuiani'	Angel	SZ 37326
'Rodrigo – Concerto for Four Guitars' – The Romeros	Philips	3677
'Guitar Concertos for Two Guitars (with Pepe Romero)	Philips	6500-918
'Classical Music for Four Guitars' – The Romeros	Philips	9500-296

Pepe Romero

PEPE ROMERO

Born – Malaga, Spain

19th March 1944

Pepe Romero began his studies on the guitar at the age of three with his father, guitarist Celedonio Romero. He was to give his first public performance with his father at the Teatro Lope De Vega in Seville, Spain, when he was only ten years old.

The Romero family moved to California in 1960 and by the time he was fifteen Pepe was regarded as a highly talented flamenco guitarist. He made his first recording as a flamenco guiratist for the Contemporary record label, at the age of fiteen, in 1959.

For almost twenty years Pepe Romero has appeared as part of the family guitar quartet, The Romeros. He also appeared as part of a duo with Celin or Angel, his older and younger brothers respectively. In more recent times Pepe Romero has appeared more often as a soloist or in a duo with his brother Angel. Together they premièred Rodrigo's 'Concerto Madrigal' for two guitars and orchestra in 1970.

Pepe Romero's only guitar teacher was his father, but he did study music both in Spain and in New York with the Basque pianist/composer Francisco De Medina. Pepe Romero has recently recorded several albums on the Philips label including six of Boccherini's guitar quintets. These recordings, together with his current concert performances, have established him as one of the great guitar virtuosi of the decade. When he is not concertizing Pepe Romero teaches at the University of Southern California. He has recently completed a guitar method entitled 'Guitar Style and Technique' which is published by Bradleys of New York.

SELECTED RECORDS

'Compositions for Two Guitars'	Philips	9500-352
'Guitar Concertos for Two Guitars' (with Angel Romero)	Philips	6500-918
'Rodrigo – Fantasia and Giuliani'	Philips	9500-042
'Famous Guitar Music'	Philips	9500-295
'Classical Music for Four Guitars'	Philips	9500-296
'Boccherini Guitar Quintets' Nos. 4 and 5	Philips	9500-621
'Boccherini Guitar Quintets' No. 1, 2 and 7	Philips	9500-985
'Boccherini Guitar Quintets' Nos. 3 and 9	Philips	9500-789
'Sor's Guitar Sonatas', Opus 22/55	Philips	9500-586
'Rodrigo for Solo Guitar'	Philips	9500-915

SELECTED READING

Pepe Romero	Article – 'Guitar' – April 1979
Pepe Romero	Article – 'Guitar Player' – January 1981

David Russell

DAVID RUSSELL

Born – Glasgow, Scotland

1st June 1953

David Russell

COURTESY TRANSBERG

Regarded as one of the greatest guitar virtuosi to have emerged in recent years David Russell was born in Scotland, and spent most of his childhood on the Spanish island of Menorca where his parents had decided to live.

Russell was attracted to the guitar at an early by the records of Andres Segovia. His father, a professional artist, was also a keen guitarist and was his son's first teacher. At sixteen David Russell, already recognized as a highly talented guitarist, moved to London, England, to study at the Royal Academy of Music. Here he twice won the 'Julian Bream Guitar Prize'. Over the years David Russell studied with several teachers, but his two main influences were Hector Quine in London, and José Tomas in Spain.

Russell's career developed rapidly after he won several of the major guitar competitions in Spain, amongst them the 'Ramirez Competition', the 'Francisco Tarrega Competition', and the 'Concurso Andres Segovia'.

David Russell spends much of his working year touring North America, most countries of Western Europe, and the United Kingdom giving recitals and master classes. He has also appeared several times for the BBC Television and Radio Services. David Russell has also been featured as part of a number of major international guitar festivals. They include the Edinburgh Festival, The Guitar Festival of Esztergrom, Hungary, the Concours of Radio France, and the Toronto Guitar Festival, Canada.

SELECTED RECORDS

'Musique Pour Basse Et Guitare'	Festival	FC 501
'Something Unique'	Overture	OR 1001
'Plays Antonio Lauro'	Guitar Masters	GMR 1001

SELECTED READING

David Russell	Article – 'Guitar' – November 1978
David Russell	Article – 'Guitar Player' – October 1981

Regino Sainz De La Maza

COURTESY GENDAI GUITAR   PHOTO KIICHI ARAKAWA

REGINO SAINZ DE LA MAZA

Born – Burgos, Spain
7th September 1896

Died – Madrid, Spain
26th November 1981

Regino Sainz de la Maza began his musical studies on the piano in his native town of Burgos. He then attended the Academy de Bellas Artes de San Sebastian, studying harmony with Beltran Pagola and piano with German Cendoya. His studies took him later to both Barcelona and Madrid where he continued to study the piano.

Madrid turned out to be an important turning point for Sainz de la Maza's career, for it was there that he began formal studies of the guitar with Daniel Fortea. It was at that time that he realized that the guitar was the instrument through which he could best display his musical talent. At the age of eighteen, Sainz de la Maza gave his first public recital at the Circulo de Belles Artes in Madrid. His performance was well received by both audience and critics alike. On the recommendation of important musicians, including Tomas Breton and Emilio Serrano, Sainz de la Maza earned a grant to further his musical studies from the municipality of Burgos.

Regino Sainz de la Maza moved to Barcelona to study composition with Enrique Morera and Jaime Pahissa. He then completed a highly successful concert tour of Spain, and this led to futher tours of South America and Europe.

When he returned to Spain, Sainz de la Maza worked with Manuel de Falla in the National Music Society, and was appointed to the newly established Professorship of Guitar at the Con-servatory of Madrid in 1935. In 1937, he went to the United States to concertise, and after the Spanish Civil War he returned to Spain to become a music critic for the Spanish daily *ABC*. Sainz de la Maza also became very involved in transcribing early Spanish works, and in doing so found himself in close contact with many of Spain's foremost musicians. In 1938 Sainz de la Maza met Joaquin Rodrigo and the Marques de Bolarque. The latter was a famous music patron and also an enthusiast of the guitar. The result of their meeting was Rodrigo's 'Concerto de Aranjuez', which he completed in the autumn of 1939. Sainz de la Maza was given the double honour of having the work dedicated to him and premièring the concerto in Barcelona on 9th November 1940. This was the first modern concerto to be written for the guitar and orchestra, and the work has since won worldwide acclaim. It is generally regarded as one of the most important pieces of modern Spanish music. Regino Sainz de la Maza was to perform the concerto a further sixty times in Europe and the Americas.

Regino Sainz de la Maza was also a very active teacher, not only in the Conservatory in Madrid, but also in private study and in master classes. He was an avid researcher on many aspects of the guitar and early Spanish music, and made numerous transcriptions as well as several original compositions. His erudition won him election to the Spanish Academy in 1958, being the first guitar player to be elected since its foundation in 1752.

SELECTED RECORDS

'Rodrigo – Concerto De Aranjuez and Fantasia'	RCA	VICS 1322
'Regino Sainz De La Maza'	Barclay	920-230

SELECTED READING

Regino Sainz De La Maza	Article – Guitar & Lute' – April 1980

SELECTED MUSIC

Alegrías	UME 16943	Rondeña	UME 19900
Canciones Castellanas	UME 22146	Sequidilla – Sevillanas	UME 16944
Cantilena	UME 15645	Soleá	UME 22145
Cuatro Fantasías del Siglo XVI	UME 18827	Zapateado	UME 19901
El Vito – New Version	UME		
Frontera de Dios	UME 20207		
Petenera	UME 20347		

GEORGE SAKELLARIOU

Born – Athens, Greece

2nd May 1944

George Sakellariou was the youngest of eight children. He was introduced to the guitar at an early age by one of his brothers.

Sakellariou studied at the Hellenikon Odeion Conservatory in Athens under Professor Charalambos Ekmetsoglou. At the age of fiteen he gave his first recital at the Parnassus Hall in Athens, and at eighteen he graduated receiving first prize for an outstanding musical performance.

George Sakkelariou emigrated to the United States in 1963 originally to study medicine at the University of California. He soon decided that music should be his career and established himself as one of the finest guitarists and teachers on the West Coast of America. In 1964 he studied privately with Andres Segovia, as well as attending some of the Maestro's International Master Classes. Sakellariou has performed throughout the United States, Canada, and South America. He has appeared in concert in many of the important universities, and also at the Carmel Bach Festival and Universidad de los Andres Bogota, Colombia. He has been a soloist with several symphony

George Sakellariou

COURTESY GEORGE SAKELLARIOU

orchestras and chamber groups in the United States. Over the years Sakellariou has made numerous appearances on the CBC Television network in Canada, and the NET Network in the USA.

George Sakellariou now lives in San Rafael, California, spending his year as a concert artist, and also teaching at the San Francisco Conservatory of Music.

SELECTED RECORD
'Music from South America'   Amat   AGS 181

SELECTED READING
George Sakellariou   Article – 'Guitar & Lute' – May 1978

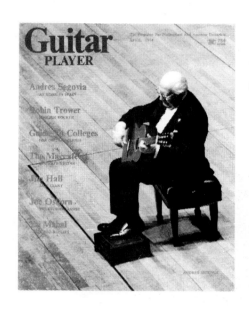

Justin Holland
1819-1887

A selection of guitar magazines.

189

Turibio Santos

TURIBIO SANTOS

Born – Sao Luis, Maranhao, North Brazil

1943

Turibio Santos was attracted to the classical guitar at the age of ten. His first teachers being Antonio Rebello and later Oscar Caceres.

In 1962 Santos gave his first recital in Rio de Janeiro, followed by a series of concerts all over Brazil. In the following year the Villa Lobos Museum invited him to play the Brazilian composer's complete 'Twelve Studies for Guitar' and 'Mystic Sextet', giving it its first public hearing. In 1964 Santos joined together with Oscar Caceres and made several tours of South America as a guitar duo. In 1965 Turibio Santos decided to establish himself in Europe. He attended master classes given by Andres Segovia in Italy and Julian Bream in England. In the same year he won the first prize in the ORTF's International Guitar Competition in Paris. His appearance later in programmes on the ORTF and the BBC, as well as his recording on disc of Villa-Lobo's 'Twelve Studies', have made him well known to European audiences. From 1965 to 1969 Turibio Santos was Professor of Guitar at the Conservatoire Municipal in Paris.

Turibio Santos has performed with many orchestras as a soloist. Included are the Monte Carlo Orchestra, l'Orchestra Philharmonic de l'ORTF, the English Chamber Orchestra, and the Royal Philharmonic Orchestra. Santos has also taken part in numerous festivals in Europe, including the fifth Croisiere Mediterranee de Musique. In 1974 he joined Yehudi Menuhin and Mstislav Rostropovitch in the opening concert for the Creation of International Funds for Musical Collabroation organised by UNESCO.

Turibio Santos established himself in North America with appearances in New York, Boston, Houston, Dallas, Minneapolis, Cincinnati and Washington DC. He was also featured at the Guitar 78 and Guitar 81 Festivals in Canada. He was recently appointed General Director of the Sala Cecilia Meireles in Brazil.

SELECTED RECORDS

'Concerto De Aranjuez – Rodrigo'	Musidisc 30	RC 894
'Villa Lobos – Twelve Studies for Guitar'	Erato	STV 70496
'Villa Lobos – Prelude and Concerto Sextour Mystique'	Erato	STV 70566
'Classiques D'Amerique Latine'	Erato	STV 70658
'Musique Francaise Pour Guitare'	Erato	STV 70767
'Musique Pour Deux Guitares' – Volume One (with Oscar Caceres)	Erato	STV 70794
'Danses Espagnoles' – Volume One	Erato	STV 70844
'J. S. Bach'	Erato	STV 70885
'Musique Bresilienne'	Erato	STV 70913
'Danses Espagnoles' – Volume Two	Erato	STV 71076
'Musique Pour Deux Guitares' – Volume Two (with Oscar Caceres)	Erato	STV 71092
'Fernando Sor'	Erato	STV 71268
'Choros Do Brasil'	Erato	ERA 9155
'Valsas et Choros'	Erato	ERA 9231
'Duo for Flute and Guitar' (with Christian Lardè, Flute)	Erato	ERA 71127

MARIA LIVIA SAO MARCOS

Born – Sao Paulo, Brazil

8th April 1942

Maria Livia Sao Marcos

Maria Livia Sao Marcos began to study the guitar at the age of five. Her first teacher was her father, Professor Manuel Sao Marcos. It was soon obvious that she had enormous musical talent and at the age of thirteen she gave her first public recital.

At the age of seventeen she was awarded a diploma with honours at the Conservatorio Dramatic E Musical in Sao Paulo. Following this she soon made her first recording.

In 1962 Maria Livia Sao Marcos went to Portugal where she played the first public performance of the guitar concerto 'Domingos Brandao'. Following this concert, which was highly acclaimed, she went to Paris, France, for several successful solo guitar recitals.

In 1964 Sao Marcos went to Santiago de Compostela in Spain to study with Andres Segovia. Later she went on to Lisbon, Portugal, for more study with Emilio Pujol.

After a highly successful career as a classical guitarist in Brazil, Maria Livia Sao Marcos went to Switzerland in 1970. Here she was offered a teaching post as Professor of Guitar at the Con- servatory of Music in Geneva, a position she has held since. A respected teacher, Maria Livia Sao Marcos still continues to give recitals in the principal cities of Europe and North and South America.

SELECTED RECORDS

'Classical Guitar and Strings'	Everest	3420
'A Internacional'	Fermata	303-1009
'Saudades do Brasil'	Fermata	303-1013
'Villa Lobos – 12 Etudes'	Fermata	305-1039
'Plays Baroque Music'	Claasic Pick Music	70-124

SELECTED READING

Maria Livia Sao Marcos	Article – 'Guitar Player' – January 1976

ISAIAS SAVIO

Born – Montevideo, Uruguay
1st October 1902

Died – Sao Paulo, Brazil
12th January 1977

Isaias Savio

Isaias Savio began his musical education at the age of nine. After studying the piano for four years, he began to study the guitar. Savio made rapid progress on his instrument, and it was soon obvious he had very special talents.

Isaias Savio became a highly successful concert artist playing througout South America. In 1931 he went to Brazil and decided to make his home there. He continued an active career as a guitarist, promoting the classical guitar throughout Brazil's cities, towns and villages.

Isaias Savio was also a fine composer. Over one hundred of his original works for the guitar have been published. Many of his composition are based on Brazilian folk melodies that he heard and learnt whilst visiting Brazilian country villages.

Towards the latter part of his life Savio devoted most of his time to teaching. He was Professor of Guitar at the Conservatorio Dramatico E Musical De Sao Paulo, the first person to hold this post. He was also Director of the Escola Violinistica Jose Do Patrocinio.

SELECTED MUSIC

A Casinha Pequenina & Minha Terra Tem Palmeiras	BR 150
Cajita de Música (Music Box)	BA 11505
Cênas Brasileiras, 1st series (seven pieces)	BR 1593
2nd series (two pieces)	MCM 0271
Celeste y Blanco – Estilo	BR 2301
Duas Guitarras – Canção Cigana	BR 1811
Nesta Rua – Theme & Variations	BR 2252
Ojos Negros (Dark Eyes, Russian Song) & A Casinha Pequenina	BA 11217
Para Nilo Brincar / 9 popular children's songs	BR 1079
Pensamientos, op. 3 – (Short Works)	R & F
Pequeña Romanza	RF 7448
Preludes Nos. 3, 4, 5, 6	BR 3193
Four Preludes Pitorescos	BR 1808
Sarabande & Gigue	BR 2170
Three Original Pieces, 1927	BR 3076
Two Pieces: Vidalita Popular, Dança de Boneca	BR 2337
Variações de Gato	BR 2302
Variations on an Infant's Theme	R & F

KARL SCHEIT

Born – Schonbrun, Austria

21st April 1909

Karl Scheit

Karl Scheit's musical studies began on the violin at an early age. Although his father was a military band conductor he did not want his son to become a professional musician.

Scheit joined a youth group when he was fifteen years old and it was then that he began to study the guitar to accompany himself when he sang. Soon afterwards the young musician realized the full potential of the classic guitar and he began to study the instrument in earnest.

Karl Scheit left his home for Vienna and began to study music theory and harmony on the guitar at the Academy of Music there. After hearing both Miguel Llobet and Andres Segovia in concert Scheit decided to make the classical guitar his career. He continued his music studies with the eminent Austrian composer N. David.

At the age of 24 Karl Scheit was appointed professor of the guitar as the Vienna State Academy, a position he still holds today. Scheit is regarded as one of the foremost guitar teachers in Europe and has published many transcriptions for guitar plus a 'Method for Guitar' in two volumes.

SELECTED RECORD
'Music for Guitar'   Turnabout   TV 341238

FRANZ SCHUBERT

Born – FRANZ PETER SCHUBERT
Lichtental, Near Vienna, Austria – 31st January 1797

Died – Vienna, Austria
19th November 1828

Franz Schubert

Franz Schubert was given a sound musical education by his father, a schoolteacher, who recognized his son's musical talents at a very early age.

Schubert learned to play the violin from his father, the piano from his brother Ignanz, and also singing at the Chapel of the Court. He befriended the poet Theodor Korner who was also an enthusiastic guitarist. Schubert became very impressed with the instrument and decided that he would master it. Within a short period of time Schubert had become an accomplished guitarist.

The classical guitar became Franz Schubert's main instrument during his early career. Before he could afford to buy a piano, Schubert conceived all his vocal compositions on the guitar, and most of his songs were written with a guitar accompaniment.

Franz Schubert lived in virtual poverty, achieving hardly any success or recognition, throughout his short life. His activities as a song writer lasted for almost seventeen years, yet it was not until 1819 that one of his songs was publicly performed, and it was not until 1821 that the first one was published Schubert is regarded as the master of the Lied, and there has been a recent revival of interest amongst guitarists in his guitar accompaniments for them. Schubert also wrote many other works for which he wrote the guitar part. In 1819 his '15 Original Dances' for flute, violin and guitar were published by Diabelli, and in 1814 he wrote a Quartet for flute, guitar, alto and cello.

Franz Schubert for many years suffered ill health. He died on 19th November 1828 at the age of thirty-one. One of Schubert's original guitars, bearing his name, is on display in the Vienna Museum.

Andres Segovia

ANDRES SEGOVIA

Born – ANDRES TORRES SEGOVIA
Linares, Granada, Spain

22nd February 1893

Andres Segovia, now approaching his ninetieth year, is one of the greatest musicians of the twentieth century and certainly the most important guitarist the world has ever known. It was because of his exceptional genius and determination that the guitar has been accepted, against very heavy prejudices, as an instrument of equal merit to any other orchestral instruments. There is not one classical guitarist in the world today who has not been influenced by Andres Segovia in one way or another.

At the age of five Andres Segovia was taken to live with his uncle in Granada. The uncle tried to encourage his nephew to learn the violin but achieved little success. Andres Segovia became fascinated with the sound of a guitar played by a flamenco guitarist who happened to be in his uncle's house. At the age of ten Segovia received his first guitar and from that moment on, despite his uncle's opposition, he devoted every spare moment to it. After his uncle's death, Segovia, who was then twelve years old, went to live with his mother and brother in Cordoba. A little later, the young guitarist decided to rent his own room so that he could fully develop his study of the guitar and music. He made friends with several musicians, including a pianist Luis Serrano who introduced Segovia to the keyboard authority De Montis. De Montis was very impressed by Segovia's transcriptions of classical masters for the guitar.

At the age of sixteen Andres Segovia left school determined to make the guitar his life. In 1909 he gave his first public recital at the Granada Art Centre. The young guitarist then went to Seville to the home of De Montis. There he met and impressed many influential people who would patronise his future concerts. Segovia stayed in Seville for over a year and played sixteen recitals whilst he was there. He then went to play in other major cities in Spain but found enormous opposition to the classical guitar from musicians and press critics alike.

In 1912 Segovia went to Madrid to make his debut in Spain's capital. There he befriended luthier Manuel Ramirez. Ramirez was so impressed with the guitarist's ability that he gave him one of his finest guitars as a gift. Segovia's Madrid concert, despite an excellent performance, was not well received. Segovia then went to Valencia where he made contact with Tarrega's most important pupil, Miguel Llobet. They became good friends and Llobet invited Segovia to his home in Barcelona. Segovia played three concerts in Barcelona and these were generally well received. On his return to Madrid Segovia was introduced to the well-known concert promoter Senõr Quesada. Quesada was greatly impressed by Segovia's musicianship and technical ability and offered to be his concert agent. The first booking that Quesada arranged for Andres Segovia was a tour of South America. This tour was highly successful. In 1920 Andres Segovia was invited to play for Queen Victoria of Spain at the Palace of Madrid, a positive sign of the young guitarist's growing reputation and enormous musical talent.

From 1920 to 1935 Segovia concertized throughout the major cities of Europe. He appeared in London in 1924, Paris in 1924, and Moscow in 1926. In 1928 he crossed the Atlantic again to make his United States debut in New York's Town Hall. Everywhere he went Segovia astounded his audiences with his performances. It was during this period that Segovia began his campaign to encourage leading symphonic composers to write for the guitar. The first to reply to Segovia's request was Moreno-Torroba. Soon after many more leading composers including Manuel Ponce, Heitor Villa Lobos, Joaquin Turina, Mario Castelnuevo-Tedesco and Joaquin Rodrigo were to compose original music for solo guitar and guitar and orchestra.

In 1938, at the outbreak of the Spanish Civil War, Segovia left Spain not to return until after the end of World War II. During these years he made his home in New York and Montevideo, Uruguay.

After the end of World War II, Segovia was instrumental in bringing about a revolution for classical guitarists. For many years Segovia had suffered with the supply of strings for his guitar. The master guitarist had been introduced to the head of the Du

Pont Chemical company by a friend. Segovia, with the help of his friend Albert Augustine, persuaded Du Pont to investigate the possibility of producing a nylon guitar string. Augustine took charge of the project and in 1947 the first nylon guitar strings were made. Another enormous step forward, instigated by Andres Segovia, had been made for the classical guitar.

During the 1950s and 1960s Segovia continued a highly successful career as a concert and recording artist. Averaging one hundred concerts a year during this period of his career, Segovia also recorded thirty albums for the Decca label. It was during this time that Segovia began his Master Classes for professional level guitarists. His annual classes in Siena, Italy and Santiago De Compostela, Spain have been attended by nearly every leading guitarist in the world today. Segovia still, at the age of 87, holds master classes in other countries as far apart as the United States of America and Japan. Once again Andres Segovia has instigated a teaching movement for the classical guitar which has ensured that the instrument has more virtuosi than it ever has had. Segovia has also encouraged and persuaded colleges and conservatories of music in every major city of the world to include the guitar in its curriculum. Today there are few colleges that do not have a Professor of Guitar.

Early on in his career Andres Segovia set himself several goals to promote the classical guitar. The seeds which had been sewn by Francisco Tarrega and Miguel Llobet were cultivated and brought to full bloom by the super human efforts of Segovia. There is little doubt he has now achieved all his goals and more. The classical guitar enjoys worldwide acceptance and popularity in all musical circles. Andres Segovia, who now lives with his family in Madrid and Switzerland for most of the year, still devotes several months each year to give concerts throughout Europe, USA, South America and the Far East. He still presides at master classes, and recently sat on the jury of the first Andres Segovia International Guitar Competition which was held in England and promoted by the Sherry Producers of Spain. Andres Segovia, whose name has become synonymous with the classical guitar, was recently described as The Patriarch of the Classical Guitar, a title that no-one could ever contest.

SELECTED RECORDS

'The Art of Segovia' 1927—1939	EMI	RLS 745 (2 LPs)
'Andres Segovia 1949'	EMI	HLM 134
'Concerto'	MCA	S-26044
'International Classics'	MCA	MACS 2359
'Andres Segovia Plays'	MCA	MACS 1354
'Recuerdos De La Alhambra' – Tarrega & Sor	MCA	S-26091
'Interprete Les Italiens'	MCA	MACS 6123
'Segovia and the Guitar'	MCA	MCF 3073
'Golden Jubilee Set' (3 LPs)	Decca	DXT 148
'Maestro'	Brunswick	SXA 4535
'Boccherini/Cassado Concerto and Bach Suite'	MCA	MACS 125
'Five Pieces from Platero and I'	MCA	MACS 1967
'Granada'	MCA	MACS 1968
'Sonata Romantica'	MCA	S-26-087
'Tansman & Mompou'	Brunswick	AXA 4532
'On Stage'	Brunswick	SXA 4550
'Mexicana'	MCA	MUCS 100
'Espana'	MCA	S-26-037
'Castles of Spain'	MCA	MACS 3045
'The Unique Art of Andres Segovia'	Decca	DL 71067
'The Guitar and I' – Volume One	MCA	MACS 3965
'The Guitar and I' – Volume Two	MCA	MACS 6281
'Nocturno'	Intercord	INT 160 815
'The Intimate Guitar' – Volume One	RCA	ARL 1-0864
'The Intimate Guitar' – Volume Two	RCA	ARL 1-1323
'Reveries'	RCA	RL 12602

SELECTED READING

Andres Segovia	Article – 'Guitar' – December 1972
Andres Segovia	Article – 'Guitar' – December 1974
Andres Segovia	Article – 'Guitar' – October 1976
Andres Segovia	Article – 'Guitar' – June 1977
Andres Segovia	Article – 'Guitar' – June 1977
Andres Segovia	Article – 'Guitar' – December 1977
Andres Segovia	Article – 'Guitar' Player' – June 1971
Andres Segovia	Article – 'Guitar' Player' – October 1971
Andres Segovia	Article – 'Guitar' Player' – February 1972

Andres Segovia	Article – 'Guitar' Player' – April 1974
Andres Segovia	Article – 'Guitar' Player' – June 1978
Andres Segovia	Article – 'Frets' – December 1981
Andres Segovia	Article – 'Guitarra' – January 1979
Andres Segovia	Article – 'Guitarra' – September 1980
Andres Segovia	Article – 'Guitarra' – Setpember 1981
'The Sound of Segovia'	'Guitar Review' No. 42, 1977
A Conversation With Segovia	'Guitar Review' No. 43, 1978
'Andres Segovia' – Bernard Gavoty	Kister (1955)
'Andres Segovia' – George Clinton	Musical New Services (1978)
'Segovia' – An Autobiography 1893-1920	MacMillan (1976)
'Andres Segovia – Contributions to the World of Guitar' – Ronald C. Purcell	Belwin Mills (1975)
'The Segovia Technique' – Vladimir Bobri	MacMillan (1972)
'The Guitar and myself'	Series of Articles – /Guitar Reviews' Nos. 4, 6, 7, 8, 10 and 13

SELECTED MUSIC

Five Short Works for the Guitar: Impromptu, Tonadilla, 3 Preludes	Kalmus
From 'Follies of My Youth'	Belwin
Five Anecdotes	
Lessons Nos. 11 and 12	
Macarena	
Two Pieces: Giga Melancólica, Neblina (a Olga)	
Prelude on Chords	Celesta

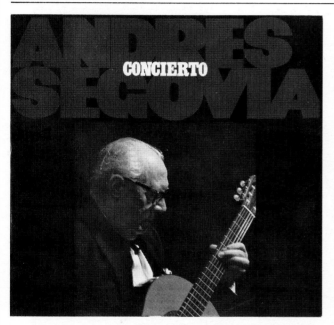

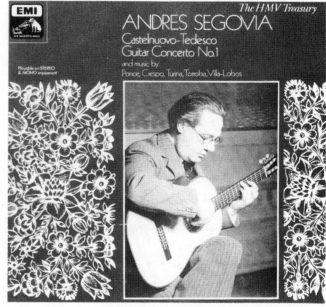

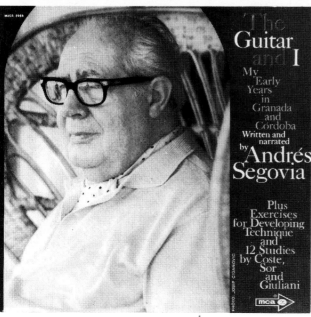

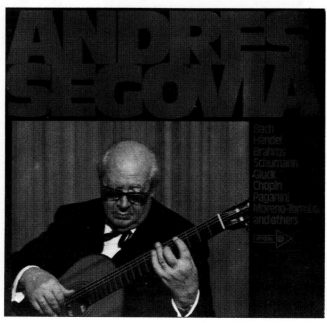

Andres Segovia

There exists a legend regarding the origin of the guitar that is more beautifully suggestive than historic fact: Apollo was running in pursuit of a beautiful nymph, gallantly repeating to her all the while: "Don't tire yourself, don't tire yourself, I promise not to catch up with you." When, finally, he did succeed in taking her into his arms, she called out to her semidivine father, who instantly changed her into a laurel tree. Apollo made the first guitar from the wood of this tree and gave it as form the graceful, curved contours that forever reveal its feminine origin. That is why the guitar is of a reserved and changeable nature, even hysterical at times; but that is also why it is sweet and smooth, harmonious and delicate. When it is played with love and skill, there issues from its melancholy sounds a rapture that holds us fast to it forever.

From my youthful years I dreamed of raising the guitar from the sad artistic level in which it lay. At first my ideas were vague and imprecise, but as I grew in years and my love for it became intense and vehement, my will to do so became more assertive, and my intentions clearer.

Since then, I have dedicated my life to four essential tasks. The first: To separate the guitar from mindless folklore-type entertainment. It was born for something more and something better. Can you imagine Pegasus drawing a cart laden with vegetable greens?

My second item of labor: To endow it with a repertoire of high quality, made up of works possessing intrinsic musical value, from the pens of composers accustomed to writing for orchestra, piano, violin, etc. The masters, in accordance with usage, had written for it with passion, but with incompetence, allowing it to sink even lower than when Flamenco *tocaores*—some of whom were wonderful within their field—strummed it. Three names stand out in the modern history of the guitar: they are Sor, Giuliani and Tárrega, although the little works of this last are not of transcendental import. The first symphonic composer to heed my request, offering to collaborate with me, was Federico Moreno Torroba; then, Falla and Turina; later, Manuel Ponce, Villa-Lobos, Castelnuovo-Tedesco, Tansman, Roussel, Cyril Scott, Rodrigo, Jolivet, Duarte, and others. Assisted by professional musicologists, I also dedicated myself to capturing delightful works written for the vihuela and the lute, and among the latter is a magnificent collection composed by Johann Sebastian Bach. Today, new works for the guitar number more than three hundred.

My third purpose: To make the beauty of the guitar known to the philharmonic public of the entire world. I began by giving concerts in Spain, disproving the truth of the saying "No one is a prophet in his own country." Theaters and music halls were filled and the public's interest and respect for the "classical" guitar grew. In 1919 I made my first tour of Latin America, and five years later the doors of the Paris Conservatory's hall opened to me. The French critics praised the guitar as an expressive medium for serious music, and mentioned the works of Bach in their words of praise. Concert societies and impresarios began to call me from London, Berlin, Vienna, Zurich, Amsterdam, Rome, Stockholm, etc. My first appearance in the United States took place in 1928, and during the summer and early autumn of that same year I undertook a tour of the Far East for the first time. Today, at seventy-seven, I continue my artistic activities throughout the civilized world. Like the poet, I can say: "I have felt the roundness of the world beneath my feet."

I am still working on my fourth and perhaps last task: That of influencing the authorities at conservatories, academies and universities to include the guitar in their instruction programs on the same basis as the violin, cello, piano, etc. I have placed pupils of mine as teachers in four conservatories in Switzerland, as well as five in Italy, two in Spain, one in England, two in Australia, two in Argentina, three in the United States, and others in Germany, Holland, France and the Scandinavian countries.

The future of the guitar is, therefore, assured. I have broken the vicious circle in which adverse fate had held it enclosed. Guitarists of worth did not appear because great composers did not write for the guitar, and the latter did not write for the guitar because it lacked virtuosos of talent. My disciples—many of whom are already famous teachers and artists—will continue my work, fervently adding their own artistic contributions to the history of this most beautiful instrument.

Sleeve notes by Segovia from his record "The Guitar and I" MCA 3965.

Andres Segovia with Tsuyoshi Horiuchi winner of the 1981 Segovia International Guitar Competition at Leeds Castle, England.

Mr. Paul Channon, Minister for the Arts (second left), greets Maestro Andres Segovia, President of the Jury of the Segovia International Guitar Competition, at the Awards Presentation during the Gala Evening given by the sponsors, the Sherry Producers of Spain, represented (fourth from right) by Mr. John Surtees, OBE, MC, MW, Chairman, Sherry Committee, Wine and Spirit Association of Great Britain and Northern Ireland. The winner, Tsuyoshi Horiuchi (Japan), Silver-medallist Paul Galbraith (UK) and Bronze-medallist Stefano Grondona (Italy) are seen on the right.

Gordon Crosskey, Anton Garcia Abril and Mrs. Abril, Bryan Buckingham (Sherry Information Bureau), Maestro Andres Segovia (President of the Jury), Agustin Leon Ara, Mrs. Galve, William Kallaway (Administrative Director), Alexandre Tansman, John Manduell and Luis Galve in the library at Leeds Castle during the 1981 Segovia International Guitar Competition sponsored by the Sherry Producers of Spain.

Peter Sensier

PETER SENSIER

Born – Ealing, London, England
20th January 1918

Died – Gateshead, England
24th September 1977

Peter Sensier was one of the most important guitar personalities in Great Britain for many years. Although his playing was generally restricted to a popular South American vocal duo 'Dorita y Pepe', for most of his career, Sensier was an authority on the classical guitar repertoire. He made many transcriptions of early lute music and classical melodies for the guitar, and he was also the original presenter of the excellent BBC Radio Three programme 'The Classical Guitar'. He was also a fine constructor of guitars and vihuelas, and a regular contibutor to BMG Magazine for many years.

Peter Sensier's first music studies were on the piano at the age of eight. After leaving school he took up the plectrum guitar and at the age of 19 was playing professionally in various dance bands. During World War II he served with the Royal Signals. He continued to play the guitar in an Army dance band, and also studied the oboe and clarinet.

In 1945 Peter Sensier returned to a career as a professional guitarist playing in several London nightclubs. In 1948 he took an interest in the classical guitar and studied it under Geoffrey Sisley, Desmond Dupré and Angel Inglesias. By 1952, Peter Sensier had gained such a wide knowledge of the instruments, he was invited to give a series of lecture-recitals at Middlesex County Schools.

In 1956, whilst working in a night club in Amsterdam, Holland, Sensier met Dorothy Holcombe. They soon found that they had a mutual interest and love of South American music and the guitar. Over the next five years the couple collected and built up a extensive repertoire of South American vocal and instrumental music.

In 1961 Dorita y Pepe made their recital debut at Wigmore Hall with great success. In the same year they visited Mexico where they were awarded a diploma, a silver plaque and a gold stauette, the much coveted 'El Pipila' for their work in spreading and popularising Latin American folk music. At about this time they became much in demand for radio and television programmes in Europe as well as Britain (where they had a 39-week series on Southern TV).

In 1964 Dorita y Pep went to Argentina and Paraquay and were invited back to Argentina for the 1965 Fifth National Festival of Artgentine Folklore in the Cosquin where they appeared beside the great folk artists of Argentina on equal terms and with great success. During that visit they also appeared in the National Festival of Poetry and Folk Music at Carlos Paz and in the first Festival of Latin American Folk Music in Salta, where they were a part of the delegation of professional Argentine folk artists.

Despite the burden of failing health, Peter Sensier continued to write about the guitar in various journals, construct many fine fretted instruments, and also broadcast for the BBC on guitar matters, until his death in 1977 at the age of 59.

SELECTED READING
Peter Sensier

Article – 'Guitar' – August 1972

ERNEST SHAND

Born – ERNEST WATSON, Hull, England
31st January 1868

Died – Birmingham, England
30th November 1924

Ernest Shand

COURTESY C. E. H. SMITH

Ernest Shand was best known to the British public as an actor and comedian, but he was also one of the best guitarists in Britain at the end of the nineteenth century. Shand studied the violin for five years and then began to teach himself the guitar. He later studied with Madame Sidney Pratten, and with her guidance made great progress on the instrument. Before he was thirty years old Shand had already written 150 compositions for the guitar many of which were published by Barnes & Mullins, Schott & Co., Weekes & Co., and Essex & Cammeyer.

In 1896, Shand opened a guitar teaching studio in Bryanston street, London. This was not to be a success as he could not get enough pupils. Although he continued to play the guitar, he never used it in his theatre appearances. He would occasionally play the guitar at concerts, some of which took place at the London Conservatoire of Music.

Ernest Shand was one of Britain's most prolific composers for the guitar. At the time of his death he had composed nearly two hundred and fifty works for the guitar, the most important of which was his 'Premier Concerto pour Guitar', op. 48. He performed this work for the first time at the Glasgow Arts Club in February 1896. He was also the author of a guitar method which was published by Barnes & Mullins of London.

NEIL SMITH

Born – Horwich, Lancashire

6th January 1945

Neil Smith

COURTESY NEIL SMITH

Neil Smith began to play the plectrum guitar at the age of sixteen. He was self-taught on this instrument and soom became a well-known dance band and session guitarist in the Lancashire area.

At the age of twenty-two, Neil Smith heard some records by Andres Segovia, and decided that he wanted to make his career on the classical guitar. He took lessons with guitarist Michael Strutt in Manchester, and also lessons in theory and harmony with pianist Robert Marsh in Manchester. Neil Smith then went on to study in London with the composer/guitarist John Duarte, and later with professors at the Royal College of Music and the Guildhall School of Music. He

gained a fellowship of the London College of Music at the end of his course.

In 1975 Neil Smith was the only Englishman invited to study in Canada with the Venezuelan guitarist Alirio Diaz in a master class recorded by CBC.

Since 1975 Neil Smith has established himself as one of Britain's finest classical guitarists.

In the United Kingdom Neil Smith has made several broadcasts on BBC radio and television, and continues an active career as a recitalist and teacher throughout Great Britain and Europe.

SELECTED RECORD
'Classical Guitar' – Neil Smith   Pennine Sound   PS 186

Fernando Sor

FERNANDO SOR

Born – JOSEPH FERNANDO MACARI SORS
Barcelona, Spain – 14th February 1778

Died – Paris, France
8th July 1839

Fernando Sor, one of the greatest guitarists and composers for the guitar the world has ever known, was born in Barcelona, Spain in 1778. He received his first musical education in singing, harmony and counterpoint at a monastery, the Escolania at Montserrat. His tutor was Father Anselma Viola. As a child Sor had played his father's guitar, and in the monastery he studied both the organ and violin as well as singing.

After he had completed his studies at the age of sixteen, Sor left the monastery and returned to Barcelona. There he joined the military academy in which he was to spend the next four years. During this time he never lost his interest in music, and at the age of nineteen Fernando Sor presented his first opera in a Barcelona theatre. By that time he was already accepted as one of Spain's most brilliant young musicians. After hearing some guitar music by Moretti, Fernando Sor decided to make the guitar his main instrument.

On a visit to Madrid Sor was commissioned by the Duke of Medina and the Duchess of Alba to write music. After the French invasion of Spain, Sor decided to enlist in Napoleon's army. On the restoration of Ferdinand IV Sor fled to Paris, France. Here, encouraged by Cherubini, Mehul and Berton, Sor resumed his musical career.

From 1815 to 1823 Fernando Sor lived in London. There his enormous talent on the guitar was fully recognised and he was highly successful as a recitalist, teacher and composer of the guitar. During his stay in London Sor composed a ballet 'Cinderella' and this was performed for the first time at the Kings Theatre, in London, in 1822. It was a great success and in the following year it was performed in Paris, and later in Moscow, Russia.

From 1823 to 1827 he lived in Russia. Here, as in London, Fernando Sor enjoyed enormous popularity. He played often for both the Imperial Royal family and Russian high society.

In 1827-28 Sor was once again living in Paris and there he decided to deovte his life totally to the guitar. Many other great nineteenth century guitarists were also living in Paris at the same time and Sor appeared often in concert with Aguado and Costé.

Fernando Sor was to spend the remaining years of his life in Paris. It was during this period that he wrote his famous guitar method. This method was originally published in Spain, and the first English translation was made by the celebrated organist and guitarist, Arnold Merrick. This English edition was published in 1827 by Robert Cocks & Co., London. It is one of the most remarkable guitar methods ever published, containing more text than music, and is a lasting memorial to the genius of Fernando Sor.

Fernando Sor composed over four hundred pieces for the guitar including studies, fantasies, themes with variations and sonatas.

SELECTED RECORDS

'Diego Blanco Plays Sor'	BIS	LP 133
'Alice Artzt Plays Sor'	Meridian	E 77006
'Turibio Santos Plays Sor'	Earto	STU 71268
'Segovia Plays Sor and Tarrega'	MCA	S 26091
'La Guitare En Duo' – Lemaigre/Lukowski	Pavanne	ADW 7016
'Rey De La Torre Plays Sor'	SMC	517

SELECTED READING

'Fernando Sor – Composer and Guitarist'	Brian Jeffrey – Tecla (1977)
Fernando Sor	Article – 'Guitar Review' No. 26, 1962
Fernando Sor	Article – 'Guitar Review' No. 39, 1974

SELECTED MUSIC

Opus 1-20, Facsimile Edition, ed. Noad	CGF 001
Complete Works for Guitar, Facsimile Edition, ed. Jeffery, 5 volums	CGF 11

FERNANDO SOR – Selected Music (continued)

First Set of Divertimenti, op. 1, ed. Jeffrey	Oxford
Second Set of Divertimenti, op. 2, ed. Jeffrey	Oxford
Third Set of Divertimenti, op. 8, ed. Jeffrey	Oxford
Fantasia No. 1, op. 7, ed. Jeffrey	Oxford
No. 2, op. 4, ed. Jeffrey	Oxford
No. 3, op. 10, ed. Jeffrey	Oxford
No. 4, op. 12, ar. Libbert	SIM
Andantino, op. 2, no. 3, ed. Scheit	UE 13941
Two Variations for the Guitar, op. 3 & 9	Kalmus
Andante Largo, from op. 5, ed. Segovia	BA 9599
Variations on a Theme of Mozart, op. 9, Segovia	GA 130
Two Minuets, op. 11, Nos. 5 & 6	GA 357
Grand Solo, op. 14 (Introduction & Allegro), ed. Azpiazu	SY 2013
Sonata, op. 15, ed. Chiese	Zerboni
Les Folies d'Espagne – Theme & Variations, op. 15A, ed. Papas	CO 100
Farewell, from op. 21	GA 350
Grand Sonata, op. 22, ed. Domandl	SIM 1322
Menuett & Rondo from op. 22, ed. Brojer	GA 450
Rondo in C Major, from op. 22	GA 362
Second Sonata, op. 25, ed. Segovia	BA 9600
Minuet, from op. 25, ed Sinópoli	BA 11837
Variations on 'Que ne suis-je la fougère', op. 26	ESC
Introduction & Variations on the air 'Marlbrough', op. 28, ed. Santos	ESC
Fantasia e Variazioni Brillanti, op. 30, ed. Ganci	

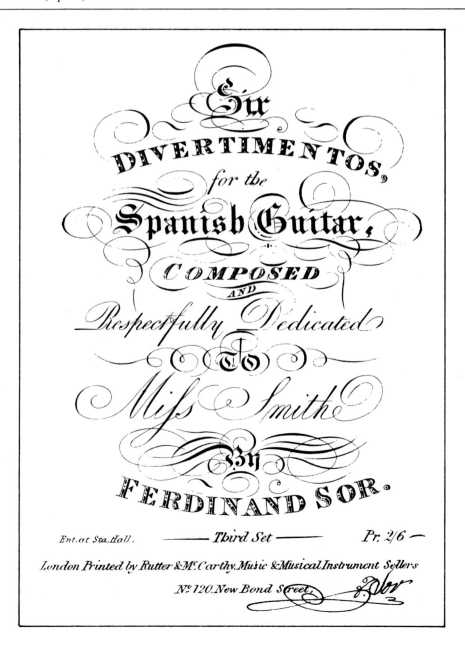

Sor's Method

FOR THE

Spanish Guitar,

TRANSLATED FROM THE ORIGINAL

BY

A. MERRICK.

LONDON:

R. COCKS AND CO., 20, PRINCES-STREET, HANOVER-SQUARE.

NEW MUSIC FOR THE SPANISH GUITAR,

PUBLISHED AS ABOVE.

INSTRUCTION BOOKS.	s.	d.	PIANOFORTE AND GUITAR.	s.	d.
NUSKE's Method, with Twenty-seven Airs	5	0	NÜSKE's Weber's Last Waltz	1	6
CARULLI's Method	4	0	——— Beethoven's ditto	1	6
VOICE AND GUITAR.			——— Alpine Melody	1	6
PELZER's Fifty National Songs ...... each	0	6	——— Souvenir's de l'Opera, 72 Airs, 12 books, ... each	2	6
HAGART's Le Papillon, 6 books ...... each	1	6	**FLUTE AND GUITAR.**		
			LE BOUQUET, Collection of elegant Airs, 6 books, each	1	6

[*W. Fowler, Printer, Cirencester.*]

Cover of Sor's famous method for Spanish guitar – English edition.

POSITION OF THE INSTRUMENT.

Having had no master, I have been obliged to reason before raising any maxim into a fixed principle.   I observed that all masters on the pianoforte agree in sitting opposite the middle of the key-board, namely the middle of the horizontal line passed over by both hands.   I considered this precept very just, because, leaving both arms equally separated from the body, no motion would be confined.   Hence I concluded that the middle part of the string (the 12th fret) should be found opposite my form of the guitar, which, describing the A as that which should be placed on the ment is too low for the left hand to be placed of requiring the guitar-makers to make any

Fig. 6.

body.   This opinion I found supported by the curve B C D A F, fig. 6, indicates the point right knee; but as in this case the instru- in the way which I find necessary, instead innovation in the instrument, I saught a

support for my right foot which, by keeping my knee higher, raised the guitar to a proper height for the left hand. Yet, in proportion as I have required more and more of the instrument, I have found it necessary to have it better fixed in its position, from which it should not deviate but when I wished.   To effect this, I have found nothing better than to have before me a table, presenting one of its corners opposite the 12th fret, allowing me to rest the point

Fig. 7.   *Fig. 8.*

B of the instrument on the right knee a little turned out, and the point C on the corner D.   By these means, finding myself placed in the position represented in figure 7. I am enabled to pass the left hand readily over the finger-board, it not being obliged to support the neck of the instrument, because the guitar is not only supported by the knee and the table, but is fixed by the weight of the right hand, which I cause to rest entirely on the point E.

I made yet another reflection on the position of the guitar.   I remarked that the French and Italians generally held it in the way represented in fig. 8; and that the line A F was always parallel to the plane on which the man appears to the eye.   That position (if I endeavoured to take it) would oblige me to advance the right shoulder in a constrained manner.   My arm, having no support, could not determine a fixed position for the hand.   The tendons acting continually to keep the arm in an unnatural position, such as the angle B C D, would make me feel difficulty in moving the joints of the fingers, and indeed often pain.   At first I said to myself that this position could only be compared to that of a pianist sitting at one end of the key-board; that the left arm being

Two pages from Sor's guitar method showing the high quality of illustration.

raised for a long time, the circulation of the blood must be affected in the parts most distant from the body; that the line C D, formed by the fore-arm indicates its continuation D E as the natural direction of the right hand, and that the latter being obliged to rise to encounter the strings, the wrist must be in a continual state of contraction in

Fig. 9.

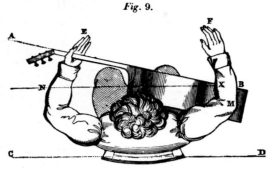

order to keep it curved. I establish as a principle that since on my left I should have only the hand beyond the line A B, fig. 9, whilst on my right, half the fore arm should be advanced, the line A B could not by any means be parallel to the line C D, if I wished to prevent displacing my right shoulder, and the parallel could only be N B. Thus placed, I found that by letting my right hand F incline naturally, it came exactly in front of the strings; that, from its form and the different lengths of the fingers, I could use to advantage the dimensions given it by nature, instead of modifying them in order to accommodate them to the proper distances; and that the point X, at the middle of the fore arm, serving me as a support, I had only to make a motion with the elbow to cause the arm of the lever X M to act in the opposite direction to that which I desired to communicate to the other arm of the lever X F.

RIGHT HAND.

The line on which the strings bear at the edge of the bridge, is a straight line, as well as that of the nut, consequently all the strings are in the same plane. If these strings were to be touched by keys or moved by quills, like the old harpsichords and spinets, all the hammers or jacks (when not set in motion) would be seen to form a straight line parallel to the strings which they were to set in vibration; and when several were made to act at once, they would always preserve a straight line parallel to the plane of the strings, and this would be one cause of uniformity in the quantity and quality of the sound. From this truth I deduced that it is necessary for the ends of the fingers of this hand to be placed in a straight line in front of the strings and parallel to the plane which they form, and I examined whether my fingers were found in that situation naturally. I saw that my fingers did not allow me to apply a straight line to touch the extremties of more than three of them, fig. I0, A B, and that if I wished to bring in the fourth, it would always be at the expense of the two which, being obliged to be bent not to over-pass the line E A (the others continuing extended), would place my hand in a constrained position, on account of the difficulty which I have always experienced in bending one single finger (excepting the thumb), if the others have not a point of support, as happens to the left hand. The joint of the thumb as well as its position cause its action to be in another direction different from that of the fingers, and, besides the possibility of pushing the string, it can approach them or recede without deranging the hand. It can slide on two succeeding strings with such a velocity as to make them both be heard together. I therefore establish as a rule of my fingering, for the right hand, to employ commonly only the three fingers touched by the line A B, and to use the fourth only for playing a chord in four parts of which the part nearest to the base leaves an intermediate string, as in example 1, Plate I.

Fig. 10. Right hand.

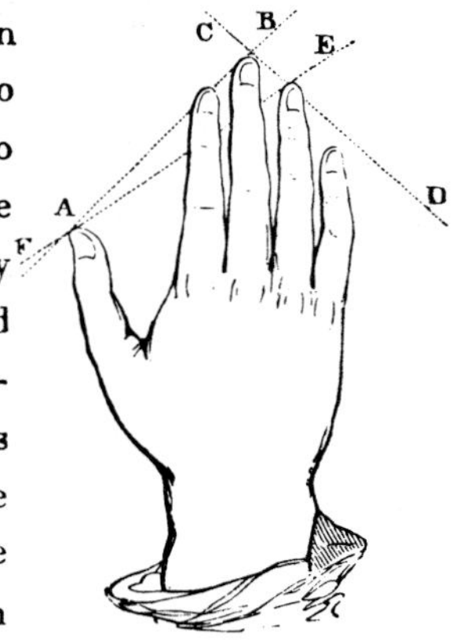

ICHIRO SUZUKI

Born – Kobe, Japan

9th May 1948

Ichiro Suzuki

Ichiro Suzuki began to play the guitar at an early age. He gave his first public recital in Kobe, Japan in March 1965 at the age of sixteen. Suzuki showed great talent and won second prize in both the 11th and 12th Tokyo International Guitar Competitions which were held in 1968 and 1969.

Since 1970, Suzuki has lived in Europe, where he has studied guitar with Andres Segovia, José Tomas, Oscar Ghiglia and Leo Brouwer. In 1974 in Valencia, Spain. At present Suzuki is music director of Palamos International Music Festival. He resides in Paris, France, and plays about 50 to 60 recitals annually in many countries including Czechoslovakia, Hungary, Poland, Yugoslavia, USSR, Japan, Australia, Africa, North and South America, Asia and the Caribbean countries. As a soloist, Suzuki has performed with the Paris Concerts Colonne Orchestre, Lyon Symphony Orchestra, the Orchestra Solistas de Cataluna, and the Tokyo Philharmonic Orchestra, amongst others.

SELECTED RECORD
'Suzuki Plays Nocturnal   CMT   1045

RENATA TARRAGO

Born — Barcelona, Spain

1927

Renata Tarrago was originally taught the guitar by her father, Graciano Tarrago, a well known professor of guitar in Barcelona. She gave her first public recital at the age of 14 and at the age of 16 won the 'Premio del Conservatorio del Liceo' with a silver medal. She was soon regarded as one of Spain's most important guitar recitalists. In 1944 she finished her studies at the Conservatory of Music in Barcelona and was then appointed Assistant Professor of Guitar to her father at the same Conservatory.

In 1948 Renata Tarrago appeared in London for the BBC in a presentation of Manuel De Falla's 'La Vida Breve'. She also appeared in a recital of popular Spanish songs in collaboration with her father and the soprano Victoria de los Angeles in London. In 1951 she won the Extraordinary Prize for guitar created by the Conservatorio del Liceo of Barcelona. Following this Renata Tarrago embarked on a concert tour of Europe which was highly successful. In 1960 she made her first tour of the United States and her performances there received high critical acclaim. In 1962 Tarrago officially represented Spain in the International Guitar Congress in Tokyo, Japan. There she won a gold medal for her performances. In 1963 she returned once more to Japan for a highly successful concert tour. During the next three years Renata Tarrago continued to give guitar recitals in most countries of the world.

In 1968 Renata Tarrago was featured with the London Philharmonic Orchestra on the soundtrack of a British film thriller entitled 'Deadfall'. In recent years Renata Tarrago has spent most of her time teaching in the Barcelona area.

SELECTED RECORDS

'La Guitarra De Renata Tarrago'	Phillips (Spain)	843 138PY
'Romance For Guitar And Orchestra' (J. Barry)	Stateside	SL 10263
'Torroba Concerto De Castille'	Erato	EFM 8080 GU
'Rodrigo Concerto/Torroba Suite'	Columbia	ML 5345
'Music of Francisco Tarrega'	Columbia	ML 5454
'Renata Tarrago'	Columbia	ML 5722

Francisco Tarrega

FRANCISCO TARREGA

Born — FRANCISCO DE ASSIS EIXEA TARREGA
Villareal De Los Infantes, Castellon, Spain
29th November 1854

Died Barcelona, Spain
5th December 1909

Francisco Tarrega was without doubt one of the greatest classical guitarists of all time. It was due to his enormous energy through the latter half of the 19th century that the way was opened for the great guitarists of the 20th century, in particular Andres Segovia, to prove to the world the enormous musical potential of the classical guitar.

Tarrega's first teacher was a local player, Manuel Gonzalez. The young guitarist's talent was first recognised when he played in public, in Villareal, a guitar concerto by Julian Arcas. In October 1874 Tarrega entered the Madrid Conservatoire of Music as a student of harmony and composition. In 1875 he was awarded the first prize for these subjects. It has been recorded that at one of Tarrega's early recitals he played half of the programme on the piano and the other half on the guitar, requesting the audience to choose which they preferred. They chose the guitar, so Tarrega decided to dedicate his life to that instrument.

Francisco Tarrega then began a highly successful career as a recitalist and teacher. He toured throughout Europe and audiences in most of the continent's major cities were able to hear his virtuoso guitar playing. He became Professor to the Guitar at the Conservatoires of Madrid and Barcelona. Among his many pupils were Emilio Pujol, Miguel Llobet, Daniel Fortea and Alberto Obregon.

Tarrega's vast knowledge of music enabled him to do two major things for the guitar. He was able to improve the technique of playing by changing the usual position of sitting, chair, footstool, legs, arms and hands, and above all the action of the fingers of each hand. The wider Torres guitar that he used also helped with the right hand position. There seems little doubt that Tarrega drew on his expert knowledge of piano playing techniques, adapting their principles to the guitar.

Franciso Tarrega's other great contribution to the classical guitar was the improvement of his repertoire. Almost all other professional guitarists at that time played nothing but their own compositions. Napoleon Costé, one of Sor's pupils made a few arrangements for the guitar of music written for other instruments, but Tarrega went much further. He transcribed works by Schumann, Chopin, Beethoven, Bach and may other great composers. He arranged a Canzonetta written by Mendelssohn for a string quartet, so that it could be played on one guitar. Tarrega also transcribed the works of several contemporary composers. He was especially successful with piano solos by Granados and Albeniz. It is said that Albeniz, on hearing Tarrega play one of his piano solos on the guitar, declare that he preferred the guitar version to his original piano version.

Francisco Tarrega has often been called the founder of the Modern Guitar School, a title well earned, although he did advocate the right hand 'no nail' technique, a technique which is today not advocated by most of the world's foremost guitarists. A man of great modesty and humbleness, Francisco Tarrega maintained his intense devotion to the guitar and music throughout his life. He died of apoplexy in 1909 at the age of 55.

SELECTED RECORDS

'Alice Artzt Plays Tarrega'	Meridian	E77026
'Segovia Plays Tarrega'	MCA	S 26091
'Rey De La Torre Plays Tarrega'	SMC	516

SELECTED READING

'Tarrega — Ensayo Biographico'	Emilio Pujol — Ramos And Alfonso (1960)
'Is There a School of Tarrega'	Article — Guitar Review No 1 (1946)

SELECTED MUSIC

'Capriccio Arabe'	Bèrben
'The Carnival of Venice'	EMB

TARREGA – Selected Music (continued)

'Complete Preludes'	UE 13408
'Danza Mora'	BA 9900
'Gavotta, Pavana, Mazurka'	Bèrben
'Gran Jota Argonesa'	BA 7924
'Gran Vals'	RF 7321
'La Alborada (Music Box)'	BA 7923
'Maria'	BA 9068
'Marieta'	BA 12075
'Danza Mora & Capricho Arabe'	GA 451
'Danza Odalisca'	BA 12074
'Eighteen Original Preludes'	BA 11365
'Pavane, ed Savio'	BR 3215
'Recuerdos de la Alhambra'	Sy 2001
'Rosita — Polka'	BA 12076
'Sueno! (Trémolo — Estudio)'	BA 11393
'Thirty Original Preludes'	BA 12720

Tarrega playing to an audience of his disciples.

Francisco Tárrega – honoured as one of Spain's foremost personalities on Spanish postage stamps 1977.

JOSÉ TOMAS

Born — Alicante, Spain

1934

Jose Thomas

José Tomas, encouraged by his father, was originally self-taught on the guitar. His first serious musical education was with the Spanish pianist Oscar Espla.

It was soon realised that Tomas was a talented player and he went to Madrid to study with Regino Sainz De La Maza. Whilst he was in Madrid Tomas met Alirio Diaz, who, after hearing the young guitarist play recommended him to go and study at te Guitar School in Siena, Italy. José Tomas went to Siena in 1955 and it was there that he first met Andres Segovia.

From 1956-1957 José Tomas was in the Spanish Army. In 1958 he went for two years to Santiago De Compastela where he worked with Emilio Pujol. He had kept contact Andres Segovia since their first meeting in Siena, and Segovia, having recognised

Tomas's exceptional teaching ability, asked him to be his assistant at his master classes. Since that time Tomas decided that he would devote most of his career to teaching, although he is a fine recitalist and has appeared in concerts throughout Europe, the Midddle East, Japan and the United States of America.

José Tomas recently changed to an 8 string guitar built by José Ramirez. This guitar has a 7th string tuned D below low E and an 8th string tuned F above low E.

José Tomas currently lives in his native town of Alicante and teaches there at the Oscar Espla Conservatory where he directs the guitar programme. He still spends his summers at Santiago De Compestala directing Segovia's master classes.

SELECTED READING
'José Tomas'

Article — 'Guitar Player' — March 1981

TERRY USHER

Born – Terence Usher
Manchester, England, 7th May 1909

Died — Manchester, England
12th April, 1969

Terry Usher

Terry Usher started to play the guitar in 1932. In 1936 he began to teach and write about the guitar for the musical press. In the same year he broadcast for the first time and was then frequently heard on the radio playing guitar solos and with various instrumental ensambles. Terry Usher heard Andres Segovia play at a concert in Liverpool in 1937. He was so impressed with Segovia's performance that he began a serious study of the classical guitar soon afterwards. Usher soon became to be regarded as one of Britain's authorities on the instrument and its music.

In 1945 Terry Usher began teaching the classical guitar and embarked on a series of lecture-recitals to musical societies under the auspices of the Halle Concerts Society and the Arts Council of Great Britain.

Usher wrote and arranged extensively for the guitar. His published compositions include 'Suite and Minuet', 'Canzoncina and Arabesque' and 'Epitaph for Manuel Ponce'. Terry Usher was a member of the Editorial Board and Editor of the Academy Section of 'The Guitar Review', New York. He was also a regular contributor on the classical guitar to BMG Magazines, and a founder member of the Manchester Guitar Circle.

On 24th March, 1954, he was appointed 'Tutor for the Guitar' to the Royal Manchester College of Music. This was probably the first appointment in Britain of a professor of the guitar to a College of Music.

Terry Usher continued his total involvement with the guitar until his death, after a stroke, in April 1969.

SELECTED MUSIC

'Canzoncina & Arabesque'	Schott
'Impromptu & Minuet'	Schott

ALBERT VALDES BLAIN

Born — Havana, Cuba

10th April 1921

In 1924 Albert Valdes Blain's parents moved to the United States of America and settled in New York City. Blain's enthusiasm for the classical guitar was aroused by the early concerts of Andres Segovia in New York.

Blain studied with the Uruguayan concert guitarist Julio Martinez Oyanguren for three years. He also studied piano and composition at the Greenwich House and the Julliard School of Music, New York.

For many years Valdes Blain was regarded as one of the foremost classical guitar recitalists in the United States. He made his debut in 1941 at the Carnegie Chamber Music Hall, and appeared in concerts throughout the North American continent for many years. He has also broadcast on both radio and television on most of the important American networks.

Roland and Albert Valdes Blain

It is as a teacher that Albert Valdes Blain has been one of the most important figures on the American guitar scene for the last few years. He has taught the classical guitar at the Greenwich House Music School, The School for Musical Education, and also the Brookland Conservatory for Music. He also has his own studios in New York City, and many of todays best known American Guitarists have studied with him.

SELECTED READING
'Albert Valdes Blain'

Article — 'Guitar Player' — November 1979

ROLAND VALDES BLAIN

Born — Havana, Cuba

1922

Roland Valdes Blain is the younger brother of Albert Valdes Blain, whose brief biography is shown above. Roland Valdes Blain originally studied with the Uraguayan guitarist Julio Martinez Oyanguren. He later went to Spain to concertize and also work in advanced study at the Royal Conservatory of Madrid with Regino Sainz de Maza. He later graduated from this Conservatory with the Grand Prize Award for concert guitar playing.

Since that time Roland Valdes Blain has toured extensively throughout the main cities of the United States, Canada, South America and Spain. He also appeared on the major radio and television networks in the United States, played and composed for various Broadway theatrical productions and appeared with several major symphony orchestras as their guest soloist.

Roland Valdes Blain currently lives in New York City, and maintains a busy career as a guitar recitalist and teacher.

SELECTED RECORD
'Guitar Masterpieces'

Sml Pr Arté SMC-546

ANDRÉ VERDIER

Born — Paris, France
1st November 1886

Died — Paris, France
13th December 1957

Andre Verdier

André Verdier studied music from the age of six. He had a fine soprano voice as a child and became a soloist in Paris churches. When his voice broke he studied the flute at the Paris Conservatoire. Later he studied the guitar under Rodriguex Aravena. Verdier met Miguel Llobet in Paris, and this great guitarist introduced him to the Tarrega method of playing.

At the age of 18 André Verdier decided to enlist in the army to make his career as a military musician. He remained in this occupation until he was 23. During his time in the army he perfected himself on the flute and also studied harmony. On returning to civilian life Verdier could not make a living as either a flautist or guitarist. He learnt to play the banjo and within a relatively short period of time was known all over Paris for his virtuoso banjo playing in nightclubs and cabarets.

André Verdier's great contribution to the classical guitar in France was his foundation, in collaboration with Emilio Pujol, of the 'Amis de la Guitare' in 1936. Verdier arranged regular meetings in his house in the Isle of St. Louis, Notre Dame, Paris. One of the first important acts of the society was a pilgrimage to the tomb of Ferdinand Sor. This had been re-discovered by André Verdier and the Danish guitarist W. Ostergoart in 1934. They arranged for a commemorative plaque to be placed on the tomb and homage was paid to the great 19th century guitarist.

In 1938, during a recital of the 'Amis de la Guitare', Verdier presented the child prodigy Ida Presti. The society made her an honorary member, and greatly helped her in her career. It was in Verdier's house that Ida Presti would meet Alexandre Lagoya years later, at another evening of lovers of the guitar.

André Verdier was a teacher of music who specialised in teaching the guitar. He was also an enthusiastic collector of classical guitars, and of guitar music and manuscripts. There is no doubt that no single person did more to promote the classical guitar in France than André Verdier.

SELECTED READING
'André Verdier'

Article — Guitar Review No. 22 1958

ROBERT J. VIDAL

Born — Paris, France

6th May 1925

Robert Vidal

COURTESY RADIO FRANCE   PHOTO ROGER PICARD

Robert Vidal is one of the most important guitar personalities in the classical guitar world today. For almost 30 years his promotions on behalf of the guitar have been quite incredible. Vidal has presented programmes on both French radio and television devoted exclusively to the guitar. He has also produced an excellent series of classical guitar records for the RCA and Erato labels. His annual 'Concours International De Guitare' (sponsored by ORTF) which is held in Paris, France, have become two of the most important annual international classical guitar events.

Robert Vidal's first venture for the guitar was his series of radio programmes for ORTF entitled 'Des Notes Sur La Guitare'. This series first began broadcasting on the 11th March 1954. In 1955 Vidal directed a series of classical guitar records for RCA Victor entitled 'The Anthology of the Guitar'. In 1969 he began a new series of records for the Erato label entitled 'Panorama De La Guitare'. This excellent series currently has 24 records in its catalogue and features many famous guitarists including Turibo Santos, Oscar Caceres, Leo Brouwer, Maria Luisa Anido, Betho Davazec, and the Pomponio/Zarrate Duo.

The first Concours International De Guitare was held in Paris in 1958. This event has gone from strength to strength and has been an important stepping stone in the career of many of today's leading classical guitarists.

Over the years Robert Vidal has presented several excellent programmes about the guitar on French radio and television. Included are 'Sortilegues Du Flamenco' (1956), 'La Guitare Et Ses Virtuoses' (1958), 'Rennaisance De La Guitare' (1959), 'L'Histoire De La Guitare' (1960), 'Le Magazine De La Guitare' (1964), 'Guitares ... Guitares' (1973) and 'Carrefour De La Guitare' (1974).

In recent years Robert Vidal's position in the guitar world as a leading authority of the instrument has led him to receiving many invitations from countries all over the world to attend, lecture and adjudicate at their guitar festivals. Vidal has travelled throughout Europe, Venezuela, Brazil, Puerto Rico, Czechoslovakia, Mexico and in November 1976 he organised the Festival Mondial De La Guitare in Martinique to which guitarists from 23 countries participated.

Robert Vidal's efforts and promotions on behalf of the classical guitar have been quite exceptional and have been applauded by Andres Segovia, Emilio Pujol, John Williams and Leo Brouwer amongst many other great classical guitarists who have recognised his vital contribution to the classical guitar.

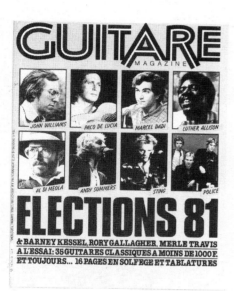

A selection of guitar magazines.

Heitor Villa Lobos

HEITOR VILLA LOBOS

Born — Rio De Janeiro, Brazil
5th March, 1887

Died — Rio De Janeiro, Brazil
17th November 1959

Heitor Villa Lobos began his musical studies at the age of six with his father, a writer and amateur musician. He first played the viola but soon mastered nearly all the orchestral instruments. Villa Lobos, at a very early age, began to improvise on popular Brazilian melodies, but his first composition was a piece for the guitar entitled 'Panqueca'.

After his father's death, when he was 11 years old, Villa Lobos became almost entirely self-taught in all aspects of music. He began to play the guitar in a small music group called choros, and at the age of 17 played the cello in theatres, cinemas, cabarets, and other small and large orchestras in Rio. At about this time he enrolled in the National Institute of Music. He had intended to study composition but soon found he did not like formal study, and left the institute. For five years he travelled Brazil, studying the music of the people and absorbing the varied landscape and picturesque style of life. He recognised it as something of his own which he would incorporate into all his compositions.

In 1918 Villa Lobos met pianist Artur Rubinstein and composer Darius Milhaud. This meeting, and his love of the music of Debussy, was to influence Villa Lobos to go to Paris, France, in 1923, It was presumed that he was going there to study European music, but he made it known that the was going there to show European musicians what he had done. Paris became excited with his music and the concerts of his music attracted worldwide attention to him. Villa Lobos lived in Paris until 1929 and it was during this period that he met Andres Segovia. The result of their meeting was that Villa Lobos would compose some of the most beautiful music in the contemporary guitar repertory.

Upon his return to Brazil Villa Lobos played an important part in the National campaign to provide general education. In 1932 he was appointed Supervisor and Director of Musical Education in Brazil and became an educator and illustrator. He invented revolutionary ideas for musical instruction and was especially interested in the development of community singing. In recognition of his achieve-

Heitor Villa Lobos

ments and instruction in choral singing the Federal Government of Brazil in 1943 made him Director of the newly founded Conservatorio Nacional de Canto Orfenico.

Villa Lobos received an impressive number of distinguished honours. In addition to a citation presented to him by the Mayor of New York for distinguished and exceptional service, he was awarded honorary degrees from several universities, was an Officer of the Legion of Honour in France, and an honorary member of the French Institute. He was also an honorary member of the American Academy of Arts and Letters, and of the Accademia di Santa Cecilia in Rome. He was also President of the Brazilian Academy.

During his lifetime Villa Lobos composed around

2,000 works. The best known of his guitar works are his 'Suite Populaire Brasilienne' (written in 1912, published 1955), 'Twelve Guitar Studies' (written in 1929, published 1952), 'Five Preludes' (written in 1940, published in 1954) and his 'Concerto For Guitar And Orchestra' which was written in 1951.

SELECTED RECORDS

'Julian Bream Plays Villa Lobos/Torroba'	RCA	CLP 1763
'Julian Bream Plays Villa Lobos'	RCA	SB 6852
'Julian Bream Plays 12 Etudes/Suite Populaire'	RCA	RL 12499
'Turibio Santos Plays 12 Etudes'	Erato	STU 1007
'Turibio Santos Plays Sextour Mystique/Preludes'	Erato	STU 70566
'Lagoya Plays Villa Lobos/Sor'	Philips	6504 131
'Ragossnig Plays Villa Lobos/Albeniz Etc'	Supraphon	1-11-1040
'John Williams Plays Villa Lobos'	Capitol	P 8497
'Yepes Plays Villa Lobos'	Deutches Grammaphon	2530-140
'Eric Hill Plays Villa Lobos'	Saga	5453
'Maria Livia Sao Marcos Plays Villa Lobos' — 12 Etudes	Fermata	305-1039
'Joseph Bacon Plays Villa Lobos'	Arch Records	S-1771
'Barrueco Plays The Music of Brazil'	Vox	FSM 53-043

SELECTED READING

'Villa Lobos'	Article — 'Guitar Player' — July 1981
'Villa Lobos'	Article — 'Guitar & Lute' — October 1980
'Villa Lobos'	Article — 'Guitar Review' — No 21 1957
'Villa Lobos'	Article — 'Guitar Review' No 29 1966

SELECTED MUSIC

'Chôros No 1'	ESC
'Prelude No 1'	ESC
'Prelude No 2'	ESC
'Prelude No 3'	ESC
'Prelude No 4'	ESC
'Prelude No 5'	ESC
'Suite Populaire Brasilienne, No 1 Mazurka — Chôro'	ESC
'Suite Populaire Brasilienne, No 2 Schottish — Chôro'	ESC
'Suite Populaire Brasilienne, No 3 Valsa — Chôro'	ESC
'Suite Populaire Brasilienne, No 4 Gavotta — Chôro'	ESC
'Suite Populaire Brasilienne, No 5 Chorinho'	ESC

Segovia and Villa Lobos and friends, Mrs. Villa Lobos is directly behind them.

LUISE WALKER

Born — Vienna, Austria

9th September 1910

Luise Walker

Luise Walker began to study the guitar at the age of eight. Her first teacher was the well-known Viennese guitarist, Zuth. She subsequently studied at the State Musical Academy in Vienna under Professor Ortner. Luise Walker was also fortunate to be able to take lessons with Heinrich Albert and Miguel Llobet, both of whom were frequent guests at her parents' home in Vienna.

From 1940 Luise Walker has devoted her life to the guitar. Over the years she has made many concert tours of Europe, Russia and the United States. She has been for many years Professor of guitar at the Viennese Staatskademie for Musik. Luise Walker is also a highly respected composer, and many of her solos, studies and arrangements have been published. Included are 'Daily Studies for the Guitar', and 'The Young Guitarist' (published by V. Hladky, Vienna).

SELECTED RECORDS

'Guitar Recital'	Supraphon	1-11-1230
'Paganini Quartet & Terzetto'	Turnabout	TV 34322S
'Guitar Music In Vienna'	Turnabout	TV 34171S

TIMOTHY WALKER

Born — Durban, South Africa

1943

Timothy Walker

COURTESY DECCA RECORD COMPANY LTD.

Timothy Walker was born in South Africa of British parents. His father was a well-known journalist, writer, broadcaster and music critic.

Walker began playing the guitar at the age of 12 to accompany himself playing the popular songs of the day. He eventually changed over to classical guitar and when Narciso Yepes first toured South Africa he invited the young guitarist to further his studies with him in Madrid. This Walker did for two years before settling in London where he gave his debut concert at the Wigmore Hall in 1970. Walker also studied with the late Ida Presti, Alexander Lagoya and John Williams. The latter recommended him for work with the 'Fires of London', a modern classical group directed by Peter Maxwell-Davies. Timothy Walker now plays regularly with this ensemble.

Timothy Walker is currently the guitarist with the London Sinfonietta and has played with the London Symphony Orchestra, the BBC Symphony Orchestra, and the Royal Philharmonic Orchestra amongst others. He has also appeared with small groups such as the Melos Ensemble, Ensemble Musique Vivants. He has concertized throughout Great Britain, Europe, South America and the United States.

Timothy Walker was the guitar soloist (playing electric guitar) in one of the 1977 Proms at the Royal Albert hall, London. In 1978 he played duets with John Williams at the Queen Elizabeth Hall, London, in a Sor Bicentenery concert. His first solo tour of the United States took place in 1978. This was followed by a tour of South America with the soprano, Mary Thomas. Walker has also composed several original pieces for the guitar, and these have been published by Belwin Mills.

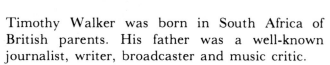

SELECTED RECORDS

'Baroque Music'	Saga	5426
'Timothy Walker — Guitar'	Decca	6-42344
'Guitar Encores'	L'Oiseau-Lyre	SOL 349
'Classical Folk Guitar'	Hyperion	A66027

SELECTED READING

'Timothy Walker'	Article — 'Guitar' — January 1974

SELECTED MUSIC

'African Light Suite'	Belwin Mills SI 115
'Fantasia Celestina'	Belwin Mills SI 120
'Prelude'	Belwin Mills SI 122

NORIHIKO WATANABE

Born — Kobe, Japan

11th September 1948

Norihiko Watanabe

COURTESY GENDAI GUITAR   PHOTO KIICHI ARAKAWA

Norihiko Watanabe is currently one of the leading classical guitar players in Japan.

Watanabe showed great progress on the guitar as a youth and became a student of Jiro Matsuda. He was also a very enthusiastic about becoming a guitar maker and studied construction of the instrument with Masaru Kohno.

In 1966 Watanabe won first prize at the Guitar Concours of Japan. In 1969 he won first prize at the prestigious Concours International De Guitare in Paris, France. His success at these competitions have established Norihiko Watanabe as one of the best classical guitarists to have emerged during the 1960s.

Norihiko Watanabe currently spends much of his time in Japan where he give recitals, teaches and is also a recording artist for the Columbia label.

SELECTED RECORDS

'Plays Villa Lobos/Tansman/Torroba'	RCA (Japan)	RVC 2272
'In Concert'	Denon (pan)	OS 7033 ND
'Guitar Recital'	RCA	GG 1001

BUNYAN WEBB

Born — BUNYAN MONROE WEBB Jnr.,
San Francisco, USA, 1936

Died — San Francisco, USA
14th November 1978

Bunyan Webb

COURTESY C. E. H. SMITH

Bunyan Webb received his Bachelor of Arts degree from South Western University in pre-medicine then decided to pursue a career in music. He continued to graduate in music at California State University at Fresno.

Bunyan Webb then studied classical guitar at the Conservatory of Valencia, Spain, and later in master classes with Julian Bream, Andres Segovia, Ida Presti and Alexander Lagoya. Following this Webb began a highly successful career as a guitar authority and teacher, and concertised throughout the United States, Europe and Japan.

Bunyan Webb made a valuable contribution to the promotion of the classical guitar in the United States of America as a Member of the Affiliated Artists programme. He acquainted a large variety of audiences with the classical guitar, and performed and recorded with guitar in duos with viola, flute, voice and harpsichord. As well as an active concert life Webb held formal teaching positions at Blair Academy at Peabody in Nashville, the University of North Carolina at Raleigh, the Inter-American University in Puerto Rico, and had given teachers' seminars for Guitar '78 in Toronto and for ASTA in New Orleans. He also held well attended master classes and workshops for classical guitar throughout the United States. Over the years Bunyan Webb had collected an extensive library of manuscripts, books and records. This collection is now housed at the San Francisco Conservatory of Music.

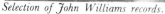
Selection of John Williams records.

John Williams

JOHN WILLIAMS

Born — JOHN CHRISTOPHER WILLIAMS
Melbourne, Australia

24th April 1941

John Williams began playing the guitar at the age of seven, receiving his first lessons from his father, Len Williams, the well known guitarist and teacher. Wiliam quickly showed himself to be a most gifted pupil and when the family moved to London in 1952 he was taken to meet Segovia who was deeply impressed by the 11 year old boy's talent. Williams began studying with Segovia and, on his recommendation, undertook a full musical education. He entered the Academia Musicale Chigiana in Siena, where Segovia himself taught at the Summer School each year. John Williams held a scholarship at the school for the following five years. During that time he gained one of its most coveted prizes and received the unprecedented honour of giving the first complete solo recital by a student of any instrument. John Williams also gave a performance of the Castelnuovo-Tedesco Concerto in Siena. On his return to England, Williams attended the Royal College of Music from 1956 to 1959, studying piano and musical theory.

On 6th November 1958, John Williams made his London debut at the Wigmore Hall. Highly successful debuts followed this, with Williams appearing in Paris, France in 1959 and in Madrid, Spain in 1961. In 1962 he toured the USSR, and visited Japan, and the United States for the first time in 1963.

During the last few years, John William's career has been developing on many diverse lines and his constant striving to cross musical barriers has led to many interesting ventures and collaborations. One of the most noted of these was his appearance at the Ronnie Scott's Jazz Club in London. In 1970 he became one of the artistic directors, with John Dankworth, Cleo Laine and Richard Rodney Bennett, of the Wavendon Theatre. In April 1970 he appeared again at Ronnie Scott's Club, on the same bill as the rock group 'Soft Machine'. Also in 1970 he took part in a Greek concert at the Royal Albert Hall, held in aid of the families of political prisoners. Later that year he recorded with the Greek singer Maria Farandouri an album of music by Mikis Theodorakis. During 1970 he also played on the soundtrack music of the film 'The Raging Moon'. He met in the studios the composer and arranger StanleyMyers, and this led to the making of John William's first popular album 'Changes' arranged and produced by Myers. Williams had already recorded several classical albums for the CBS label.

Several important composers have dedicated works to John Williams. Andre Previn's Guitar Concerto' was given its world premier in November 1971 under the direction of the composer, at the London Symphony Orchestra Gala Concert. Stephen Dodgson has also written several works for Williams, including the 'Partita' in 1964 and 'Fantasy Division' in 1969.

John Williams, more than any other living guitarist, has managed to bridge many musical barriers. In the last two years his classical/rock fusion group 'Sky' received an enormous popular success. Likewise his concert appearances and recordings with the popular jazz singer Cleo Lane have attracted vast audiences who never previously appreciated the classical guitar. John Williams continues to give strictly classical recitals, including some guitar duo concerts with his countryman Julian Bream, a constant reminder that John Williams is one of the greatest classical guitar virtuosi the world has ever known.

SELECTED RECORDS

'Guitar Recital' — Volume One	Ace of Diamonds	SDD R328
'Guitar Recital' — Volume Two	Ace of Diamonds	SDD R328
'Twenty Studies for Guitar' — F. Sor	Pathé-Marion	C-065 93404
'Virtuoso Music For Guitar'	CBS	72348
'John Williams/William Brown — Songs and Poems with Guitar'	CBS	61126
'Two Favourite Guitar Concertos'	CBS	72439
'More Virtuoso Music For Guitar'	CBS	72526
'John Williams Plays Two More Guitar Concertos'	CBS	72661
'Haydn Guitar Quartet/Paganini Trio'	CBS	72678

JOHN WILLIAMS – Selected Records (continued)

'Virtuoso Variations For Guitar'	CBS	72728
'John Williams Plays Spanish Music'	CBS	72860
'Songs and Guitar Pieces by the Theodorakis' (with Maria Farawdouri)	CBS	72947
'Music For Guitar and Harpsichord'	CBS	72948
'Gowers Chamber Concerto/Scarlatti Six Sonatas'	CBS	72979
'Rhapsody by Patrick Gower/Five Preludes-Villa Lobos'	CBS	73350
'André Previn Guitar Concerto/Ponce Concerto Del Sur'	CBS	73060
'Music From England, Japan and Latin America'	CBS	73205
'John Williams and Friends'	CBS	73487
'Bach: Complete Lute Music	CBS	'79203
'Rodrigo Concerto/Villa Lobos Concerto'	CBS	76369
'Duo — Paganini and Giuliani For Guitar and Violin' (with Itzhak Pearlman)	CBS	76525
'Castelnuovo Tedesco/Dodgson/Arnold Guitar Concerto'	CBS	76634
'John Williams Plays Barrios'	CBS	76662
'Arnold and Brouwer Guitar Concertos'	CBS	76715
'John Williams Plays Manuel Ponce'	CBS	76730
'Together' Duo with Julian Bream	RCA	SB 6862
'Together Again' Duo with Julian Bream	RCA	ARL1 0456
'Live' Duo with Julian Bream	RCA	RL 03090(2)
'Boccherini Quintets'	CBS	6671
'Bach For Guitar and Organ' — with Peter Hurford	CBS	37250

SELECTED READING

'John Williams'	Article — 'Guitar' — August 1973
'John Williams'	Article — 'Guitar' — September 1973
'John Williams'	Article — 'Guitar' — August 1977
'John Williams'	Article — 'Guitar' — August 1978
'John Williams and Sky'	Article — 'Guitar' — July 1979
'John Williams'	Article — 'Guitar Player' — February 1977
'John Williams'	Article — 'Guitar Player' — November 1980

LEN WILLIAMS

Born — LEONARD ARTHUR WILLIAMS
London, England

11th August 1910

Len Williams

COURTESY C.E.H. SMITH

Len Williams began to play the piano at the age of six and by the time he was 14 was already playing professionally in a dance band. After three years he gave up his career as a professional musician and became an assistant in the fretted instrument firm of John Alvey Turner in London. It was there that Williams became interested in the guitar after hearing some records by jazz guitarist Eddie Lang.

Williams studied both plectrum and fingerstyle guitars, taking lessons with Mario Maccaferri, who was resident in London at that time, on the latter. It was Maccaferri who made Williams aware of Andres Segovia, and soon he preferred playing the classical guitar, although professionally he played and taught the plectrum guitar.

In 1939 Len Williams emigrated to Australia where he established himself as a teacher at Suttons, in Melbourne. He was house guitarist for radio station 3DB, and soon became very well known as a plectrum guitar soloist and teacher. In 1946 he decided to give up the plectrum guitar and con-

centrate on the classical guitar, and as a result did much to popularise the instrument in Australia.

Williams decided to return to England in 1952 and soon established his famous Spanish Guitar Centre in London. Since that time hundreds of pupils have passed through his school, many of which have become fine players ad teachers of the classical guitar. There is no doubt that Len Williams' most famous pupil is his son John, who has become one of the most successful guitar virtuosi of all times. In addition to his teaching activities Len Williams developed a new classical guitar trio, consisting of bass-guitar played by Desmond Dupré; standard Spanish guitar played by Robert Wilson; and himself playing the Tarina soprano guitar.

In recent years Len Williams has devoted most of his time to the study of monkeys having sold his interest in the Spanish Guitar some years ago. He has made his home close to the monkey sanctuary at Looe in Cornwall, England.

SELECTED READING
'Len Williams'
'The Dancing Chimpanzee' — Len Williams

Article — 'Guitar' — October 1978
Allison and Busby 1980

Leo Witoszynskyj

LEO WITOSZYNSKYJ

Born — Vienna, Austria

23rd June 1941

Leo Witoszynskyj began to play the guitar at an early age. He completed his studies with Luise Walker at the Vienna Academy of Music with honours. He later studied with Andres Segovia and Narciso Yepes. At international competitions in Liege, Paris and Vercelli he was a finalist and prizewinner. In 1968 he won the 1st International Competition for Guitar in Alessandria, Italy.

Since that time Leo Witoszynskyj has maintained an active career as a recitalist in most countries of Europe, the Near East, Venezuela and the United States. He made his United States debut in 1974 in the Carnegie Recital Hall, New York. As a soloist Witoszynskyj has played with many leading orchestras including the BBC Concert Orchestra, the Birmingham Symphony Orchestra, and the Vienna Symphony Orchestra.

In 1974 Leo Witoszynskyj was appointed Professor at the Hochschule for Musik in Graz, and in 1980 elected as its Assistant Director. He combines his working year as a teacher at this important music establishment, and as an international recitalist.

SELECTED RECORDS

'International Guitar'	Music for Pleasure	CFP 122
'Music For Guitar and Piano'	Turnabout	TV 34728

SELECTED READING

'Leo Witoszynskyj'	Article — 'Guitar' — March 1975

KAZUHITO YAMASHITA

Born — Tokyo, Japan

25th March 1961

Kazuhito Yamashita

COURTESY GENDAI GUITAR   PHOTO KIICHI ARAKAWA

Regarded as potentially one of the greatest classical guitar virtuosi that Japan has produced, Kazuhito Yamashita was a child prodigy. His first public recital in Japan was at the MY Studio in Tokyo in 1974.

Yamashita first came to public notice when he won the Kyushu 18th Guitar Competition in 1972. In 1976 he won the 19th Tokyo International Guitar Competition which was sponsored by the Japanese Federation of the Guitar. Following on his great successes in Japan, Kazuhito Yamashita went to Europe in 1977. Here at the age of 16 Yamashita

won first prize in three important competitions, the Ramirez Guitar Competition, Santiago de Compostela, Spain, the 10th Concorso Internazionale Chiterra Classica, Alessandria, Italy, and the 19th Concours International de Guitare, organised by the Radio/Television France in Paris.

Kazuhito Yamashita now leads a busy life as a recitalist both in Europe and Japan. He has an exclusive recording contract for RCA Victor of Japan, and six of his recordings have already been released.

SELECTED RECORDS

'Romance de Amor'	RACE	RDC-8
'Guitar Recital'	Victor	SJX-9538
'Concierto de Aranjuez'	RCA	RUC-2280
'Guitar Recital II'	Victor	SJX-9544
'Yamashita Plays Bach'	RCA	RCL-8014
'Pictures at an Exhibition/Kazuhito Yamashita'	RCA	RCL-8042

SELECTED MUSIC

Mussorgsky/K. Yamashita, Pictures at an Exhibition for Guitar	Gendai Guitar Co Ltd.

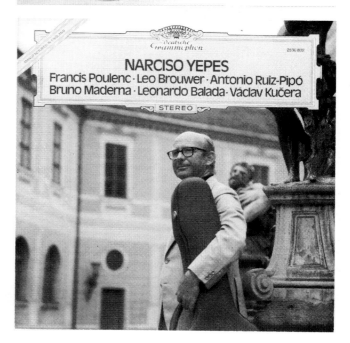

A selection of Yepes records.

Narciso Yepes

NARCISO YEPES

Born — NARCISO GARCIA YEPES
Lorca, Spain

14th November 1927

Narciso Yepes was given his first guitar at the age of four by his father, and he took his first real lessons on the instrument at the age of six.

In 1940 Narciso Yepes began his studies at the Conservatory of Music in Valencia, and in 1943 Vicente Asencio, the pianist and composer became his teacher. Asencio's approach to music had a great influence in developing Yepe's guitar style.

In 1946, Ataulfo Arganta, the head of the Spanish National Orchestra, became aware of the 19 year old guitarist, and Yepes was invited to come to Madrid. The following year, Yepes debuted as a soloist with the orchestra in the performance of Joaquin Rodrigo's 'Concierto de Aranjuez'. By 1948 Yepes was established as a guitarist of international importance and made his first European tour. In 1950 he gave his first concert in Paris, and this performance was highly acclaimed. In 1952 Narciso Yepes achieved international fame as a composer and interpreter for the music to René Clement's film 'Jeux Interdits'. During the next few years he continued to devote part of his career to composing more film music. The major part of his working year was devoted to expanding his concert career into nearly all countries of the world. In 1957 he made his first South American tour, in 1960 his Japanese debut, and 1964 his first appearance in the United States of America.

Since 1963 Narciso Yepes has played a 10 string classical guitar of his own design. Yepes commissioned José Ramirez to design a special instrument with four additional low-resonance strings tuned at c, b-flat, a-flat and g-flat. The purpose of this new instrument was, through the extra bass strings, that a more balanced or equalised group of sounds could be produced than with the traditional six string guitar.

Since the middle 1960s Narciso Yepes has resided in Madrid, Spain, and divides his year between concertising and teaching. He is also a major recording artist for the Deutches Gramaphon Company.

SELECTED RECORDS

'Rodrigo Guitar Concerto And Fantasia'	Decca	SPA 233
'Musique Espagnole Pour Guitare'	Ace of Clubs	ACL 907
'Narciso Yepes'	Decca	105-018
'Fernando Sor — 24 Studies'	Deutsche Gramaphon	139 364
'Musica Catalana'	Deutsche Gramaphon	2530 273
'Bacarisse/Halffter Concertos'	Deutsche Gramaphon	2530 326
'Ohana/Ruiz Pipo Works With Orchestra'	Deutsche Gramaphon	2530 585
'Twentieth Century Guitar Music'	Deutsche Gramaphon	2530 802
'Narciso Yepes'	Deutsche Gramaphon	2531 113
'Telemann Guitar Duos'	Deutsche Gramaphon	2531 350

SELECTED READING

'Narciso Yepes and the 10-String Guitar'	Article — 'Guitar' — August 1974
'Narciso Yepes''	Article — 'Frets' — February 1980
'Narciso Yepes''	Article — 'Guitar Player' — March 1978

MILAN ZELENKA

Born — Prague, Czechoslovakia

4th June 1939

Milan Zelenka

COURTESY SUPRAPHON

Milan Zelenka is regarded as one of Czechoslovakia's leading guitarists. As a student he won first prizes and meals in the Moscow and Vienna International Guitar contests. Since 1957, he has been constantly concertising; not only in Czechoslovakia, but all over Europe. He has been on many tours all over Russia, Hundgary and Germany.

He is a graduate of Prague Conservatory of Music. Zelenka now ranks, with his many international appearances, as one the most active representatives of Czech guitar playing. As a student he won first prize at international concourses and competitions in Moscow (1957) and Vienna (1959). Apart from an extensive concert activity, in which Zelenka frequently performs original Czech modern works many of which have been written especially for him, he spens much of his year teaching the guitar.

Critics speak in superlative terms and consider Milan Zelenka one of the world's outstanding guitarists.

He is a member of the Concert Artists Union and has made recordings with the State Music Editor and Artia. Milan Zelenka is active as an editor and lecturer on his chosen instrument, and is currently Professor of guitar at the Prague Conservatory of Music.

SELECTED RECORDS

'Guitar Concerto'	Rediffusion	ROY 2004
'Moderni Ceske Skaldby'	Supraphon	1-11-0969
'Guitar Recital'	Supraphon	SUB 10373

THE CLASSICAL GUITAR
ITS DUOS, TRIOS, QUARTETS
AND MORE

Duo Presti-Lagoya, probably the greatest classical guitar duo of all time.

THE CLASSICAL GUITAR
ITS DUOS, TRIOS, QUARTETS
AND MORE

The main section of this book has dealt with the foremost classical guitarists and guitar personalities since 1800. A prominent feature of the instrument's development since that time has been guitarists playing in duos, trios and other combinations of the instrument.

In the 19th century Dionisio Aguado appeared in concert several times in a duo with Fernando Sor. The 20th century has seen a succession of great guitarists performing as a duo. Francisco Tarrega with Daniel Fortea, Miguel Llobet and Maria Luisa Anido, Emilio Pujol and Mathilde Cuervas, Renata and Graciano Tarrago, and, regarded by many as the greatest guitar duo of all time, Ida Presti and Alexandre Lagoya. The Romero family quartet, often called the royal family of the guitar,

first achieved worldwide fame in the 1950s, since then this remarkable family of guitarists have established themselves as the most outstanding guitar quartet of all time.

In more recent times Turibio Santos has recorded and concertised with Oscar Caceres, and likewise Julian Bream with John Williams. All these great guitarists are included individually in the main section of the book.

This section of the book deals with the most important of those groups of guitar players, not previously mentioned in the book, who have established themselves as a vital part of the evolution of the classical guitar outside the sphere of the solo guitar.

SERGIO AND EDUARDO ABREU

The two Brazilian brothers , Sergio (born June 1948) and Eduardo (born September 1949), originally studied the guitar with their grandfather Antonio Rebello. They were then tutored by the Argentinian guitarist and lutenist Adolfina Raitzin Tavora, who had studied with Andres Segovia.

Their duo playing began in 1963 when they enjoyed enormous success in tours sponsored by the Brazilian Government. Individually both brothers won high honours in contests both in Brazil and in Europe.

This duo, regarded by many critics as the finest since Presti and Lagoya, split up after Eduardo decided to make his career in another profession. Sergio Abreu, whose biography is shown earlier in this book, is now a prominent guitar soloist of international renown.

Sergio and Eduardo Abreu

SELECTED RECORDS

'The Guitars of Sergio and Eduardo Abreu'	CBS	61262
'The Guitars of Sergio and Eduardo Abreu'	Ace of Dimaonds	SDD 219
'Two Concerts For Two Guitars'	CBS	61469

NICOLAS AND ILSA ALFONSO

Nicolas Alfonso was born in Santander, Spain on the 6th December 1913. He studied music and the guitar in both Madrid and Barcelona. At the end of his studies Alfonso became a successful recitalist on the guitar in Spain and throughout Europe. In 1950 he settled in Brussels, Belgium, establishing himself as a highly successful teacher, composer and editor of guitar works. Schott Frères of Brussels have published most of his original works and transcriptions, including a two volume guitar method.

In 1965 Nicolas Alfonso was appointed professor of the newly founded Guitar Department of the Royal Academy of Music in Brussels.

For many years Alfonso has concertised and recorded in a successful guitar duo with his wife Ilsa (born 15th February 1933.)

SELECTED RECORDS

'Concerto Pour Deux Guitares'	Erato EFM	8040
'Musique Espagnole Pour Deux Guitares'	Zephyr	Z05

Nicolas and Ilsa Alfonso

THE ROMEROS

The Romeros are the most famous guitar quartet of all time. This family quartet consists of Celedonio Romero and his three sons Celin, Angel and Pepe. The main section of the book has already included biographies of Celedonio, Angel and Pepe, as they have all achieved individual success outside this famous guitar group. Celin, born in Malaga in 1936, has at this time devoted his whole professional career as an integral part of the quartet. When not working with the quartet Celin is on the faculty of the University of California at San Diego.

Since the Romeros settled in the United States of America in 1958 they have been enthusiastically received throughout the North American continent for their solo, duo and quartet performances. In 1967, they commissioned Joaquin Rodrigo to compose his 'Concerto Andaluz' for four guitars and orchestra. Since that time several other important composers, including Frederico Moreno

Torroba, have dedicated works to them. For over 20 years this outstanding group of guitarists have entertained audiences all over the world.

SELECTED RECORDS

'European Court Music'	Philips (Universo)	6582-001
'Compositions for Two Guitars'	Philips	9500-352
'Classical Music for Four Guitars'	Philips	9500 296
'Rodrigo Concertos Andaluz/Aranjuez	Mercury	75021
'An Evening With the Romeros'	Mercury	75022
'Royal Family of the Guitar'	Mercury	75027
'Vivaldi Concertos'	Mercury	75054

SELECTED READING

The Romeros	Article – 'Guitar Player' – April 1972
The Romeros	Article – 'Guitar & Lute' – September 1978

THE THOMATOS GUITAR TRIO

The Thomatos Guitar Trio was founded in 1974 by Spiro Thomatos, professor of guitar at the Zurich Conservatory in Switzerland.

The trio consists of Marlies Waespe, guitar teacher at the Winterthur Conservatory of Music, Antonio Valero, who also teaches at the Winterthur Conservatory, and Spiro Thomatos.

Spiro Thomatos

SELECTED RECORDS

'Serenade Music For Three Guitars'	Spectrum	SR 109

Frankfurt Guitar Duo

FRANKFURT
GUITAR DUO

This German guitar duo, Michael Teuchert and Olaf Van Gonnissen, was founded in 1971. Since their first public recital in 1972 they have established themselves as one of the finest guitar duos in the world today.

Michael Teuchert was born in 1948 in Frankfurt on Main, West Germany. The son of a well known guitar teacher, Heinz Teuchert, Michael Teuchert began to play the guitar at the age of four and gave his first public recital as a soloist at the age of eight in Frankfurt on Main. He later continued his studies at Dr Hochs Conservatory at the Academy of Tokunst in Darmstadt.

Olaf Van Gonnissen was born in 1954 in Tiengen. He began to play the guitar at the age of eight and later also completed his musical studies at Dr Hochs Conservatory in Frankfurt. It was there that he met Michael Teuchert.

SELECTED RECORDS

'Renaissance Music'	Soloist Stereo	1176
'Virtuoso Guitar Music'	Soloist Stereo	1175
'Frankfurt Guitar Duo'	Soloist Stereo	1174

HENRI DORIGNY
AND AKO ITO

Henri Dorigny was born in France in March 1939. He began the study of the guitar in Nice where he improved his knowledge of the instrument with the duo Presti-Lagoya at the Academie Internationale d'Eté. He attended various master classes and in 1963 was appointed as the Professor of Guitar at the Conservatoire Regional de Musique of Nice. He also began to perform widely as a guitar soloist. In 1966, whilst still attending the master classes of Presti-Lagoya, he met Ako Ito, whom he later married. They began performing as a guitar duo throughout France. They made many appearances on radio and television and have made several recordings.

In 1970 they made their first international tour of Japan, including an appearance with the Tokyo Philharmonic Orchestra. Since then they have appeared regularly throughout Europe, the United States and Canada.

Ako Ito was born in Japan, December 1942. She began to study the guitar as well as the piano and voice at an early age. Her talent soon became evident and at the age of 18 she went to the United States to continue her music studies and to give numerous concerts as a guitar soloist. She studied

in France and in Canada with the duo Presti-Lagoya, and in the United States and Spain with Andres Segovia. She married Henri Dorigny in 1967 and now lives with him in Nice. She was made Professor of Guitar at the Academic de Musique Rainier III in Monaco, a position she still holds.

SELECTED RECORDS

'Danses Espagnoles Pour Deux Guitares'	SFP	31-102
'Compositions For Two Guitars'	Delos	FY 008

EVANGELOS
AND LIZA

Evangelos and Liza

Evangelos and Liza, also known as the Athenian guitar duo, consists of Evangelos Assimakopoulos and his wife, Liza Zoi.

Both began, in 1954, their advanced studies on the guitar in the National Conservatory of Athens under the direction of Dimitri Fampas. At the end of their studies, each graduated and took First Prize with honours. Both guitarists gave their debut solo recitals in Athens in 1959. One year later they took the first two prizes in the International contest in Naples and, in 1962 both were appointed as Professors of the Guitar in the National Conservatory in Athens.

The duo was founded in 1963 and Evangelos and Liza were married in 1965. For three years they were awarded scholarships to study with the Presti-Lagoya duo in France and also in Spain with Andres Segovia who encouraged composers such as Castelnuovo Tedesco to write works especially for them.

Since their arrival on the international music scene in 1967 Evangelos and Liza have played concerts in the major cities of Great Britain and Europe, in addition to Greece. They have also appeared regularly on television and radio. Since 1969 they have also made a number of extensive tours of North America.

SELECTED RECORDS

'Musique Baroque Pour Deux Guitares'	Edici Ed	21290

SELECTED READING

'Evangelos & Liza'	Article — 'Guitar' — August 1977
'Evangelos & Liza'	Article — 'Guitar' — August 1980
'Evangelos & Liza'	Article — 'Guitarra' — July 1980

POMPONIO
AND ZARATE

Pomponio and Zarate

Jorge Martinez Zarate was born in Buenos Aires, Argentina, on the 1st October 1923. He became interested in music at an early age, and later began to study at the National Conservatory of Music in Buenos Aires where he studied guitar with Maria Luisa Anido. Soon after he left the Conservatory, Zarate married guitarist Graciela Pomponio, and they were soon gave their first duo concert.

Jorge Martinez Zarate, as well as appearing throughout the world as a concert artist with his wife, is a highly respected teacher of the guitar. He was appointed Professor of the Guitar at the Music School of Santa Fe, and later became Professor of the Guitar at the National Conservatory of Music in

Buenos Aires. Zarate is also a composer and has made over 600 transcriptions for one, two and four guitars.

Graciela Pomponio was born on the outskirts of Buenos Aires, Argentina, 12th April 1926. Like most of the talented classical guitarists in Argentina at that time, Pomponio came to study with Maria Luisa Anido. Pomponio had already made her first public recital on the guitar at the age of eight.

She entered the National Conservatory of Music in Buenos Aires and studied the guitar, harmony and the theory of music. After completing her studies Graciela Pomponio became the Professor of Guitar at the Music School of the National University of Littoral.

Whilst studying at the National Conservatory of Music in Buenos Aires, Pomponio met Jorge Martinez Zarate. They married in 1948 and since that time have appeared together throughout the world, with great success, as the Pomponio-Zarate duo.

SELECTED RECORDS

'Moreno Torroba'	Erato	STV 70549
'Masters Of The Guitar' — Volume Two	RCA	RB 6599
'Masters Of The Guitar' — Volume Three	RCA	?? ????

ITALIAN GUITAR TRIO

The Italian Guitar Trio was founded in 1969 by three guitarists from Florence, Italy — Alfonso Borghese (1945), Roberto Frosali (1940) and Vicenzo Saldarelli (1946). All three studied in Florence with guitarist Alvaro Company.

All three guitarist currently teach guitar in the music conservatories of Pesaro, Ferrara and Modena.

SELECTED RECORDS

'Trio Chitarristico Italiano'	RCA	RL 31277 (Italy)
'Trio Chitarristico Italiano'	RCA	RL 31521 (Italy)

THE OMEGA GUITAR QUARTET

The Omega Guitar Quartet was formed by Gilbert Biberian in 1969. At its inception it was the only classical guitar quartet in existence in England. Although nothing had been written specifically for a guitar quartet at that time, the repertoire has now considerably grown. The group's repertoire includes not only transcriptions of various renaissance and baroque works, but also a variety of new compositions written especially for the guitar quartet. The Omega's use of requintos — guitars tuned to a fourth higher — transformed the Omega Quartet's sound into something comparable to a string quartet. The Omega gave many concerts throughout Britain and also appeared in Italy at the International Guitar Festival in Florence. In 1975 they made two tours of North America. The original group consisted of Colin

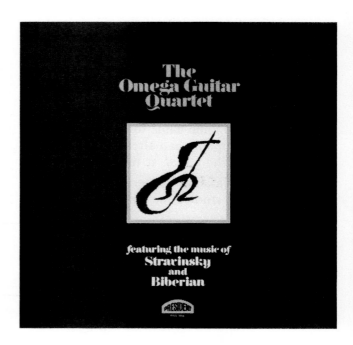

Downs (born 1949), Gregory Pickler (born 1949), Bernard Watson (born 1949), and its founder Gilbert Biberian.

SELECTED RECORDS
'Omega Guitar Quartet'   President   PTLS 1066

SELECTED READING
'Omega Quartet'   Article — 'Guitar' — August Vol 6

THE ENGLISH GUITAR QUARTET

The English Guitar Quartet was formed by Simon Munting (born 1947) early in 1978. Following on the success of the Omega Quartet this group built up a large and varied repertoire including pieces by Praetorious, Vivaldi, Telemann, Handel, Haydn, Debussy and de Falla. All the arrangements for the group were made by members of the quartet. In addition to normal concert repertoire, which included music interspersed with explanation and background detail. The original English Guitar Quartet consisted of Simon Munting, Peter Martin (born 1957), Alexander MacDonald (born 1950) and Colin Thompson (born 1954).

TARRAGO GUITAR QUARTET

The Tarrago Guitar Quartet was founded in 1971 by four Barcelona guitarists, Laura Almerich, Manuel Calve, Jordi Codina and Josep Jan Henriquez. This quartet has appeared throughout Europe with great success and has inspired several leading Spanish composers to write pieces especially for them, including Joaquim Homs, Antonio Ruiz Pipo, Leonard Balada and Charles Guinovart.

THE TOKYO NIIBORI GUITAR ENSEMBLE AND ORCHESTRA

The Nihon Guitar Music Academy is the most well known music academy in Japan, which conducts a full scale academic guitar education. This Academy, which is directed by Hiroki Niibori, adopts graduate school, college and high school systems in their methods of education which focus on the guitar.

The Academy has approximately 200 students, most of which are aged between 15 and 23. A special feature of this institute is that the students not only learn to play solo guitar, but also in duets, ensembles, concerto, and as part of a guitar orchestra. In order to achieve a full orchestral sound students of the academy who are members of the Niibori Guitar Orchestra use alto, cembalo, contrabass, guitaron and bass guitars as well as the standard six-string guitar.

The Niibori Guitar Ensembles and Orchestra have achieved popular success in Japan playing over 400 concerts a year. Recently they have made several recordings including one of Vivaldi's 'Four Seasons' arranged for the ensemble.

Niibori Guitar Ensemble

SELECTED RECORDS

'The Four Seasons/Vivaldi'	Fontec	5016
'Niibori 'Live' With Jorge Cardoso'	Apassionato	8009

Robert Brightmore

THE CLASSICAL GUITAR
THE OTHER CLASSICAL GUITARISTS

The early 19th century has often been called the golden age of the guitar but few musicologists would disagree that the real golden age of the classical guitar is now. The major part of this book deals with the most important classical guitarists and guitar personalities since 1800. Needless to say the classical guitar scene is now so vast that there are thousands of guitarists all over the world who, for one reason or another, have not yet received wide public recognition for their contribution to the instrument.

This section of the book pays tribute to these guitarists by including photographs of a few of those who seem likely to achieve fame in the very near future. The last few pages of this section have been reproduced, with kind permission of Kallaway Limited, from the programme of the Segovia International Competition held under the sponsorship of the Sherry Producers of Spain, in England, in October 1981. These pages show the 43 entrants to this prestigious competition and as such give the reader an excellent précis of those guitarists from whom many of tommorow's great virtuoso guitarists will probably emerge.

Douglas Rogers

Lynn Gangbar

Benjamin Verdery

Anthea Gifford

Pedro-Jose Ibanez

Eric Hill

Gregg Nestor
Sarabande

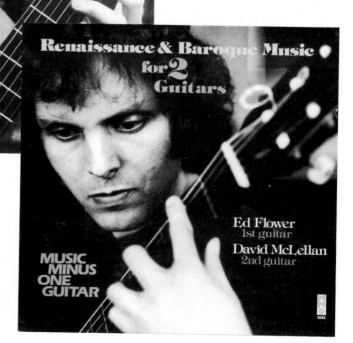

PRESSED FLOWER

Renaissance & Baroque Music for 2 Guitars

Ed Flower 1st guitar

David McLellan 2nd guitar

MUSIC MINUS ONE GUITAR

259

Gentil Montana
Hommage à Augustin Barrios Mangore

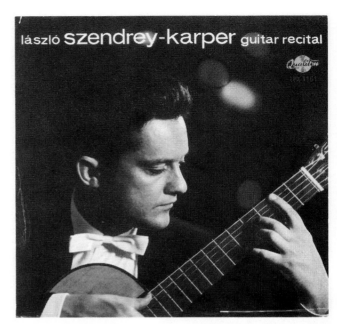

lászló szendrey-karper guitar recital

Suite murciana
Manuel Diaz Cano

CANTO DE VIDA
Y ESPERANZA
CANCION
NAPOLITANA
PRELUDIO EN EL ESTILO
DE LOS VIEJOS MAESTROS
FANTASIA
AMERICANA
ESTUDIO n° 34
DOS CANCIONES
POPULARES
ESPAÑOLAS

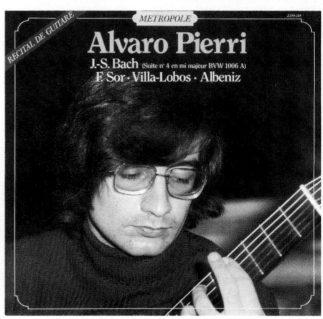

RECITAL DE GUITARE   METROPOLE
Alvaro Pierri
J.-S. Bach (Suite n° 4 en mi majeur BVW 1006 A)
F. Sor · Villa-Lobos · Albeniz

JOHN ARRAN   CASTLES OF SPAIN

LA CHITARRA DAL '500 AD OGGI
dalla trasmissione televisiva:
"MUSICA INSIEME"

GÖRAN SÖLLSCHER

J.S. Bach Fuga g-moll BWV 1000 · Preludium fuga och allegro Ess-dur BWV 998
Fernando Sor Morceau de concert op. 54 · Sonat C-dur op. 15

STEREO

Masayuki Hirayama
Gitarre – Recital

Romantic Melodies for Classic Guitar
MACHIKO KIKUCHI

GITARRENMUSIK
Turina · Tárrega
Sor · Ponce · Villa Lobos

Sonja Prunnbauer

JÜRGEN
SCHÖLMANN

LUCIEN
BATTAGLIA
INTERPRETE
LES

MAITRES D'AMERIQUE LATINE

CARLO AMBROSIO plays Giuliani

GIULIANATE, Opus 148: Scherzo, Amoroso, Malancolia & Risoluzione
VARIATIONS, Opus 45 & 38

Spanish Baroque

Guitar Duo

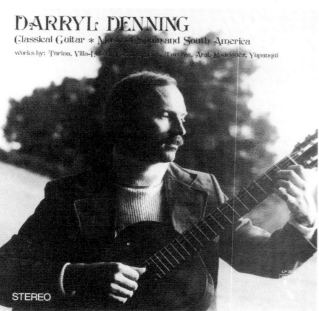

DARRYL DENNING
Classical Guitar * Music of Spain and South America
works by: Turina, Villa-Lobos, Ponce, Sor, Tarrega, Aral, Rodriguez, Yupanqui

STEREO

John shane howell

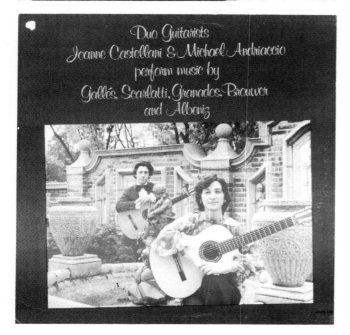

Duo Guitarists
Joanne Castellani & Michael Andriaccio
perform music by
Gallés, Scarlatti, Granados-Brouwer
and Albeniz

in his recording debut

Doug

262

Segovia International Guitar Competition

Sponsored by the

Sherry Producers of Spain

Jury

Andrés Segovia

President

Anton Garcia Abril · Agustin Léon Ara

Gordon Crosskey · Stephen Dodgson

Luis Galve · John Manduell

Alexandre Tansman

Administrative Director

William Kallaway

Leeds Castle

Kent

England

9–13 October 1981

Presentation and Management: Kallaway (Consultants and Management) Ltd, London

Title Page of programme for Segovia International Competition 1981.

Competitors

Colin ARENSTEIN
UK
Aged 27

1

Studied at the London College of Music, winning a Performance Prize and FLCM Performance Diploma. While still a student, he gave the first performance of his own Guitar Concerto. Has also studied with Carlos Bonell, Gilbert Biberian and Robert Boyle. Gave his first professional London concert at Leighton House.

Arnaldur ARNARSON
Iceland
Aged 22

2

Educated at Umea Music School, Sweden, and Tonskoli Sigursvein D. Kristinssonar in Iceland. Now studying guitar with Gordon Crosskey at the Royal Northern College of Music. Professional experience includes recitals in Iceland, Sweden and England, and appearances on Icelandic radio and television, and Finnish television.

Dominic BERTUCCI
Canada
Aged 23

3

Began studying classical guitar at the age of seventeen, and studied music at the University of Windsor, Ontario. Currently studying at the University of North Carolina with Michael Lorimer, in whose Master Classes he has also taken part. Professional experience includes a series of recitals in Ontario, and concerts in the USA.

David BOND
USA
Aged 19

4

Began studying classical guitar at the age of nine; now studying at the Manhattan School of Music with Sharon Isbin. Has taken part in Master Classes with Manuel Barrueco, Abel Carlevaro and Phillip Roesheger. Awards include a scholarship to the Manhattan School of Music.

David BREAUGH
USA
Aged 21

5

Studied at Montana State University; Master Classes with Michael Lorimer and Christopher Parkening. Has also studied in the UK with (among others) John Duarte and Stephen Dodgson. Also studied at Santiago de Compostela in 1976. Professional experience includes concerts in the USA, England and Sweden.

Eduardo CASTAÑERA
Argentina
Aged 25

6

Began studying the guitar at the age of seven, first performing in public at the age of nine. Awards include first prizes at competitions in Brazil (1975), Ecuador (1976), and Venezuela (1977), and second prize in the Radio France Competition in Paris (1979). Professional experience includes concerts in Uruguay, Brazil, Ecuador and Venezuela; in Europe he has given concerts in France and Spain.

Charles CAVANAUGH
USA
Aged 24

7

Has studied with Jose Tomas, Pepe Romero and Manuel Barrueco (among others). Now studying at North Texas State University. Professional experience includes concerts in Minnesota and Texas; he was Artist-in-residence at the Austin Symphony Project in 1977, and has been awarded first prize in the American String Teachers' Competition. He is also a composer, and has featured his own works in recitals.

Claudio DAIBAN
Argentina
Aged 23

8

Began studying the guitar at the age of ten, and was awarded second prize at the Guitar Competition of the National Guitar Association at the age of sixteen. He has frequently been seen on radio and television both in Argentina and in Spain, and has given recitals and chamber concerts in Buenos Aires. He has played in Israel, and in the UK has worked at the Yehudi Menuhin School and the Purcell School of Music (1980); he is now a postgraduate student at the Royal College of Music.

Lucio DOSSO
Italy
Aged 23

9

Studied with Sergio Notaro at the Centro Romano della Chitarra, where he is now teaching. Has also studied with Oscar Ghiglia and Jose Tomas, and regularly takes part in Master Classes at the Accademia Musicale Chigiana in Siena. He has performed in numerous public concerts.

Five pages from programme for Segovia International Competition 1981, showing details of competitors.

10 **Alexander DUNN**
USA
Aged 26

Studied at the San Francisco Conservatory. He is a member of the Conference on Contemporary Music Ensemble at the Aspen Music Festival, where he has also been Staff Vocal Accompanist since 1977. Professional experience includes chamber music and recitals, including appearances in Los Angeles, San Francisco and New York, and orchestral concerts in San Francisco.

11 **Tom DUPRÉ**
UK
Aged 22

Tom Dupré is the son of the late Desmond Dupré, the lutenist and viola da gamba player. He began studying the guitar at the age of fourteen, and graduated from the Royal Academy of Music, where he studied with Hector Quine. Professional experience includes concerts in London, and appearances at the King's Lynn and Stour Festivals, and on BBC local radio.

12 **Eliot FISK**
USA
Aged 27

Began studying the guitar at the age of seven. Studied at Aspen with Oscar Ghiglia, at Banff with Alirio Diaz, and at Yale, where he now teaches guitar; he is also on the faculty of the Aspen School of Music. His extensive professional experience includes recitals and orchestral concerts throughout the USA, Europe, Israel and South America; in addition he gives duo recitals with the soprano Victoria de los Angeles. Recordings include music of Baroque, classical, Latin American and twentieth century composers.

13 **Paul GALBRAITH**
UK
Aged 17

Studies piano and guitar at Chetham's School of Music, and guitar with Gordon Crosskey at the Royal Northern College of Music. Has taken part in Master Classes with Alirio Diaz and John Williams. Awards include third prize in the BBC's Young Musician of the Year Competition (1980). Concert experience includes appearances in Scotland and England.

14 **Jose Maria GALLARDO DEL REY**
Spain
Aged 20

Studied at the Conservatorio Superior de Musica in Seville with America Martinez. Has also studied with Jose Tomas. He has given recitals throughout Spain and has appeared on Spanish radio and television. He won prizes at Musica en Compostela in 1979 and 1980, and was awarded the Silver Medal at the Concurso Internacional de Ejecucion Musical Maria Canals earlier this year.

15 **Paul GREGORY**
UK
Aged 25

Began playing the guitar at the age of twelve, and has studied with Robert Sutton and Carlos Bonell. He has given several concerts in London both as soloist and in chamber music ensembles, and has made two BBC recordings. Awards include second prize at Valencia, and first prize in the International Andrés Segovia Competition at Mallorca (both 1978).

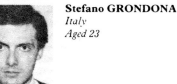

16 **Cheryl GRICE**
UK
Aged 28

Studied at the Royal Northern College of Music with Gordon Crosskey. Awards include first prize in the Concurso Internazionale di Chitarra Classica in Italy, and first prize (shared) in the Lanchester International Guitar Competition in England (both 1974). Concert appearances include the premieres of Wilfred Joseph's concerto *Saratoga* at the Queen Elizabeth Hall, and of Quaranta's *Divigazioni* on Italian television. In 1978 she took part in a BBC Television Master Class with Julian Bream, and she has made two recordings for BBC Radio 3.

17 **Stefano GRONDONA**
Italy
Aged 23

Began studying guitar at the age of nine. Studied with Sergio Notaro, and attended Master Classes with Oscar Ghiglia at Gargnano and Siena, and with Julian Bream at Montepulciano. Awards include first prize at the Castelnuovo-Tedesco Competition in Parma (1975), and at the Citta di Alessandria Competition (1978), and second prize at the Andrés Segovia Competition in Mallorca in 1979 and 1980. Professional experience includes many recitals in Italy, and concerts for Italian television. He recently made his first recording.

18 **Forbes HENDERSON**
UK
Aged 29

Studied at the Royal Northern College of Music with Gordon Crosskey and John Williams. Professional experience includes concerts with the London Sinfonietta, Nash Ensemble and Ballet Rambert, and appearances at festivals in the UK, Holland and Norway. Awards include first prize at the Lanchester International Guitar Competition (1972). He has appeared on BBC Television in a Master Class with Julian Bream, and has made a record which includes works by Stephen Dodgson and John Duarte.

19 **Tsuyoshi HORIUCHI**
Japan
Aged 23

Began playing the guitar at the age of twelve. Studied with Nobutaka Nakagawa for four years, during which time he won the fourth Japanese Guitar Competition in Osaka. He is now studying with Hector Quine at the Royal Academy of Music, where in 1980 he was awarded the Julian Bream Prize.

20

Yoshinobu IWANAGA
Japan
Aged 28

Began studying the guitar at the age of nine in Japan. Since 1976 he has studied in Europe, with Alberto Ponce and Nadia Boulanger. Awards include first prize in the first Japanese Guitar Competition (1974), first prize at the Gargnano International Guitar Competition in Italy (1977), and second prize in the Twentieth International Guitar Competition in Paris (1978). Professional experience includes recitals in Italy, France and Belgium.

21

Timothy KAIN
Australia
Aged 30

Studied at the Canberra School of Music; graduate work with Jose Tomas in Spain, at the Royal Northern College of Music with Gordon Crosskey and John Williams, and summer schools with (among others) Oscar Ghiglia, Alirio Diaz and Jose Tomas. Has been awarded several study scholarships. Professional experience includes numerous solo and chamber music concerts in Australia; recitals in Eire, Canada and the USA; recitals and orchestral concerts in the UK including four concerto performances with the Halle Orchestra (1980).

22

Helen KALAMUNIAK
UK
Aged 30

The daughter of a Ukrainian guitar teacher, she studied at the Royal Northern College of Music with John Williams and Carlos Bonell, and studied lute with Diana Poulton. As a member of a quartet, she played in a Nadia Boulanger Master Class, and also toured the UK and appeared in the First International Guitar Festival in Florence. London appearances include duo recitals with her husband Charles Ramirez.

23

Dietmar KREŠ
Austria
Aged 18

Began studying the guitar at the age of nine, giving his first recital at the age of fifteen in Graz, Austria. Studied at the Graz Academy of Music with Heinz Irmler. Awards include first prize in the Austrian Jugend Musiziert Competition (1977 and 1979), and third prize at the International Guitar Competition in Paris (1980). He has appeared on radio and television.

24

Wlodzimierz LERNER
Poland
Aged 23

Educated in Cracow; studied music at the Primary and Secondary Schools of Music with Wanda Dubinska-Kopec and Jerzy Dylag. Now a fourth-year student at the Academy of Music where he works under the direction of Krzysztof Kossakowski. Concert experience includes recitals for music clubs and other organisations in Poland.

25

Jesper LÜTZHØFT
Denmark
Aged 24

Began playing the guitar at the age of fifteen, also studying organ and piano. Entered the Royal Danish Conservatory in 1977; since then, he has given an increasing number of concerts in Denmark both as soloist and in chamber music ensembles. Has also studied with (among others) John Williams and Alexandre Lagoya.

26

Christopher LYALL
UK
Aged 28

Studied with Julian Byzantine, and with Patrick Bashford at the Royal College of Music, where he also studied lute and cello. Professional experience includes solo recitals and chamber music concerts. He has broadcast for BBC radio and television, and made his London debut at the Wigmore Hall.

27

Gregg NESTOR
USA
Aged 26

Studied with (among others) Michael Lorimer, Pepe Romero, John Duarte and Alirio Diaz. Awards include two scholarships, and first prize in the San Diego Symphony Young Artists' Competition (1973). Professional experience includes recitals, chamber music concerts and orchestral concerts in Europe and the USA, with premiere performances of works by Duarte and Castelnuovo-Tedesco.

28

Stefan NESYBA
Austria
Aged 26

Began playing the guitar at the age of thirteen. Studied at the Fachhochschule für Musik in Lübeck, and at the Musikhochschule Lübeck where he now teaches. While a student, was awarded fourth prize in the national Jugend Musiziert Competition in Germany. In 1977 he took part in a Master Class with Julian Bream in Liechtenstein. Has given concerts in Finland, Sweden and Denmark, and has broadcast for Deutschlandfunk Köln.

29

Marinko OPALIĆ
Yugoslavia
Aged 29

Studied music with the Yugoslav guitarist Milan Grakelić, and in Venice with Angelo Amato. Professional experience includes recitals, radio broadcasts and television appearances in Yugoslavia. Awards include first prize at the International Competition in Bardolini, Italy (1979).

Victor PELLEGRINI
Argentina
Aged 23

30

Studied guitar with Juan Carlos Zemp and Ines Panero de Zemp. Awards include four first prizes in national competitions in Argentina; second prize at the Palestrina Competition (1979); first prize in the Alirio Diaz Competition in Venezuela (1979); third prize in the Andrés Segovia Competition in Mallorca (1979 and 1980). Professional experience includes radio broadcasts in Argentina and Brazil, and concerts throughout South America and in Spain.

Charles RAMIREZ
UK
Aged 28

31

Began studying the guitar at the age of fourteen with William Gomez, later studying at the Royal College of Music, where he is now Professor of Guitar. Made his London debut in 1974 and has since given concerts both in the UK and abroad, including a series of Master Classes in Israel. He regularly broadcasts for BBC Radio 3, and also gives duo recitals with his wife Helen Kalamuniak.

Ruben RIERA
Venezuela
Aged 24

32

Began playing the guitar at the age of ten, attending the Real Conservatorio de Musica in Madrid, and later studying in Venezuela with Rodrigo Riera. He is now studying at the Guildhall School in London with John Duarte. Awards include third prize in the Alirio Diaz Competition in Venezuela (1976). Professional experience includes numerous radio broadcasts and recitals as well as appearances on television. He gave the world premiere performance of Duarte's first guitar concerto in Venezuela earlier this year.

Stephen ROBINSON
USA
Aged 28

33

Music and guitar studies in the USA, and Master Classes with (among others) Oscar Ghiglia, Angel Romero, Manuel Barrueco and Jose Tomas. Awards include first prize in the Carmel Classical Guitar Festival Competition in California (1978); he is a finalist in the Concours International de Guitare which takes place in late October in Paris. Professional experience includes numerous concerts throughout the USA; he was Assistant Guitar Instructor at Yale University for a year, and now holds the same post at Florida State University.

Francesco ROMANO
Italy
Aged 24

34

Studied guitar with Sergio Notaro, and obtained scholarships to attend Master Classes with Oscar Ghiglia and Bruno Battisti D'Amaro. He teaches guitar at the Tommaso Ludovico da Vittoria School in Rome. Professional experience includes numerous solo recitals in Italy; he is also a member of the Boccherini Ensemble. He has recorded broadcasts for both Vatican and Italian Radio.

Dante ROSATI
USA
Aged 22

35

A graduate of Mannes College of Music, New York, where he studied with Leonid Bolotine; also studied with Vito Cuscuna, Jose Franco and Herbert Levine. Master Classes with Oscar Ghiglia and Eliot Fisk. Awards include Stuyvesant Music Award (1977). He has extensive concert experience in the USA, and appeared at Carnegie Hall earlier this year. He is a Faculty Member of the American Institute of Guitar in New York.

Robert SECRIST
USA
Aged 25

36

Began studying the guitar at the age of eleven. Has attended Master Classes with Oscar Ghiglia in Aspen and Siena. Awards include the Silver Medal at the Alirio Diaz Competition in Venezuela (1979). Many concerts in the USA, including a Carnegie Hall recital. His first solo recording was released in December 1980.

Steven SMITH
UK
Aged 21

37

Began studying the guitar at Salford Music Centre, and is now attending the Royal Northern College of Music, where he is a pupil of Gordon Crosskey. He takes part in concerts and theatre productions at the College, and also plays the mandolin and banjo. He is a member of an ensemble specialising in children's concerts and musical education.

David TANENBAUM
USA
Aged 25

38

Studied guitar in New York and Baltimore, and with Michael Lorimer at the San Francisco Conservatory. Awards include first prize in the Carmel Classical Guitar Festival Competition in California (1977), and second prize in the International Guitar Festival Competition in Toronto (1978). His numerous appearances throughout the USA include five New York solo recitals. He has broadcast on radio and television in the USA and Canada, and was guitar soloist for the Joffrey Ballet in the USA and the USSR.

David THORNTON
UK
Aged 22

39

Studied music at the University of Lancaster, and studied guitar with John Arran. He was awarded a Countess of Munster Musical Scholarship to travel to the USA, where he studied in New York with Alice Artzt. He has also worked with (among others) Julian Byzantine, John Duarte and Gordon Crosskey. Professional experience includes concerts and festival appearances throughout the UK, and regular broadcasts on radio.

40 **Zoltán TOKOS**
Romania
Aged 29

Studied at the Conservatory of Music in Cluj, Romania, and at the Ferenc Liszt Conservatory in Budapest where he is now resident. He also spent a year at the Athens Conservatoire. Awards include a Diploma at the International Maria Canals Competition in Spain (1981). Professional experience includes recitals, orchestral concerts, radio and television appearances both in Romania and Hungary.

41 **Gerald TOLAN**
UK
Aged 24

Studied classical guitar with Hector Quine at the Guildhall School; while still a student, performed Richard Rodney Bennett's Guitar Concerto at the Camden Festival. Professional experience includes London concerts and radio broadcasts; he appeared on BBC Television in a Master Class with Julian Bream. His first record, of two suites written for him by Ronald Binge, was released in 1978.

42 **Bryan TOWNSEND**
Canada
Aged 30

Studied at McGill University, and with Jose Tomas, Pepe Romero and Manuel Barrueco (among others). Professional experience includes solo recitals, orchestral concerts and radio broadcasts in Canada; he gave the Canadian premiere of Henze's *El Cimarron*. He is Head of the Guitar Department at the Victoria Conservatory of Music.

43 **Robert WETZEL**
Holland
Aged 27

Born in Holland, he has spent most of his life in the USA, where he began studying guitar at the age of fifteen. He has studied for several years with the Romero family, in particular with Angel and Pepe Romero. He made his professional debut as a member of the Romero Quartet in 1977, playing both guitar and lute. He has given solo recitals throughout the USA.

"At the beginning of my career, I set myself four tasks: to redeem the guitar from flamenco and other folkloric amusements, to persuade composers to create new works, to show the real beauty of the classical guitar and to influence schools of music and conservatoires to teach guitar at the same dignified level as the piano, violin and 'cello.

"It is for the classical guitar, to which I have devoted my life, and to help young guitarists, that I and my friends from the Sherry City of Jerez have come together to create this Competition. It is a particular pleasure to me that it will take place in the beautiful Leeds Castle with its Spanish association."

Spanish Embassy, London *8 October 1980*

THE CLASSICAL GUITAR
ITS COMPOSERS

Federico Moreno Torroba

THE CLASSICAL GUITAR

ITS COMPOSERS

During the 19th century the repertory for classical guitarists consisted mainly of their own compositions and those of other guitarists. Sor, Giuliani and Paganini were the most outstanding of these and to a lesser extent Aguado, Costé and Regondi, amongst others, also proved themselves to be talented composers. Towards the end of the 19th century Francisco Tarrega extended the range of music available for the guitar considerably with his numerous transcriptions of works by important 19th century composers like Mendelssohn, Albeniz and Granados. Tarrega's lead in this field was followed in the 20th century by Emilio Pujol, Miguel Llobet Andres Segovia. Subsequently more and more classical guitarists made their contribution in this field so that today a great portion of the guitarist's repertoire consists of transcriptions of works originally written for other instruments. The works of J. S. Bach (1685-1750), D. Scarlatti (1685-1757), I. Albeniz (1860-1909), and E. Granados (1867-1916) are amongst these composers whose works have been most successfully transcribed for the guitar. A vast library of music originally written for the lute, vihuela and early guitar has also been transcribed successfully for the classical guitar. The most important of these composers are John Dowland (1562-1626), Alonso de Mudarra (1508-1580), Francesco Corbetta (1612-1681), Gaspar Sanz (1640-1710), Luis Milan (1500-1561), Enriques de Valderrabano (1500-1547), Adrian de Roy (1520-1598), Diego Pisador (1509-1557), Francois Campion (1686-1748), Sylvius Leopold Weiss (1686-1750), Robert de Visée (1660-1720), and Luis Narvaez (1500-1551). Their works are often included in the concert programmes of guitarists today.

It was during the 1920s that Andres Segovia began his great campaign to encourage leading contemporary composers to write for the guitar. In fact the first major composer to do this was Manuel de Falla. He wrote the guitar solo 'Homenaje Pour Le Tombeau De Claude Debussy' in 1920, fulfilling an earlier promise to Miguel Llobet. The first two great composers to answer Segovia's call were Joaquin Turina and Federico Moreno Torroba. Turina's 'Fandanguillo' and Torroba's 'Suite Castellana' were both published in 1926. They were the first of many important works written by these Spanish composers especially for the guitar. Since that time more and more great contemporary composers have written important works for the guitar. These compositions together with those written by great 20th century guitarist/composers like Barrios, Antonio Lauro and Heitor Villa Lobos, have now given the guitar a repertory equal to most other solo instruments.

This section of the book is devoted to biographies of the most important of these 20th century composers who have made such a vital contribution to the evolution of the classical guitar since 1800.

Mario Castelnuovo-Tedesco with Vahdah Olcott Bickford at 40th Anniversary dinner of American Guitar Society.

COURTESY C. E. H. SMITH

MALCOLM ARNOLD

Born — MALCOLM HENRY ARNOLD
Northampton, England

1921

As a child Malcolm Arnold studied the violin and trumpet. he won a scholarship at the Royal College of Music and joined the London Philharmonic Orchestra as a trumpet player. Arnold studied orchestration with Gordon Jacobs and in 1943 his overture 'Beckus and Dandiprat' was a great success. This established him as a gifted composer and later in 1948 he was awarded the Mendelssohn Scholarship which enabled him to study in Italy for one year.

Since that time he has composed orchestral music including several symphonies and a great deal of highly successful incidental music for films, including the theme music for 'The Bridge on the River Kwai'. Malcolm Arnold composed a 'Serenade for Guitar and Strings' in 1955, and in 1959 he wrote his 'Guitar Concerto (opus 67)' which was dedicated to Julian Bream.

SELECTED RECORDS

'Serenade' — John Williams	CBS	76634
'Guitar Concerto' (opus 67) — Julian Bream	RCA	SB 6826

RICHARD RODNEY BENNETT

Born — Broadstairs, Kent, England

1936

Richard Rodney Bennett won a scholarship to the Royal Academy of Music in 1953. There he studied with Lennox Berkeley and Howard Ferguson. In 1957 Bennett went to Paris to study with Pierre Boulez for two years, having been awarded a scholarship by the French Government. In 1965, he was elected Composer of the Year by the Composers' Guild of Great Britain.

In 1968 Richard Rodney Bennett composed five short impromptus, for solo guitar, and in 1970 he completed his Concerto for Guitar which he dedicated to Julian Bream.

SIR LENNOX BERKELEY

Born – Oxford, England

1903

Lennox Berkeley is partly of French descent. Although his general education was completed at Oxford, Berkeley completed his music education in Paris as a pupil of Nadia Boulanger.

Lennox Berkeley, who was knighted in 1974, is without doubt one of Great Britain's most important composers of the 20th century. He has written for the piano, chamber music, orchestral music and several operas. For the past 25 years he has been the Professor of Composition at London's Royal Academy of Music.

With the encouragement of Julian Bream, Berkeley has written several compositions for the guitar. The first was his 'Sonatina' (1957), 'Songs For Half Light' (for Peter Pears and Julian Bream), 'Theme And Variations' and more recently his 'Guitar Concerto'. This concerto was commissioned in 1974 by the City of London Festival. The work was dedicated to and given its premier by Julian Bream.

SELECTED MUSIC
'Sonatina for Guitar'   JWC
'Theme and Variations'   JWC

BENJAMIN BRITTEN

Born — Lowestoft, England
22nd November 1913

Died — Aldeburgh, England
4th December 1976

Benjamin Britten started to compose at the age of five. He was taught the piano and viola. By the time he was 14 he had shown that he was a talented composer. In 1927 he studied composition with Frank Bridge and a few years later won an open scholarship in composition to the Royal College of Music.

Benjamin Britten soon established himself as one of Britain's finest 20th century composers. In 1963 Britten composed his 'Nocturnal' for guitar. Several years earlier he had promised Julian Bream that he would write a work for the guitar. The famous 'Nocturnal' based on a 16th century song of John Dowland, was first performed by Julian Bream at the 1964 Aldeburgh Festival.

MARIO CASTELNUOVO-TEDESCO

Born — Florence, Italy
3rd April 1895

Died — Beverley Hills, California, USA
16th April 1968

Mario Castelnuovo-Tedesco was of Spanish/Jewish origin. He began to study the piano with his mother at the age of nine and almost immediately began to compose. At the age of 13, he entered the Cherubini Conservatory in Florence where he studied the piano with Edgar Samuel de Valle. He also studied composition with one of Italy's foremost composers, Ildebrando Pizzetti. Before he reached the age of 20, the young composer was acclaimed not only in Italy but throughout Europe.

In 1925 Castelnuovo-Tedesco won the National Prize for his opera, 'La Mandragola', performed for the first time in 1926 at La Fenice in Venice. In 1931 his ballet, 'Bacco in Roscanam' was performed at La Scala in Milan. In 1932 Castelnuovo-Tedesco first met Andres Segovia at the International Festival of Venice. It was there that Segovia asked the composer to write a piece for the guitar, the result was Tedesco's first piece for the guitar which is entitled 'Variations' (attraverso i secoli) opus 71. Over the next few years Tedesco continued to write several pieces for the guitar, and once again at the request of Andres Segovia Tedesco wrote a concerto for guitar and orchestra. This he did in 1938 when he wrote his Concerto in D (opus 99). This composition, which was dedicated to Andres Segovia, was the last composition that Tedesco would write in Italy.

After the Fascist government in Italy started its anti-Semitic campaign, Tedesco and his family decided to leave Italy. They emigrated to the United States in 1939, and after spending a year in New York, Tedesco went to California to live and work in Beverley Hills. During his early years there he wrote scores for motion pictures but later devoted himself mainly to teaching composition and orchestra.

In 1961 Andres Segovia introduced Tedesco to the guitar duo team of Ida Presti and Alexandra Lagoya. They inspired him to produce a series of works for two guitars: the 'Sonatina Canonica' (opus 196), 'Twenty-Four Preludes and Fugues for the Well Tempered Guitar' (opus 199) and the 'Concerto for Two Guitars and Orchestra' (opus 201).

Castelnuovo-Tedesco was prolific composer. Included amongst his works are six operas, five oratorios, numerous orchestral pieces, including overtures for 11 Shakespeare plays, over 100 piano works, over 400 songs, more than 100 choral pieces and a great amount of chamber music for varied instrumental combinations. Mario Castelnuovo-Tedesco composed almost 100 works for the guitar. One of his last and most beautiful is Platero (opus 190) for narrator and guitar.

SELECTED RECORDS

'Guitar Concerto No 1' — Andres Segovia	EMI	HLM 7134
'Concerto For Two Guitars' — The Abreu Duo	CBS	61469
'Platero And 1' — Andres Segovia	MCA	MACS 1967
'Platero And 2' — Andres Segovia	MCA	S-26 087
'Music of Castelnuovo-Tedesco' — Beppe Ficara	C&M	PNL 059

SELECTED READING

'Mario Castelnuovo-Tedesco	Article — 'Guitar' — February 1978
'Mario Castelnuovo-Tedesco	Article — 'Guitar Review'— No 37 1972

SELECTED MUSIC

'Aranci in Fiore, ed Segovia'	Ricordi
'Aria Da Chiesa'	Bèrben
'Ballatella, on the Name of Christopher Parkening, op 170/34'	Farfisa
'Canción Argentian, on the Name of Ernesto Bitetti, op 170/41'	Bèrben
'Canción Cubana, on the Name of Hestor Garcia, op 170/39'	Bèrben
'Canción Venezolana, on the Name of Alirio Diaz, op 170/40'	Bèrben

'CanzoneCalabrese, on the Name of Ernest Calabria, op 170/48' Bèrben
'Canzone Siciliana, on the Name of Mario Gangi' Bèrben
'Capriccio Diabolico (Homage to Paginini)' Ricordi
'Escarraman — A Suite of Spanish Dances from the 16th century
    (after Cervantes)' Bèrben
'Estudio, on the Name of Manuel Lòpez Ramos' Bèrben
'Homage to Purcell — Fantasia, on the Name of Ronald and Henry
    Purcell, op 170/46' Bèrben
'Japanese Print, on the Name of Jiro Matsuda, op 170/46' Bèrben
'Passacaglia, Omaggio a Ronacalli, op 180' Bèrben
'Platero y Ko, op 190 (for Narrator and Guitar)' Bèrben
'Romanza, on the Name of Oscar Ghighlia, op 170/37' Farfisa
'Rondo, op 129' GA 168
'Sonata (Omaggio a Boccherini)' GA 149
'Suite, op 133' GA 169
'Tarantella' Ricordi
'Tarantella Campana, on the Name of Eugene Di Novi, op 170/50' Bèrben
'Tonadilla, op 170, No 5' GA 191
'Tre Preludi al Circeo, op 194' Farfisa
'24 Caprichos de Goya, op 195' Bèrben
'Variations à travers les siècles' GA 137
'Variations Plaisantes, ed Gilardino' Bèrben
'Volo D'Angeli, on the Name of Angelo Gilardino, op 170/47' Bèrben
'Concerto for 2 Guitars and Orchestra, op 210 (Piano reduction)' Bèrben
'Fantasia for Guitar and Piano, op 145' GA 170
'First Concerto for Guitar and Orchestra in D, op 99 (Piano reduction)'GA 166
'Second Concerto in C, op 160 (Piano reduction)' GA 240
'Sèrènade, op 118 (Piano reduction), ed Behrend' GA 167

Fine drawing of Castelnuevo Tedesco on music cover.

STEPHEN DODGSON

Born — London, England

17th March, 1924

Stephen Dodgson

Stephen Dodgson studied at the Royal College of Music, which he left in 1950 after receiving a scholarship to study in Italy.

On his return to England he has been active as a composer, teacher, lecturer and broadcaster, and is closely concerned with the work of the Composers' Guild of Great Britain. He has twice been the recipient of Royal Philharmonic Society Prizes.

Stephen Dodgson's orchestral works include concertos for harpsichord, viola da gamba, viola, piano, cello and bassoon. He has also written a large amount of chamber music, and his compositions for guitar include two sets of solo pieces, a trio with flute and cello, a concerto, a partita, and a set of songs.

SELECTED RECORDS

'Dodgson Guitar Concerto No 2 — John Williams'	CBS	76634
'Dodgson Guitar Concerto No 1 — John Williams'	CBS	72661

SELECTED READING

'Stephen Dodgson'	Article — 'Guitar' — March 1973

SELECTED MUSIC

'Fantasy-Divisions'	Bèrben
'Legend for Guitar'	G 123
'Partita for Guitar'	Oxford
'Partita No 2 for Guitar'	Oxford

MANUEL DE FALLA

Born — Cadiz, Spain
23rd November 1876

Died — Alta Gracia, Argentina
14th November 1946

Manuel De Falla was a pupil of Felipe Pedrell who was regarded as founder of the Modern National Spanish school. Although Falla wrote only one piece specifically for the guitar, 'Homenaje Pour Le Tombeau De Claude Debussy', several other of his compositions have been very successfully transcribed for the guitar becoming part of the standard repertoire for the instrument.

Falla's opera 'La Vida Breve' won the prize for the best national opera. For eight years Falla lived in Paris where he befriended Debussy, Ravel and Dukas. Falla was a keen student of native folk song and many of his compositions had a distinct Andalucian flavour. He arranged several festivals in Spain to maintain the cultivation of native folk song.

In 1939, horrified by the events of the Spanish Civil War and also suffering from serious ill health, Falla went to Argentina where he decided to settle. He died there in 1946 at the age of 70.

Manuel de Falla

SELECTED RECORDS

'Manuel de Falla — Ernesto Bitetti'	Hispavox	S60-207

SELECTED READING

'Manuel De Falla'	Article — 'Guitarra' — May 1979
'Manuel De Falla'	Article — 'Guitar Review' No 41 — 1976
'Manuel De Falla — On Music and Musicians'	Boyars 1979
'Manuel De Falla — Ronald Crichton'	Chester 1976
'Manuel De Falla — Burett James'	Gollancz 1981

SELECTED MUSIC

'Homenaje — 'Le Tombeau de Claude Debussy', ed Llobet'	JWC
'Omaggio — Por le Tombeau de Debussy, tr Llobet'	Ric 129390
'Miller's Dance and Dance of the Corregidor, ed Behrend'	JWC
'Récit du Pêcheur and Chanson du Feu Follet, from 'El Amor Brujo', tr Pujol'	JWC

FEDERICO MORENO TORROBA

Born — Madrid, Spain

3rd March 1891

Federico Moreno Torroba has the distinction of being the first composer to heed Andres Segovia's request for one of the great contemporary symphonic composers to write especially for the guitar.

Torroba's first music teacher was his father, the organist José Lopez Ballesteros. His musical talent was obvious at an early age and he enrolled into the National Conservatory of Music where he studied extensively with Conrado del Campo, a celebrated musical pedagogue of that period.

Torroba's compositions are regarded by some critics as being milestones in Spanish music in the three creative media into which he chose to direct his talents. These are the orchestra, the guitar and the Spanish Zarzuela. The National Orchestra of Madrid has successfully and repeatedly presented such symphonic works of Torroba's as 'Capriccio Romantico' and the 'Cuadros Castelanos'. Torroba's Zarzuelas are regarded to be oriented to the great tradition of Spanish theatre art form. Federico Moreno Torroba has written many works for the guitar since his meeting with Andres Segovia many years ago. Included are his 'Pieces Caracteristiques' in two volumes, 'Sonatina in A Major', 'Burgalesa in F Sharp' and his 'Castles of Spain Suite'. In 1974 Torroba wrote his 'Dialogos' for guitar and orchestra dedicated to Andres Segovia, and in 1976 he wrote his 'Concierto Iberica' for four guitars and orchestra dedicated to the Romero Quartet. Torroba also wrote a 'Concierto En Flamenco' for flamenco guitar and orchestra dedicated to and played by Sabricas with the Concert Orchestra of Madrid. These compositions firmly established Torroba as one of the greatest composers for the guitar of the 20th century.

SELECTED RECORDS

'Concierto Iberico/Dialogos' — The Romeros	Philips	9500 749
'Piezas Caracteri Sticas' — Angel Romero	Angel	37312
'Julian Bream Plays Torroba/Villa Lobos'	HMV	CLP 1763
'Moreno Torroba' — Duo Pomponi-Zarate	Erato	STV 70549
'Two Concertos For Guitar' — Sabicas/Tarrago	Erato	EFM 8080

SELECTED MUSIC

'Aires de la Mancha'	GA 235	'Scherzando'	BA 10041
'Alpujarrena'	BA 10840	'Serenata Burlesca'	GA 115
'Burgalesa'	GA 113	'Sonatina'	BA 10042
'Castles of Spain'	Cadencia	'Sonatina (New Edition), ed Segovia'	CO 168
'Characteristic Pieces', Book I'	Ga 113	'Suite Castellana'	GA 104
Book II'	GA 134	'Triptico: Pintoresca, Romance, Festiva'	UME
'Contradanza'	AMP	'Verbenera'	UME
'Five Pieces: Zapateado, Capricho, Improvisaciòn, Sevillana, Romancillo''	GA 234	'Vieja Leyenda'	UME
'Jaranera'	UME		
'Jota Levantina'	AMP		
'Madrileñas — Suite: Tirana, Copla, Bolero'	Música del Sur		
'Madraños'	AMP		
'Mi Farruca'	BA 10841		
'Molinera'	AMP		
'Nocturno'	GA 103		
'Preludio'	GA 114		
'Punteado y Taconeo Clásico'	ESC		
'Romance de los Pinos, ed Segovia'	Cadencia		

MANUEL PONCE

Born — MANUEL MARIA PONCE, Fresnillo, Mexico
8th December 1886

Died — Mexico City, Mexico
24th April 1948

Manuel Ponce began composing at the age of seven and by the time he was 12 years old was playing the Cathedral organ. After studying at the National Conservatoire of Music in Mexico City he went to Italy and Germany in 1904 to study the piano and composition. On his return to Mexico in 1908 Ponce was appointed Professor at the Conservatory of Music. For a few years Ponce had made a special study of the folk music of Mexico and by 1912 the influence of this music was seen in some of his compositions. In 1925 he returned to Europe and lived in Paris, France. There he studied composition and orchestration with Paul Dukas. It was during his stay in Paris that Ponce met Andres Segovia, and his life long association with this great guitarist was to be the determining factor for most of his guitar compositions.

In 1931 the Mexican Government arranged for him to make a tour of several South American Republics by aeroplane. It was during this tour that Ponce conducted the first performance of his 'Concerto del Sur' for guitar and small orchestra on 4th October 1941 at Montevideo, Uruguay. The guitarist on this

Manuel Ponce

occasion was Andres Segovia himself. In 1936-37 Ponce founded and edited the journal 'Cultura Musical' in Mexico City. His guitar works, which included 24 preludes. three popular Mexican songs, a Mazurka, amongst many other pieces, laid the foundation and set standards for future Latin American composers.

SELECTED RECORDS

'John Williams Plays Manuel Ponce'	CBS	76730
'Concierto Del Sur' — John Williams	CBS	73060
'Sonata Meridional' — Andres Segovia	EMI	HLM 7134
'Sonata Romantica' — Andres Segovia	MCA	S-26-087

SELECTED READING

'Manuel Ponce — A Tribute'	'Guitar Review' No 7-1948

SELECTED MUSIC

'Mazurka, arr Almeida'	No 93
'Preludes 1-6'	GA 124
'Preludes 7-12'	GA 125
'Preludio'	GA 112
'Scherzino Mexicano'	Southern
'Six Short Preludes'	Southern
'Sonata Clásica'	GA 122
'Sonata Mexicana (Sonata No 1), ed López Ramos'	Southern
'Sonata Romántica'	GA 123
'Sonata III'	GA 110
'Sonatina Meridional'	GA 151
'Suite: Preambule, Courante,, Sarabande,Gavotte I and II, Gigue'	Southern
'Thème, Varié, et Finale'	GA 109
'Three Popular Mexican Songs'	GA 111
'24 Preludes for Guitar, ed Alcázar from the original manuscripts	TEcla
'Two Pieces: Scherzino Mexicano, Giga Melancólica, ed Papas	CO 199
'Valse'	GA 153
'Variations on Folia de España, and Fugue'	GA 135

JOAQUIN RODRIGO

Born — Sagunto, Province of Valencia, Spain

22nd November 1902

Joaquin Rodrigo with his wife.

Joaquin Rodrigo, though blind from early childhood, studied music in Valencia and later went to Paris, as had other famous Spanish musicians including Albeniz, Falla and Turina. In 1927, he entered the Ecole Normale de Musique in Paris as a pupil of Paul Dukas. At that time Dukas occupied, as a teacher and composer, a leading position among musicians in Paris, and he exerted, together with Manuel de Falla and the Spanish pianist Ricardo Vines, a lasting influence on the young composer.

Joaquin Rodrigo continued to study with Dukas until 1932. In the next four years Rodrigo travelled extensively, principally in Switzerland, Germany and Austria. With the outbreak of the Spanish Civil War in 1936, Rodrigo returned permanently to live in his home land. He eventually took up residence in Madrid and it was there in 1938 that he met guitarist Regino Sainz De La Maza and music patron the Marques De Bolarque. The result was his 'Concerto de Aranjuez' which was performed for the first time on 11th December 1940, in Madrid by Regino Sainz De La Maza. This concerto, which was dedicated to Regino Sainz De La Maza, brought Rodrigo immediate worldwide fame, and

has over the years become one of the most popular pieces of classical music.

Joaquin Rodrigo continued his association with other guitarists and was to write some of the most beautiful guitar music of all time. In 1954 he wrote his 'Fantasia Pour un Gentilhomme' which was dedicated to Andres Segovia. After this an association with the Romero family, whom he knew in Madrid before they left for the United States, encouraged him to write in 1967 the 'Concerto Andaluz for Four Guitars', in 1968 the 'Concerto Madrigal for Two Guitars' and in 1971 his 'Elogio De La Guitarra' which was dedicated to Angel Romero.

SELECTED RECORDS

'Concierto Madrigal' — Angel And Pepe Romero	Philips	6500 918
'Concertios Anduluz And Aranjuez' — The Romeros	Philips	SAL 3677
'Elogia De Guitarra' — Angel Romero	Angel	S 37312
'Fantasia Pour Gentilhombre' — Angel Romero	EMI	SD 3415
'Rodrigo Concierto Aranjuez' — Narciso Yepes	Decca	SPA 233
'Rodrigo' — Pepe Romero	Philips	9500-915

SELECTED MUSIC

'Bajando de la Meseta (Por losCampos de España) No 2'	SCH 99
'Concierto de Aranjuez (Guitar part only)'	AP 425
'Elogio de la Guitarra, ed Gilardino'	Bèrben
'Four Easy Pieces from the Album of Cecilia'	UME 19440
'Invocation et Danse, Homage à Manuel de Falla, ed Diaz'	EFM
'Junto al Generalife, ed Behrend'	UME 21788
'Por Los Campos de España, En Los Trigales, Entre Olivares'	EMM
'Sarabande Lointaine'	ESC
'Sonata a la Españalo'	ESC
'Sonata Giocasa'	JWC
'Three Little Pieces'	ESC
'Three Spanish Pieces: Fandango, Passacaglia, Zapateado'	GA 212
'Two Preludes for Guitar'	ESC
'Concierto de Aranjuez (Piano reduction): Score'	AP 424

Christopher Parkening discussing manuscript with Joaquin Rodrigo.

GUIDO SANTORSOLA

Born — Candosa di Puglia, Italy

18th November 1904

Guido Santorsola was taken to Brazil with his family at the age of five. There he began to study the violin and by the time he was nine years old he was already performing in public. It was in San Paulo, Brazil that Santorsola received his early music education. He studied composition with Agostino Cantu and Lamberto Baldi. He later went to Europe for work in Naples and also at the Trinity College of Music in London.

In 1931 Santorsola moved to Montevideo, Uruguay, where he still lives, and in 1936 he became a Uruguayan citizen. He has performed extensively in string ensembles, both as a soloist with the orchestra and also as a conductor. He is the Director of the Escuela Normal de Musica in Montevideo. An early interest in the guitar became fully developed when a lasting friendship with Andres Segoviawas made during Segovia's stay in Montevideo during World War II.

Guido Santorsola has written almost two dozen works for the guitar and also text on the harmonic principles applied to the guitar. He has also written a 'Concerto for Two Guitars and Orchestra' (1966) which was dedicated to Sergio and Eduardo Abreu.

SELECTED MUSIC

'Chôro No 1 and Valsa Chôro'	CO 245
'Giga'	BR 3082
'Preludio No 2'	BR 2795
'Ringraziamento and Tempo di Minuetto'	CO 242
'Sarabanda'	BR 3081
'Sonata No 2, Hispanica'	Bèrben
'Sonoridades 1971: Four Latin American Pieces'	Bèrben
'Sonoridades 1971: Sonata No 4 (Italiana)'	Bèrben
'Three Airs of Court: Preludio, Aria, Finale (Giga)'	CO 219
'Concertino for Guitar and Orchestra (Piano reduction)'	Southern

ALEXANDRE TANSMAN

Born — Lodz, Poland

12th June 1897

Alexandre Tansman first came to prominence following a concert of his music in Paris in 1921. It was during his stay in Paris that Tansman met Andres Segovia. Since that time Tansman has written a number of important works for the guitar.

Alexandre Tansman, although born in Poland, has lived and travelled widely in the United States, Europe and Asia. Originally influenced by his countryman pianist/composer Chopin, Tansman's compositions reflect the wide experience of his travels together with his own strong lyrical individuality. His works include operas, ballets, orchestral, choral and chamber music as well as concerti and solo instrumental music.

In 1952 his composition 'Cavatina' for solo guitar was a prize winner at the International Music Competition in Siena, Italy.

SELECTED RECORDS

'Tansman and Mompou' — Andres Segovia	Brunswick	AXA 4532
'Musique de Cour' — For Guitar and Orchestra — Sonja Prunnbauer	Schwann	VMS 2062E

SELECTED MUSIC

'Cavatina'	GA 165
'Danza Pomposa'	GA 206
'Mazurka'	GA 116
'Pezzo in Modo Antico, ed Gilardino'	Bèrben
'Suite in Modo Polonico'	ESC
'Twelve Easy Pieces'	ESC
'Variations on a Theme of Scriabin'	ESC

JOAQUIN TURINA

Born — Seville, Spain
9th December 1882

Died — Madrid, Spain
28th December 1949

Joaquin Turina was one of Spain's most outstanding musicians of the 20th century. He was not only a composer, but a fine pianist and conductor. He greatly admired the guitar and wrote several pieces for solo guitar which he dedicated to Andres Segovia. Best known of these are 'Fandanguillo', 'Rafaga Sonatina', 'Hommage A Tarrega'. His best known chamber work 'La Oracion Del Turero' was originally written for four guitars.

SELECTED MUSIC

'Fandanguillo, ed Segovia'	BA 12928 and GA 102
'Homage a Tárrega'	GA 136
'Ráfaga'	GA 128
'Sacro-Monte, ed Azpiazu'	Salabert
'Sevillana — Fantasia, ed Segovia'	GA 158
'Sonatina (Sonata in D)'	GA 132

A LIST OF MORE PROMINENT 20th CENTURY COMPOSERS, WHO ARE NOT GUITARISTS, WHO HAVE WRITTEN FOR THE CLASSICAL GUITAR

Ambrosius, Hermann (1897)
Amy, Gilbert (1936)
Angerer, Paul (1927)
Apostel, Hans Erich (1901-1972)
Artner, Norbert (1922-1971)
Auric, Georges (1899)

Bacarisse, Salvador (1898-1963)
Balcom, William (1938)
Bartolozzi, Bruno (1911)
Baumann, Herbert (1925)
Baur, Jurg (1918)
Berg Gunnar (1909)
Bettinelli, Bruno (1913)
Bialas, Gunter (1907)
Bolling, Claude (1930)
Bondon, Jacques (1927)
Borup-Jorgensen, Axel (1924)
Boulez, Pierre (1925)
Bressen, Cesar (1913)
Burghayser, Jarmil (1921)
Burkhard, Willy (1900-1955)
Burkhart, Franz (1902)
Bussotti, Sylvano (1931)

Cardew, Cornelius (1936)
Cerf, Jacques (1932)

David, Johann Nepomuk (1895-1977)
David, Thomas Christian (1925)

Einem, Gottfried Von (1918)
Erbse, Heino (1924)

Farkas, Ferenc (1905)
Feld, Jindrich (1925)
Fheodoroff, Nikolaus (1931)
Fricker, Peter Racine (1920)

Gefors, Hans (1952)
Genzemer, Harald (1909)
Ghedini, Giorgo Frederico (1892-1965)
Ginastera, Alberto (1916)
Gowers, Patrick
Gnattali, Radames (1906)
Guarnieri, Camargo M. (1907)

Halffter, Cristobal (1930)
Halffter, Ernesto (1905)
Hallnias, Hilding (1903)
Hartig, Heinz Friedrich (1907-1969)

Hasenohrl, Franz (1885-1970)
Haubenstock-Ramati, Roman (1919)
Harris, Albert (1916)
Haug, Hans (1900-1967)
Henze, Hans Werner (1926)
Humel, Gerald (1931)

Ibert, Jacques (1890-1962)

Jelinek, Hanns (1901-1969)
Jolivet, Andre (1905-1974)

Kagel, Mauricio (1931)
Kelterborn, Rudolf (1931)
Klebe, Giselher (1925)
Kont, Paul (1920)
Kotonsku, Wlodzimierz (1925)
Kounadis, Arghyris P. (1924)
Kovats, Barna (1920)
Krenek, Ernst (1900)
Kronsteiner, Joseph (1910)
Kubizek, Augustin (1918)
Kucera, Vaclav (1929)

Lacerda, Osvaldo (1927)
Lampersberg, Gerhard (1928)
Lechthaler, Josef (1891-1948)
Leukauf, Robert (1902)
Linde, Hans-Martin (1930)

Maderna, Bruno (1920-1973)
Malipiero, Gian Francesco (1882-1973)
Martin, Frank (1890-1974)
Migot, Georges (1891)
Milhand, Darius (1892-1974)
Miroglio, Francis (1924)
Mittergradnegger, Gunther (1923)
Molleda, José Munoz (   )
Mompoe, Frederico (1893)
Morancon, Guy (1927)

Nielson, Tage (1929)
Noro, Takeo

Obrovska, Jana (1930)
Ohana, Mauricio (1914)

Petrassi, Goffredo (1904)
Pfister, Hugo (1914-1969)
Porrino, Ennio (1910-1959)
Poulenc, Francis (1899-1963)
Previn, Andre (1930)

Rawsthorne, Alan (1905-1971)
Rebay, Ferdinand (1880-1971)
Reitz, Heiner (1925)
Roussel, Albert)1869-1937)
Ruders, Paul (1949)
Ruiz-Pipo, Antonio (1934)

Schibler, Armin (1920)
Schonberg, Arnold (1874-1951)
Schwertberger, Gerald (1941)
Searle, Humphrey (1915)
Seiber, Matyas (1905-1960)
Siegl, Otto (1896)
Skorzeny, Fritz (1900-1965)
Sojo, Vincente Emilio (1887-1974)
Sprongl, Norbert (1892)
Stravinsky, Igor (1882-1971)
Surinach, Carlos (1915)
Suter, Robert (1919)

Tippett, Michael (1905)

Uhul, Alfred (1909)
Uray, Ernst Ludwig (1906)

Vlad, Roman (1919)

Walton, Sir William (1902)
Webern, Anton (1883-1945)
Weiss, Harald (1949)
Wissmer, Pierre (1915)

Zbinden, Julien-Francois (1917)
Zehm, Friedrich (1923)
Zimmermann, Bernd Alois (1918-1970)

David Russell with Spanish composer Vicente Ascencio.

THE CLASSICAL GUITAR
ITS MAKERS

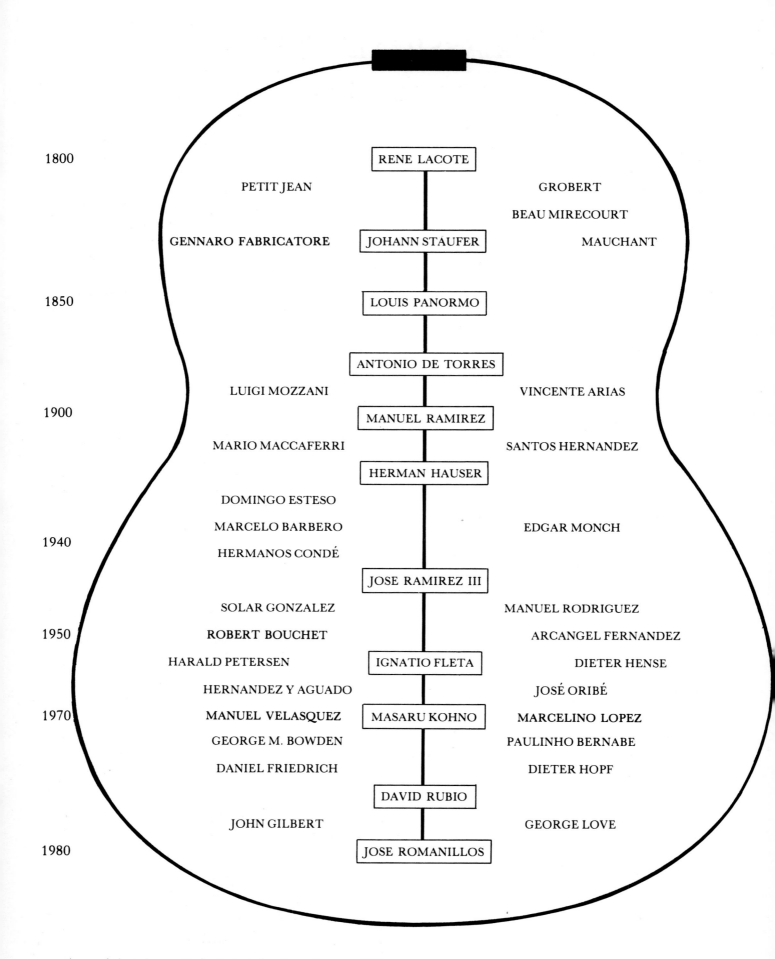

1800

RENE LACOTE

PETIT JEAN

GROBERT

BEAU MIRECOURT

GENNARO FABRICATORE

JOHANN STAUFER

MAUCHANT

LOUIS PANORMO

1850

ANTONIO DE TORRES

LUIGI MOZZANI

VINCENTE ARIAS

1900

MANUEL RAMIREZ

MARIO MACCAFERRI

SANTOS HERNANDEZ

HERMAN HAUSER

DOMINGO ESTESO

MARCELO BARBERO

EDGAR MONCH

1940

HERMANOS CONDÉ

JOSE RAMIREZ III

SOLAR GONZALEZ

MANUEL RODRIGUEZ

1950

ROBERT BOUCHET

ARCANGEL FERNANDEZ

HARALD PETERSEN

IGNATIO FLETA

DIETER HENSE

HERNANDEZ Y AGUADO

JOSÉ ORIBÉ

1970

MANUEL VELASQUEZ

MASARU KOHNO

MARCELINO LOPEZ

GEORGE M. BOWDEN

PAULINHO BERNABE

DANIEL FRIEDRICH

DIETER HOPF

DAVID RUBIO

JOHN GILBERT

GEORGE LOVE

1980

JOSE ROMANILLOS

A general chart showing the finest classical guitar makers since 1800.

286

THE CLASSICAL GUITAR SINCE 1800
ITS GUITAR MAKERS

As has already been pointed out the evolution of the guitar since 1800 shows a parallel development and growth of the guitarist, guitar repertory and the instrument itself. Historically the luthier and the guitarist have always worked closely together to improve the sound and volume of the guitar.

In the 19th century Sor worked with Panormo, Carulli with Lacote, Legnani with Staufer, Madame Sidney Pratten with Panormo, and Arcas and Tarrega with Torres. It was the joint efforts of these great guitar figures that led to the ideas that contributed to the development of the guitar as we know it today.

In the 20th century Andres Segovia has over the years worked with several important guitar makers. Included are the Ramirez family, Hauser and Fleta. In more recent times Julian Bream has encouraged luthiers David Rubio and José Romanillos. It was with Andres Segovia's encouragement and advice that luthier Albert Augustine was to develop the first nylon guitar string, a vital step forward for the classical guitarist in 1948.

This section of the book spotlights the most important guitar makers since 1800.

STAUFER

Johann George Staufer (sometimes spelt Stauffer) (1778-1853), was one of the foremost guitar makers of the 19th century. Staufer's workshops were in Vienna, Austria, and many important guitarists including Regondi, Mertz and Schubert used his guitars. Luigi Legnani also used Staufer's guitars and he suggested several methods of improved construction to Staufer. Staufer eventually produced large quantities of this guitar bearing the label — Legnani model.

Johann Staufer was the inventor of the guitar with a detachable neck and also the arpeggione. The arpeggione, sometimes called the guitar amour, was a mixture of the guitar and cello and first appeared in 1824. Although Schubert was quite taken with the instrument, he wrote a sonata in A minor for it, the arpeggione, which was a bowed instrument, did not achieve much success.

Johann Staufer composed a few pieces for the guitar and was also a publisher of guitar solos.

Staufer Guitar

LACOTE

René-Francois Lacote (1785-1855) was born at Mirecourt, France. He made guitars for the most famous players of his day including Fernando Sor and Carulli.

A writer in the 'Giulianiad' magazine (1833) commented: "The superiority of Lacote's guitars consists in their symmetrical proportions; in the quality of the wood; in the mathematical exactness of the frets, neck and head; and in their general workmanship". On some of his earlier labels Lacote described himself as a pupil of M. Pone. Later labels read 'Lacote and Cie' (Company) and gave particulars of some of the many medals and decorations that he won at the great exhibitions.

Lacote guitars have lute type fingerboards with top frets let into the table of the guitar. Others have the wood scalloped out between the frets, whilst later instruments often have an enclosed machine head. Fine guitars of the Lacote type are sometimes found without labels and these were probably made by apprentices of Lacote.

Lacote Guitar

PANORMO

Panormo guitars were made by the sons and grandsons of Vincenzo Panormo, who was born at Monreale, Sicily, 30th November 1734.

Vincenzo Panormo was regarded as one of Italy's finest violin makers. He moved to England in 1777 and settled in London with his family. Three of his four sons — Joseph, Louis and George — were to become leading guitar makers.

Joseph Panormo had a workshop in Church Street, Soho, London. Fernando Sor, in 1809, left him his Spanish made guitar (probably a Jose Martinez of Malaga) to copy. The result was a blend of Spanish design and Italian craftsmanship. This guitar became the basis of later models to be made by Louis, and other members of the Panormo family.

Louis Panormo had a shop at 46 High Street, Bloomsbury, London and together with several members of his family developed a prosperous guitar making business. Louis Panormo eventually emigrated to New Zealand, but the business continued under the management of his brother George and nephew George junior. In all, Panormo guitars were made in London for around 70 years.

Panormo Guitar

Their output was approximately seven-ten guitars per week for a good portion of this period. The Panormo family offered a selection of quality instruments including basic models to high quality recital instruments. They were used by many of the top players of the day.

SELECTED READING
'Louis Panormo'

Article — 'Guitar' — June 1975

TORRES

Don Antonio de Torres Jurado was born in San Sebastian de Almeria, Spain on 18th June 1817. He died there on 19th November 1892. He is the man to whom we owe the modern concert guitar.

It was whislt Torres was working for the guitar maker José Pernas in Granada, that he was approached by one of the foremost classical guitarists of the time, Julian Arcas. Arcas had for some time been unhappy with the sound and volume of his guitar and put several ideas to Torres about improving the instrument.

It was with Torres' craftsmanship and ingenuity that the proportions of the classical guitar became enlarged from the original small 19th century bodied guitar to the type of guitar we know today. After Arcas, Torres worked with Francisco Tarrega and developed an instrument which has become the basis of all today's classical guitars.

Torres made guitars in two distinct periods. The first period lasted from 1850-1869. Then Torres retired from guitar making to open a china shop. He returned to guitar making in 1880 and continued to construct many fine instruments until his death in 1892. Torres never signed the labels of his guitars and only numbered those of the second period.

Antonio Torres

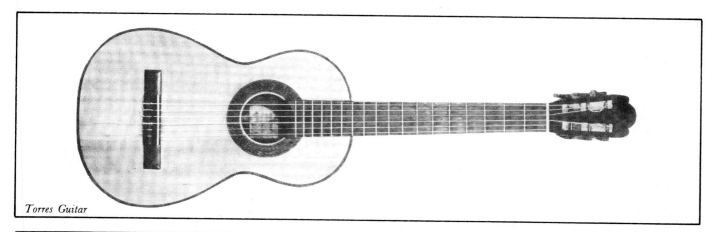

Torres Guitar

SELECTED READING
'Torres and the First Generation'
'Torres'

Article — 'Guitar' — October 1973
Article — 'Guitar Review' — No 16 — 1954

Herman Hauser II

HAUSER

It was Joseph Hauser, in the late 19th century, who was the first member of the Hauser family to make musical instruments. Joseph Hauser was a talented composer and an accomplished zither player. He won many medals and presentations from the German state for his outstanding achievements in music.

It was his son Herman Hauser Snr who extended his father's instrument making profession. He built a vast selection of string instruments including lutes, viols, zithers, violins and guitars. The first guitars he built were similar to the small bodied mid 19th century French guitars. In the late 1920s Herman Hauser was fortunate to have the great guitar player Andres Segovia as a guest in his house. Segovia was very impressed with the workmanship of Hauser's guitars, and suggested that Hauser should make a guitar of the same size as his Ramirez. Within a short period of time Hauser had built a new size guitar of exceptional sound and quality. Segovia was to use this guitar for many years establishing Hauser as one of the foremost guitar makers of the 20th century.

Since Hauser's death, his son Herman Hauser Jnr and grandson Herman Hauser III have carried on the great tradition of guitar making. Hauser guitars remain one of the most sought after brands by classical guitarists in the world today.

Current Workshop Address
Herman Hauser, 8386 Reisbach an der Vils, Bayern, West Germany.

SELECTED READING
'Herman Hauser'

Article — Guitar & Lute' — May 1978

BOUCHET

Robert Bouchet's early training was as a painter in his home town of Paris, France. Although he played the guitar from 1932 it was not until 1946 that he made his first guitar. Bouchet had befriended a Spanish guitar maker who lived in Paris called Ramirez. After losing his own guitar Bouchet decided to try and make one himself. On his regular visits to the workshop of his luthier friend, Bouchet had observed all the various stages of guitar making. The artist had always been good at making things and found that he had no problem in constructing a guitar. Friends were so impressed with his first instrument that Bouchet soon received orders for more of his guitars.

Robert Bouchet did not have a very large output of his instruments, but his reputation grew very quickly and many top players came to buy a guitar from him. Included were Ida Presti, Alexandre Lagoya, Emilio Pujol, Oscar Ghiglia, Turibio Santos, Manuel Lopez Ramos and Julian Bream.

Robert Bouchet, now 80 years old, rarely makes any guitars. He lives in the countryside on the outskirts of Paris, and devotes most of his time to painting.

Current Workshop Address
Robert Bouchet, 189 Rue Ordener, Paris 18, France.

SELECTED READING
'Robert Bouchet'

Article — 'Guitar' — February 1973

RAMIREZ

The Ramirez guitar is one of today's most popular guitars for concert guitarists. Under the management of Jose Ramirez III and Jose Ramirez IV, the Ramirez workshops in Madrid employ around 17 luthiers with several assistants. Their annual production at the moment is around 1,000 concert models which are exported all over the world, and are in constant high demand.

The Ramirez tradition dates back to the second half of the 19th century when Jose Ramirez I set up a workshop in Madrid. As a child he had been apprentice guitar builder to Francisco Gonzalez. In his Madrid workshop Jose Ramirez I, now recognised as a master luthier, taught his younger brother, Manuel Ramirez and also Julian Gomez Ramirez and Enrique Garcia.

It was Manuel Ramirez who gave Andres Segovia one of their finest guitars as a gift, after hearing him play, when the guitarist was still in his teens and unknown. For many years Segovia, on his concert tours throughout the world, only played the Ramirez guitar. Since that time the name Ramirez is synonymous with the best in classical guitars.

Over the years the Ramirez workshop has had many apprentices who in turn became some of the greatest guitar makers the world has known. Included are Santos Hernandez, Domingo Esteso, Marcelo Barbero, Manuel Rodriguez, Manuel

Jose Ramirez III

Contreras and Paulino Bernabe. As a result the Ramirez workshops, now managed by third and fourth generation members of the Ramirez family, can be considered a vital part in the development of the classical guitar.

Current Workshop Address
Jose Ramirez, Conception Jeronima 2, Madrid 12, Spain.

SELECTED READING

'Jose Ramirez III'   Article — 'Guitar Player' — April 1973
'Jose Ramirez III'   Article — 'Guitar & Lute' — May 1979
'Ramirez Guitars'   Article — 'Frets' — January 1982

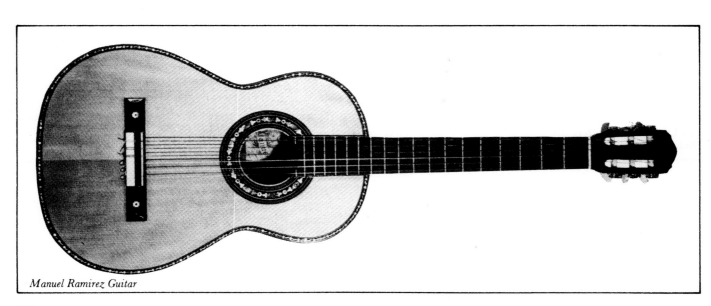

Manuel Ramirez Guitar

FLETA

Ignacio Fleta, regarded by many as the greatest guitar maker of the 20th century, was born in Huesca, Spain on 31st July 1897. He died in Barcelona, Spain on 11th August 1977. Ignacio Fleta's father was a joiner, and it was from him that Fleta learned many aspects of joinery. As a youth Fleta was fascinated by music and at the age of eight he was able to play the bandurria and the guitar. At the age of 13 he went to Barcelona and learned the basics of guitar construction from a French luthier. He worked in the luthier's workshop with his two brothers and studied violin, cello and bass-viol making as well.

In 1927 Ignacio Fleta opened up his own workshop in Barcelona. The first instrument that he made was the cello, but soon was making guitars and violins as well. From 1939-1945 he reproduced a collection of old instruments for the musical society 'Ars Musica'. The collection included the gothic harp, fiddle, lute, vihuela, and other instruments right through to the modern guitar. The brilliance of his construction of these instruments brought Fleta worldwide fame.

In 1955 Ignacio Fleta heard Andres Segovia for the first time. The luthier was so impressed by Segovia's music he decided from that moment on he would only build guitars. In 1957 Fleta built the first of three guitars which Andres Segovia would play in his recitals all over the world. Since that time over 700 guitars have been made in the Fleta workshop. Many of these are owned by today's foremost guitarists, including John Williams, Oscar Caceres, Turibio Santos, Alberto Ponce, Ernesto Bitetti and Alexandre Lagoya.

Since Ignacio Fleta's death in 1977, his two sons, Francisco (born 22nd July 1925) and Gabrielle (born 21st December 1929), have carried the business on with equal success.

Current Workshop Address
Ignacio Fleta y hijos, Calle de los Angeles 4, Barcelona, Spain.

Fleta Guitar

RUBIO

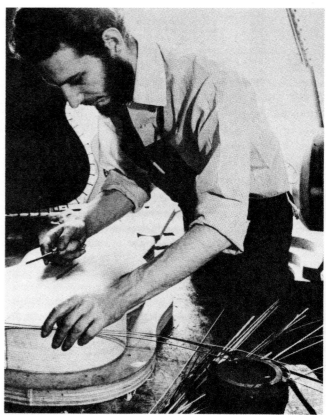

David J. Rubio was born in London, England in 1934. He originally decided to become a doctor, but before he qualified had already decided that this was not the career for him. Rubio went to Spain to study flamenco guitar, as at that time felt he would like to be a professional player of the instrument. He settled in Madrid and usually spent his day practicing in the guitar workshop of Sabrinos de Esteso. It was there that Rubio developed an interest in guitar making, and during his three year stay in Madrid Rubio was able to serve a full apprenticeship as a guitar maker.

In 1961 David Rubio moved to New York City and continued to study guitar construction with a maker by the name of Amedeo. In 1963 Amedeo died and Rubio set up his own workshop. He began to build guitars and lutes of exceptional quality, and soon his reputation was such that top quality guitarists, including Julian Bream, were to become his customers.

In 1967 Rubio returned to England and set himself up in Duns Tew, Oxford as a master builder of guitars and lutes. He also began to construct stringed instruments of the baroque period including viols, cellos and harpsichords. In recent years David Rubio has concentrated on harpsichords and in fact left the construction of guitars to other members of

David Rubio

his workshop, namely Paul Fischer and Edward B. Jones.

Current Workshop Address
David J. Rubio, The Ridge House, Duns Tew, Oxford, England.

SELECTED READING

'David Rubio' Article — 'Guitar' — October 1972
'David Rubio' Article — 'Guitar' — August 1976
'David Rubio' Article — 'Guitar & Lute' — January 1979

Rubio Guitar

KOHNO

Masaru Kohno learnt his craft as a guitar maker from Spanish luthier Arcangel Fernandez. Kohno spent a period of six months in the Madrid workshops of Fernandez studying in great detail the construction of the classical guitar. On his return to Tokyo, Japan, Kohno established his own workshops for guitar making. These today produce some of the finest classical guitars in the world.

In 1967 Masaru Kohno won first prize for guitar making at the Liège Concourse National Des Guitares. This established Kohno as a maker of world importance and since that time many leading guitar recitalists have used his guitars exclusively.

Current Workshop Address
Masaru Kohno, Nishiikebukuro 5-27, Toshimaku, Tokyo, Japan.

Masaru Kohno

COURTESY GENDAI GUITAR PHOTO KIICHI ARAKAWA

ROMANILLOS

José Romanillos was born in Madrid in 1932. Prior to his coming to Great Britain his only real interest in the guitar was a player. By profession he was a woodworker and he had tried repairing some guitars belonging to his friends.

When he arrived in London in 1959 he could not afford to buy himself a guitar. He therefore decided to build one. With the help of a guitarist friend, Romanillos completed his first guitar in six months. Following this first effort friends encouraged Romanillos to continue building guitars. He returned to Spain in 1964 for three years during which time he made some more guitars. Returing to England in 1967 Romanillos brought two of his guitars with him. Guitarists Carlos Bonell and Gilbert Biberian were very impressed with them

and Romanillos decided to give up his regular job as a cabinet maker to devote himself entirely to guitar making.

In 1970 Romanillos showed one of his guitars to Julian Bream who was so impressed that he helped the young guitar maker to set up a workshop near his home in Semley, Dorset. With the help and encouragement of Julian Bream, Romanillos developed a new classical guitar which has become very much sought after by classical guitarists all over the world.

Current Workshop Address
José Luis Romanillos, The Bungalow, East End Farm, Semley, Dorset, England.

SELECTED READING

José Romanillos	Article — 'Guitar' — December 1972
José Romanillos	Article — 'Guitar' — June 1978
José Romanillos	Article — 'Guitar' — December 1980

ALBERT AUGUSTINE

Albert Augustine (1900-1967) was the pioneer of the nylon string for the guitar. As such he may be regarded as one of the most important figures in the evolution of the classical guitar.

It was with the encouragement of Andres Segovia that Albert Augustine, luthier and patron of the arts, began to research the possibilities of developing a nylon guitar string. Before 1947 guitarists used gut treble strings and metal wound silk floss basses. These strings were unreliable, difficult to tune, and soon wore out or broke, even after limited use. During and after World War II the supply situation of good strings for all instruments became very difficult. Segovia, together with Albert Augustine, discussed the matter with a top rank executive of the Du Pont Chemical Company. It was he that would make available to Augustine monofilament nylon originally developed for the manufacture of fishing lines. In 1947 Albert Augustine's workshops in New York produced the first commercially available nylon guitar strings. Since that time the 'Augustine' brand of guitar strings has remained a leader amongst the many brands of classical guitar strings available today.

For much of his life Albert Augustine experimented in the building of guitars and completed several fine instruments before his death in April 1967. His New York workshop, under the supervision of Frank Haselbacher, continues to this day to produce fine classical guitars. The Augustine string business continues to prosper under the management of his wife Rose Augustine. Other prominent

Albert Augustine with Andres Segovia

COURTESY AUGUSTINE STRINGS

brands of classical guitar strings favoured by the world's best players include 'Savarez' and 'Concertiste' produced in France and 'D'Addario', 'Aranjuez' and 'La Bella' produced in the USA.

CLASSICAL GUITAR CONSTRUCTION – SELECTED READING

'Manual of Guitar Technology' — Franz Jahnel — Das Musikinstrument (1981)
'Classical Guitar Construction' — Irving Sloane — Dutton (1966)
'Guitar Repair' — Irving Sloane — Dutton (1973)
'The Classical Guitar, Design and Construction' — McLeod and Welford — Dryad (1971)
'Make Your Own Spanish Guitar' — A. P. Sharpe — Clifford Essex (1957)
'Classic Guitar Making' — Arthur E. Overholtzer — Brock (1974)
'Guitar Review'— Magazine No 28 — 'A-Z of Guitar Construction' — New York (1965)
'Make Your Own Classical Guitar' — Stanley Doubtfire — Gollancz (1981)
'Making Musical Instruments — The Guitar' — Jose Romanillos — Faber and Faber (1979)

THE CLASSICAL GUITAR
ITS SCHOLARS

Ronald Purcell

Richard Stover

THE CLASSICAL GUITAR SINCE 1800

ITS SCHOLARS

Another vital contribution to the evolution of the classical guitar since 1800 has been its numerous scholars. These scholars are those guitarists who have dedicated themselves to research and education rather than to the concert platform.

In the early 19th century a professional soldier Francois De Fossa, who was also an enthusiastic amateur guitarist, was to be instrumental in preserving Luigi Boccherini's guitar quintets (written towards the end of the 18th century under the patronage of the Marquis de Benavente) for future generations. Dionisio Aguado also attributes the formulation of the rules for the production of artificial harmonics on the guitar to Francois De Fossa. Since that time there have been many more classical guitar enthusiasts who have devoted every spare moment to the research and to historic documentation of the classical guitar. The main section

of this book has already discussed in detail several guitar personalities like P. J. Bone, Alexander Bellow, Domingo Prat and André Verdier, who devoted their lives to the guitar. The early guitar, that is the instrument prior to 1800, has two outstanding British scholars in James Tyler and Harvey Hope. Both are fine guitarists who have made great contributions in researching this particular field of the modern instrument's development. Other fine guitar scholars are Josef Powrozniak in Poland, Eli Kassner in Canada and the late Boris L. Volman in Russia. This section is devoted to the most important guitar scholars of recent years. Their enormous contribution to the classical guitar (and that of many other not so well known guitar scholars all over the world) is often overlooked by the majority of classical guitar lovers.

MARIO ABRIL

Mario Abril was born in Havana, Cuba in 1943. He spent his early years in the small city of Sagua La Grande where he studied music theory, music literature, piano, violin and the guitar under the guidance of his mother. In 1961 he took part in the ill-fated Cuban Bay of Pigs invasion and was captured. During his 22 months imprisonment he met the well known Cuban guitarist Hector Garcia who was also a political prisoner. Garcia became Abril's teacher and for several years after their release from prison, the two musicians worked together in the United States of America.

Mario Abril earned a Bachelor's Degree in Guitar from the University of Albuquerque, New Mexico and a Ph.D Degree in music theory from the Florida State University School of Music. For many years Abril performed extensively throughout North America as a guitar recitalist. He is currently an Associate Professor of Guitar and Music Theory at the University of Tennessee, Chattanooga. He has written articles for several guitar magazines including Guitar Review, and has had many books of guitar solos and transcriptions published by Hansen House.

JOHN GAVALL

John Gavall was born in Liverpool, England, in 1919. He was educated at Malvern and earned his MA at Peterhouse.

From the early 1950s he was a frequent performer on radio and television in Great Britain, and it was from that time that he became a very active protaganist of the guitar as an ideal instrument for the dissemination of musical knowledge and education.

In 1954 he became a full time music teacher. Between 1955 and 1962 he was appointed Music Adviser to the West Riding of Yorkshire Education Authority. In 1962 as a guitarist, in competition with such traditional applicants as organists, pianists and conductors, Gavall took over as Senior Music Adviser for all of the thousand or more schools and colleges of the West Riding Education Authority. In this position John Gavall directed the musical activity and teaching for all schools in one of the largest counties of Great Britain. This was the first time that a guitarist had gained such an important position in musical education in Great Britain.

Over the years John Gavall has also been responsible for a large number of publications for the guitar. The most important of these are probably his five volume set 'Learning Music Through The Guitar' which is published by Belwin Mills. Gavall wrote this set of books to prove that the guitar had enormous potential for music education and that it should be a serious part of all teacher training.

In 1972 John Gavall was appointed Lecturer in Music at Moray House College in Edinburgh. From that time Moray House offered tuition and harmony through the guitar, and also the techniques of teaching guitar to large groups of adults or college students. Gavall has also been involved in guitar education by the means of closed circuit television.

There is no doubt that John Gavall has been one of the most important figures in Great Britain for the promotion of the guitar over the last 30 years.

ANGELO GILARDINO

Angelo Gilardino was born in Vercella, Italy in 1943. He studied the guitar with local teachers from an early age, and later studied music with Giuseppe Rosetta at the Viotti Institute in Vercelli. There he studied theory, musical history, tableture, conducting and accompaniment. He eventually achieved very high standards in all these subjects and since 1965 has been Professor of Guitar at the Viotti Institution.

Gilardino is not only an excellent musicologist for he also developed an active career as a soloist throughout Europe. He gave his first public performance at the age of 16 and many well known composers, including Asencio, Berkeley, Castelnuovo-Tedesco, Duarte, Rodrigo and Ruiz-Pipo, have

dedicated works to him.

When the house of Berben, a long established and distinguished publishing house in Italy, was looking for a new editor for its guitar music, Gilardino was highly recommended by many eminent musicians, including Castelnouvo-Tedesco. The bulk of the Berben collection of guitar music over the past few years has been edited and fingered by Gilardino and guitarists throughout the world are aware of the remarkable contribution of Angelo Gilardino to contemporary guitar music. Gilardino is also a respected writer on contemporary music and the guitar and has written many articles on these subjects for various magazines throughout the world.

FREDERIC V. GRUNFELD

Frederic Grunfeld was born in Berlin, Germany on the 2nd June 1929. He was trained in both music and art at the University of Chicago from where he graduated. He began his career as a critic on the radio in the 1950s when he introduced a new programme entitled 'Music Magazine' on WQXR radio station. Grunfeld has been involved in several volumes of Time-Life Great Music Series, and has also written several important music books including 'The Art and Times of the Guitar' (Macmillan),

which is one of the finest general histories of the guitar ever written.

For several years Grunfeld worked in Europe as a cultural correspondent of 'The Reporter' and his essays on the art have appeared regularly in 'Horizon' and 'Queen' magazines. Since 1961 he has lived in Spain where, although not a performer, he retains an avid interest in the guitar. He has contributed articles to guitar magazines including 'Guitar Review' of New York.

THOMAS F. HECK

Thomas Heck was born in Washington USA on the 10th July 1943. Heck began to study the classical

guitar in Paris, where he lived whilst his father was stationed for a number of years with the USA State

Department. On returning to the United States Heck entered Notre Dame, where he received his BA degree. He went on to spend a year at the Academy of Music in Vienna, following which he entered the graduate programme at Yale University. In 1970 he earned his PHD degree in Music History there.

In recent years Thomas Heck has established himself as a foremost historian, teacher and authority of the guitar. He is an editor and regular contributor of Soundboard magazine an excellent quarterly magazine published in California devoted to the classical guitar.

OLIVER HUNT

Oliver Hunt (born 26th June 1934) studied the guitar at the Guild Hall School of Music in London with Adele Kramer in 1958. He also studied privately with Julian Bream. Hunt then went on to continue his musical studies in theory and composition at the Royal Academy of Music with Sir Lennox Berkeley and James Illiff eventually winning the William Wallace Exhibition for Composition.

Oliver Hunt, who is currently Professor of Guitar at the London College of Music, has composed a wide variety of works including solo works for guitar, piano and organ as well as choral, orchestral and chamber music. One of his most recent works is the 'Barber of Baghdad Suite' (1976) written for English guitarist Robert Brightmore. He has also written an excellent text book for guitarists entitled 'Harmony for Guitarists'.

SELECTED READING
'Oliver Hunt'   Article — 'Guitar' — March 1977

BRIAN JEFFERY

Brian Jeffery was born in London, England on the 13th November 1938. He was educated at Oxford and holds a doctorate in French and a degree in musicology. He was a lecturer in French at the University of St. Andrews and Visiting Professor in the Department of French at the University of California at Berkeley and at Santa Barbara, and at the University of Warwick. Over the years he has had many scholarly articles, books and reviews, mainly in the fields of Renaissance literature and

music, published. His biography of Fernando Sor, and also his compilation of the complete works of Fernando Sor, published by Tecla, are some of the most important books of interest to classical guitarists to have been published in the last few years.

Brian Jeffery has also performed as a solo lutenist and guitarist. He has appeared on both radio and television in Great Britain, and has accompanied various singers on recital tours of the British Isles.

SELECTED READING
'Brian Jeffery'   Article — 'Guitar Player' — July 1979

FREDERICK NOAD

Frederick Noad was born on the 8th August 1929 in Blankenberg, Belgium. He now lives in Los Angeles and is the author of several successful books including 'Playing The Guitar', and 'The Guitar Songbook'. He has been a regular contributor to several guitar magazines including the prestigious

Guitar Review, and his two series of guitar instructional programmes have been shown on educational television on both coasts of the United States of America. Noad is regarded as one of the foremost authorities and teachers of the classical guitar in the United States of America today.

THEODORE NORMAN

Theodore Norman was born on the 14th March 1912 in the United States of America. He first studied the violin with Wily Hess, and composition with Adolph Weiss. He played first violin in the Los Angeles Philharmonic Orchestra from 1935 to 1942.

Norman became interested in the guitar while composing his ballet, 'Metamorphosis', using a guitar in the entire composition. Today he is regarded worldwide for his music for the guitar and also as a gifted teacher.

After study with the well known guitarist Aurio Herrero in Madrid, Spain, Norman wrote 10 pieces for the guitar in the 12 note system. These pieces were the first of this type ever to be published. Later he went to Europe travelling throughout Spain, France and Italy, meeting the continent's leading classical and flamenco guitarists. He was also heard on French radio giving a guitar recital.

After returning to the United States, Norman played the guitar part in Pierre Boulez's 'Le Marteau sans Maitre', and Schoenberg's 'Serenade', recording both works for Columbia records.

Theodore Norman has many guitar books to his credit and is regarded as one of the foremost teachers of the instrument in the United States of America today.

MATANYA OPHEE

Matanya Ophee was born in Jerusalem, Israel, in 1932. He took up the guitar in 1955 and has studied the instrument in many parts of the world since.

In 1965 Matanya Ophee settled permanently in the United States of America. By profession he was a full time air line pilot, but for many years devoted the bulk of his spare time to researching the repertoire of guitar chamber music and editing music which is out of print. He has recently written a definitive work on Boccherini's guitar quintets which also reveals the importance of the early 19th century guitarist Francois De Fossa. This book is published by Matanya Ophee's own publishing company - Editions Orphée — which is based in Boston, USA. Ophee also writes articles for various guitar magazines including the prestigious 'Guitar Review'.

SELECTED READING
'Boccherini's Guitar Quintets' – Matanya Ophée   Editions Orphée (1981)

RONALD C. PURCELL

Ronald Charles Purcell was born on 5th October 1932 in San Jose, California, USA. He first began to play the guitar at the age of seven, but it was not until he was in Europe at the age of 18 that he discovered the classical guitar. It was then that he started an intense study of the instrument and amongst his teachers over the next few years were to be several noteable guitarists including Andres Segovia, Emilio Pujol, Alirio Diaz and Oscar Ghiglia.

Purcell studied at the Free University of Berlin and the Los Angeles Conservatory of Music where he received his BM degree in composition in 1961. He was a composition student of Mario Castelnuovo-Tedesco for a number of years, and he also studied with the noted musicologist of Hispanic music, Mario Santiago Kastner. Ronald Purcell is the author of a book devoted to Segovia's contribution to the guitar, and also a discography of lute and guitar records. He is also a regular contributor of articles to guitar magazines including 'Soundboard'. He was recently appointed President of the American Guitar Society and he is also the first President of the Guitar Foundation of America which was founded in 1973. Since 1975 he has acted as the guitar consultant for publishers Belwin Mills and has completed more than 35 solo and ensemble music publications for guitar.

Ronald Purcell is one of the United States most highly regarded guitar authorities. He currently teaches guitar, lute, vihuela and other courses at the California State University at Northbridge and also at the California Institute of Arts.

HECTOR QUINE

Hector Quine was born in London on the 30th December 1926. He received his general education at Hextable College in Kent. He intitally studied music privately with Penelope Englehart. Quine, whose principal instrument is the guitar, was appointed Professor of the Guitar at the Trinity College of Music in London in 1958. The following year he was Professor at the Royal Academy of Music in London, and since 1966 has been Professor at the Guild Hall School of Music in London. Hector Quine has also been principal guitarist at the Royal Opera House, London since 1954.

Hector Quine is highly regarded in Great Britain as one of the leading teachers and editors of guitar music. He currently edits most of the guitar works for Oxford University Press in Great Britain. His works include some studies and exercises for the guitar composed jointly with Stephen Dodgson, the well known English composer.

RICHARD STOVER

Richard Stover was born in Clinton, Iowa, USA in 1945. He has been one of the major figures in the re-discovery of most of the guitar works of Agustin Barrios Mangoré. These have been published and distributed worldwide by Belwin Mills.

Stover was raised in California. He began to study the guitar when he was an exchange student in Costa Rica. On his return to the United States he studied with Japanese guitarist Ako Ito in San Francisco.

In 1966 Stover travelled to Spain and there he studied with José Tomas, at Santiago de Compostela. In 1966-1967 he studied Spanish literature and poetry at the Faculty of Philosophy and Letters at the University of Madrid. During this time he furthered his guitar studies with Jorge Fresno.

In 1967 Richard Stover travelled throughout Argentina for over a year. On his return to the United States of America he continued his guitar studies at various guitar courses for a period of a few years. In 1969 he studied with Manuel Lopez Ramos, in 1970 with Rey De La Torre, and in 1978 with Leo Brouwer. In 1975 Stover earned his Bachelor of Arts, with an independent major in Latin American Ethnomusicology, at the University of California in Santa Cruz.

Between 1975-1979 Stover was Associate in Music at the University of California, Santa Cruz. At the same time he was a Visiting Lecturer at the Merrill College, UCSC. He currently teaches at California State University at Northridge.

Richard Stover founded his own publishing firm, Gringo Publications, some years ago. Through this he edited a large number of compositions for the guitar by a diversity of composers from both South and North America.

He is also a regular broadcaster, author of many articles for guitar magazines, and has appeared in concert in most parts of the North American continent both as a soloist and with his ensemble Los Gringos. He has recently formed a recording company, El Maestro, which has amongst its releases several important albums including collections of the original recordings of Barrios and Miguel Llobet.

GRAHAM WADE

Graham Wade was born on the 18th January 1940, Coventry, England. He began to play the guitar at the age of 13 after originally playing the piano. Whilst studying at Cambridge University for a degree in English literature, Wade continued his guitar studies with guitarist Jerzy Jezewski and Julian Byzantine.

After graduating from University Wade made the guitar his career and gave recitals throughout Great Britain in Universities, Music Societies, Schools and Colleges. He also appeared as a soloist and in a guitar duo with his wife. He has published a guitar method in two volumes with recorded cassettes and this was published by ICS (International Correspondence Schools) with great success. For several years Wade was a regular contributor to BMG magazine.He is currently Professor of Guitar at the City of Leeds College of Music and is the author of a book 'Traditions of the Classical Guitar' published by John Calder in 1980.

THE CLASSICAL GUITAR

ITS PLAYERS AND ITS PERSONALITIES SINCE 1800

INDEX

ITS DUOS, TRIOS, QUARTETS AND MORE

ITS COMPOSERS
(WHO ARE NOT GUITARISTS THEMSELVES)

ITS GUITAR MAKERS

ITS SCHOLARS

SOURCES OF INFORMATION
AND SUPPLIES

GUITAR MAGAZINES

Guitar Player
20605 Lazaneo
Cupertino
CA 95014
USA

Frets
20605 Lazaneo
Cupertino
CA 95014
USA

Guitar World
79 Madison Avenue
New York
NY 10016
USA

Guitar & Lute
1229 Waimanyu Stret
Honolulu
Hawaii 96814
USA

Guitar Review
409 East 50th Street
New York
NY 10022
USA

The Sound Board
6538 Reefton Avenue
Cypress
California 90630
USA

Guitar
Musical Services Ltd
3 Bimport
Shaftesbuty
Dorset
UK

Il 'Fronimo'
Edizioni Zerboni
20138 Milano
Via MF Quintallano 40
ITALY

Guitarre
BP87-08
75360 Paris
Cadex 08
FRANCE

Gendai Guitar
2-12-4 Ike-Bukuro
Toshima-Ku
Tokyo
JAPAN

Guitar Music Monthly
1-4-1 Asagaya-Minami
Suginami-ku
Tokyo
JAPAN

Classical Guitar
Ashley Mark Publishing Company
Saltmeadows Road
Gateshead NE8 3AJ
UK

Le Guitariste Magazine
Edits Folk International
43 Rue Leon Frot
75011 Paris
FRANCE

Guitarra Magazine
3145 West 63rd Street
Chicago
Illinois 60629
USA

Guitarre/Laute
Verlagsgesellschaft MBH
Postfach 41-04-08
5000 Koln 41
W. GERMANY

Jaleo
Flamenco Magazine
Box 4706
San Diego
CA 92104
USA

Mundo Guitarristico
1091 Moreno 1287
3 Er Piso Dept 'O'
Buenos Aires
REP. ARGENTINA

SHOPS FOR CLASSICAL GUITARS/BOOKS/RECORDS/MUSIC

GREAT BRITAIN

Spanish Guitar Centre
36 Cranbourn Street
London WC2H 7AD
Guitars/Music

The Guitar Shop
Musical New Services
3 Bimport
Shaftesbury
Dorset
Guitars/Music/Books/Records

Bristol Spanish Guitar Ctr
2 Elston Road
Bristol BS7 8DA
Guitars/Music/Books/REcords

Midlands Spanish Guitar Ctr
44 Nottingham Road
New Basford
Guitars/Music/Books

W. & G. Foyle Ltd
119-125 Charing Cross Road
London WC2
Books/Music/Records

Blackwells Music Shop
38 Holywell Street
Oxford OX1 3SW
Books/Music

Ivor Mairants Musicentre
56 Rathbone Place
London W1P 1AB
Guitars/Music/Books/Records

Northampton Guitar Studios
46 Brookland Road
Northampton NN1 4SL
Guitars/Music

Guitar Record Centre
Mail Order
9 The Drive
Kingsley
Northampton
Records

J. G. Windows Ltd
1-7 Central Arcade
Newcastle upon Tyne 1
Guitars/Music/Books/Records

Gordon Simpson Ltd
Stafford Place
Edinburgh
Guitars/Music/Books/Records

HMV Shop
363 Oxford Street
London W1
Records

Direction Ltd
97-99 Dean Street
London W1
Records

USA

Joseph Patelson Music House
160 West 56 Street
New York
NY 10019
USA
Music/Books/Records

Vitali Import Company
5944 Atlantic Blvd
Maywood
California 90270
USA
Books

Noah Wolfe
115 West 57th Street
New York
NY 10019
USA
Guitars

Dauphin Company
PO Box 5137
Springfield
IL 62705
USA
Guitars/Music

Barnes & Nobles Classical Record Store
128 5th Avenue
New York
USA
Records

King Carol's
11 West 42nd Street
and 1500 Broadway 43rd Street
New York
USA
Records

Schirmers
586 5th Avenue
New York 10017
USA
Books/Music/Records/Guitars

Jim Forrest
Guitar Music Mail Order
PO Box 5311
Garden Grove
CA 92645
USA
Music/Books

Antigua Casa
Sherry-Brenner Ltd
3145 West 63rd Street
Chicago
Illinois
Guitars/Music/Records/Books

Spanish Music Centre
319 West 48th Street
New York City
NY 10036
Mail Order Books/Records

The Bold Strummer
1 Webb Road
Westport
CT 06880
Mail Order Books/Music

Gringo Publications
7100 Fullbright Avenue
Canoga Park
CA 91306
Mail Order Records/Music

Celesta Publishing Co
PO Box 560603
Kendall Branch
Miami
Florida 33156
USA
Music

Guitar Studio
1433 Clement Street
San Francisco
CA 94118
USA
Guitars/Books/Music/Records

International Guitar Shoppe
5169 Baltimore
La Mesa
CA 92041
USA
Guitars

Paragon Music
1510-C Walnut Street
Berkeley
CA 94709
USA
Guitars/Music

Theodore Front
155 North San Vincente Blvd
Beverley Hills
CA 90211
USA
Mail Order Music/Books

Sam Goody's
1290 Avenue of the Americas
New York
USA
Records/Music

Record Hunter
507 5th Avenue
New York 10017
USA
Records

Rose Discount Record Store
165 West Madison
Chicago
USA
Records

SWEDEN

Gitarren
Skanstorget 10
Gothenburg
Guitars/Music/Books/Records

SPAIN

Centro De La Guitarra
Calle Montenegro 10
Palma De Mallorca
Guitars/Music/Records/Books

Bowden Music
Cl Huerto De Torrella 13
Palma De Mallorca
Guitars/Music/Records/Books

FRANCE

La Flute De Pan
55 Rue De Rome
Paris 75008
Books/Music/Records

Academie Internationale De Guitare
23 Passage Verdeau
75009 Paris
Guitars/Books/Music/Records

Oscar Music
20 Rue Duperre
75009 Paris
Music/Books/Records

Libraire Musicale De Paris
68 Bis Rue Reaumir
75003 Paris
Music/Books

FNAC (Several Stores)
Including:
Rue De Raennes & Forum Centre
Les Halles
Paris
Books/Records

ITALY

G. Ricordi & Co
Via Salomone 77
Milan
Music/Books/Records/Guitars

JAPAN

Yamaha Music Store
Central Ginza
Tokyo
(branches throughout Japan)
Guitars/Books/Music/Records

NETHERLANDS

P. J. Richter & ZN
Hoof Straat 121-123
Amsterdam Z
Records

Broekmans & Van Poppel
Baerlestraat 92-04
Amsterdam Z
Books/Music

GERMANY

HeinerViertmann
5000 Koln 1
Lubecker Strasse 2
Guitars/Books/Music

Die Zupfgeige
Adlerstrasse 43
7500 Karlsruhe
Guitars

Steinway Haus
Coloonaden 29
2000 Hamburg
Guitars/Music/Books/Records

Norbert Giebel
4920 Lemgo 1
Brette Strasse 4
Guitars

SWITZERLAND

Dennis Roshard Guitar Studio
Satmpfen Bachstrasse 110
8006 Zurich
Guitars/Music

Aux Gitarres
Theaterstrasse 7/3
CH-4051 Basel
Guitars/Music

Music Hug
Limmatquai 26-28
80001 Zurich
Guitars/Music/Records/Books